C000241607

For Aïda

  Hope you enjoy the book.
Was great to meet you!

                    Musab

ON THE SCALE OF THE WORLD

The publisher and the University of California Press Foundation gratefully acknowledge the generous support of the Constance and William Withey Endowment Fund in History and Music.

ON THE SCALE
OF THE WORLD

The Formation of Black Anticolonial Thought

‖‖‖

MUSAB YOUNIS

UNIVERSITY OF CALIFORNIA PRESS

University of California Press
Oakland, California

© 2022 by Musab Younis

Chapter 5 reproduces material from Musab Younis, "Race, the World and Time:
Haiti, Liberia and Ethiopia (1914–1945)," *Millennium: Journal of International
Studies* 46, no. 3 (2018): 352–70, doi: 10.1177/0305829818773088.

Library of Congress Cataloging-in-Publication Data

Names: Younis, Musab, 1988– author.
Title: On the scale of the world : the formation of black anticolonial thought /
    Musab Younis.
Description: Oakland, California : University of California Press, [2022] |
    Includes bibliographical references and index.
Identifiers: LCCN 2022005980 (print) | LCCN 2022005981 (ebook) |
    ISBN 9780520389168 (cloth) | ISBN 9780520389175 (ebook)
Subjects: LCSH: Anti-imperialist movements—20th century. |
    Authors, Black—Political and social views.
Classification: LCC JC359 .Y68 2022 (print) | LCC JC359 (ebook) |
    DDC 325/.32—dc23/eng/20220701
LC record available at https://lccn.loc.gov/2022005980
LC ebook record available at https://lccn.loc.gov/2022005981

Manufactured in the United States of America

31 30 29 28 27 26 25 24 23 22
10 9 8 7 6 5 4 3 2 1

For my parents

We have been called a moron race, infant race, senile and a dying race . . . ! Economic and political and social subordination confronts our race in the land of its birth, and in the lands of its sojourn. In Africa as well as in America and Europe and Asia we are a race most submerged, most despised; we are classed among the so-called "Minority Groups," "Retarded Races," "Backward Races". . . .

Sometimes we revolt against the idea; sometimes we quietly or even unconsciously accept it. But as a very stubborn fact it ever stares us in the face. The so-called virile and progressive races say to us, "You moribund creatures must speedily give place, make place for us. Your survival will contaminate the life, the culture and civilisation, of the quality which we want to evolve upon this planet."

WEST AFRICAN PILOT, February 8, 1938

Contents

Acknowledgments

IT WOULD BE IMPOSSIBLE to adequately express my gratitude to the countless people whose assistance and generosity have made this book possible. Nevertheless I would like to thank in particular Andrew Hurrell for his unstinting advice—first as teacher, then as doctoral supervisor, and finally as colleague—and Robbie Shilliam, who sustained interest in the project over several of its iterations. I must also gratefully acknowledge the intellectual environment created by my colleagues and students at Queen Mary University of London, as well as at the University of London Institute in Paris.

This book builds on several years of doctoral research funded by the UK Economic and Social Research Council. At Oxford University I benefitted from the financial assistance of the Department of Politics and International Relations, the Scatcherd European Scholarship, the Vice Chancellor's Fund, and St. Catherine's College. The Department of History and

Civilization at the European University Institute in Florence hosted me as visiting researcher during my doctoral studies, exposing me to debates and ideas in global history. Sudhir Hazareesingh, Karma Nabulsi, and Stephen Tuck read and commented perceptively on the thesis at different stages.

All those who helped me access material at libraries and archives in Dakar, Accra, Cape Coast, Porto Novo, Oxford, London, Paris, Edinburgh, New York, Rome, Florence, Marseille, and Aix-en-Provence have my lasting gratitude. My preparation for the research trip to West Africa was made easier with the assistance of Festus Asaaga, Hélène Neveu Kringelbach, Martine Ndiaye, and Martin Rosenfeld. Several historians responded patiently to my questions about archives, and were in other ways generous and supportive. My deepest thanks to Hakim Adi, Jonathan Derrick, Richard Drayton, Leslie James, Robin D. G. Kelley, J. S. Spiegler, and Romain Tiquet. The elegant map of the Atlantic was drawn for this book by Martin Lubikowski.

This book has been immeasurably improved by the comments of those who read some or all of the manuscript, including Adam Elliott-Cooper, Brent Hayes Edwards, Merve Fejzula, Adom Getachew, Kojo Koram, Arun Kundnani, Katherine McKittrick, Alexandra Reza, Rahul Rao, and Satnam Virdee. Jonathan Jacobs was, especially, a sympathetic and meticulous interlocutor over many years and versions of this work. His textual improvements permeate every paragraph. Thanks, finally, to Niels Hooper and Naja Pulliam Collins at University of California Press, as well as to Caroline Knapp, for expertly guiding this project to its finished form.

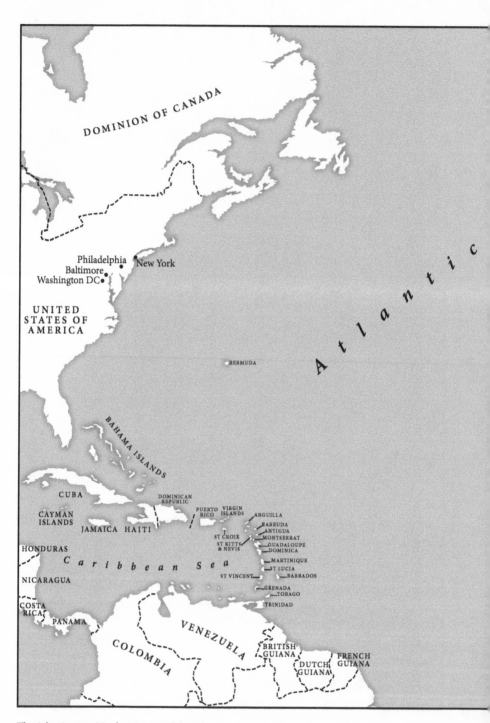

The Atlantic, 1920. Map by Martin Lubikowski.

INTRODUCTION

SEVEN MONTHS AFTER THE END of the First World War, a writer for a Sierra Leonean newspaper reflected on how "the multifold and complex parts of the grand machinery that is to control the movements of the 'world to be'" were "being fitted up" by the war's victors in Paris.[1] Excluded from the Paris Peace Conference, a group seeking to represent the interests of Africans and those of African descent had held its own conference in the same city—the Pan-African Congress—to try to influence this process of worldly reorganization. "It needs no saying," continued the Sierra Leonean writer, extending the mechanistic metaphor,

> that the Resolutions passed by the [Pan-African] Congress, on behalf of the 200,000,000 Negros [sic] of the world . . . are, from the Negro's point of view, further parts that are to be adjusted to that machinery in order to give added placidity to the movements of the reconstructed world.[2]

Thinking on the scale of the world was not unusual in interwar Sierra Leone. Journalists and editorialists regularly looked beyond what they called "our own small corner" of the world, especially where "the future of the black races" was concerned.[3] They commonly observed that the "natives of West Africa have entered into the whirl of the wheels of the world's progress," as one editorialist put it in 1919. But this entry into the world had confronted Africans with a problem. While they had become more confident that "there is no reason why they should not enjoy the world as other people," they had also been forced to see that "the race barrier is being erected everywhere" and that "at no time has white prejudice against the African been more keen than at present."[4]

These depictions of a world-spanning political machinery were written in a small West African city under British colonial rule. Yet they were reflective of widespread efforts across the Black Atlantic to understand politics in global perspective. If some traditions of Black writing dating back to the 1880s had already set their sights on the "entire global system," as Robin D. G. Kelley has shown, a wide-angle focus came to dominate Black Atlantic political thought during the 1920s and 1930s.[5] Across the print circuits of the Atlantic emerged a shared sense among Black writers that, as the *Gold Coast Leader* put it in 1919, "there is a greater world, a greater force, beyond us, which is shaping our destiny."[6] The Caribbean-born, Harlem-based autodidact and activist Hubert Harrison, writing the same year, insisted that "the Negroes of the Western World" needed to "acquaint themselves with what is taking place in the larger world" since "our problem here is really a part of a great world-wide problem."[7]

A sense of hopefulness and even exhilaration at the shrinking of the world was common in newspapers of the Black Atlantic. Journalists and editors exclaimed that "the world is *now* an open world—absolutely open."[8] They declared that the "narrow patriotism of past days is fast vanishing," looked forward to the "unity of the entire human race," and marveled at how "distance is being annihilated and contact between men of different nationalities is on the increase."[9] "After all," explained the *Gold Coast Leader* in 1927, "humanity is one, and the world has contracted tremendously. The weak are coming together more and more, if not physically, in sentiment and common understanding, and the latter is more powerful in the affairs of men than armies and fleets. The cry of a contracted world is for liberty and justice."[10]

But the history of this way of thinking about the world has fallen from view in recent years. It has become harder to think about globality without remembering its complicity in the colonial drive for omniscience. Though virtually all human cultures have produced depictions of the whole world, those that rose to dominance in the modern era conceptualized the world in order to rule it.[11] That vision of globality was imperial in both origin and effect, sweeping away diverse cosmologies. It was the basis of capitalism, a restless system operating on a "constantly extending scale."[12] And it was tied to a human drive for environmental supremacy whose destructiveness is now everywhere apparent. Yet if there are good reasons to see globality in terms of the mastering gaze of the Apollonian eye—*urbs et orbis terrarium*, the pacified universal empire imagined by Augustinian Rome—this is only a partial view.[13] It misses in particular the existence of a "surreptitious counter-narrative" of the world that has quietly followed in the wake of its dominant counterpart.[14]

This book is an attempt to come to terms with the idea of the world across interwar cultures of Black Atlantic internationalism and nationalism. It focuses on an archive of English- and French-language anticolonial writing produced by Black writers in France, the United States, and West Africa. As the exclusion of the Pan-African Congress delegation from the Paris Peace Conference suggests, much of the world's population was not expected to participate in the business of planetary reorganization. But many Black intellectuals rejected the notion that the domain of the global was restricted to an imperial elite. They saw a theory of global order as necessary for the liberation of Africa and its scattered diasporas. By thinking on the scale of the world, they developed a distinct strategy for considering the problem of imperial rule. This was a connective, comparative, and relational approach. It was resolutely antiprovincial. It was skeptical of claims to national or imperial uniqueness. It challenged received wisdom on boundaries by insisting on seeing individuals, groups, nations, regions, and empires in planetary perspective. In this way, it sought to rectify imperialism's cartographical lopsidedness: "that it is always the natives who don't have the maps," as Edward Said pointed out, "and the white people who do."[15]

The most pressing reason to think on the scale of the world was to comprehend—in order to resist—the formidable power of race, the principal ideology of nineteenth- and twentieth-century colonialism. Simultaneously ideology and structure, race operated in starkly temporal ways. To be racialized was to be sealed in the past, alienated from the present, written out of the future, or seen as always slipping back to a prehistoric state. Since the idea of race was premised on a totalizing classification of all of humanity, this temporal matrix mapped spatially onto the whole world. Joining the colonized individual to the world through race—an immobilization in both space and time—was essential to imperial power. Anticolonial thought sought at bottom to escape the spatial and temporal fixities of imperial discourse. For that to happen, the world had to be articulated as the scale on which the politics of race was premised.

By thinking about the world from the perspective of pan-African liberation, Black writers illuminated the hierarchies of race that did not simply exist on a global scale but in an important sense *produced* that very scale. Operating in a constitutive relationship with the national and imperial units of political organization into which the planet was divided, race emerged in this view as a deleterious but cohesive form of global cohesion. Race hierarchically stabilized a restless and changing world, protecting the spoils of the planet's original bifurcation. In the process, it revealed the interpenetration of scales, from the imperial to the global, which may have seemed opposed to one other, but which actually produced one another. By seizing upon and subverting pro-imperial globalisms, Black writers did not only conjure a critique of the world. They also indicated a method for understanding oneself as political in relation to the world. It was only by accessing the scale of the global, they suggested, that race could be grasped and turned against itself. The conjugation of the world thus provided a route to conceptualizing race as the basis for political action—allowing people to "occupy the discursive site of injury," in Judith Butler's formulation—without necessarily creating an essentialized or naturalized identity.[16] Yet by the same token, where the world slipped from view, or was lost or obscured, counterreadings of race could come to resemble dominant narratives.

Reflecting on the imprint of the globe on the racialized body, Black anticolonial writers produced an archive about the implication of the individual in matrices of power. Their insights on this question, which focused in particular on the eliminatory drive of colonial sovereignty with respect to the colonized body—rendered peripheral, trapped and isolated by its interpellation as "native"—hint at a fascinating and underappreciated prefiguration of later attempts to connect experiences of embodied oppression to world-scale processes. Black interwar writers suggested, in different ways and often through fiction and poetry as well as directly political writing, that intimate experiences of race—what Fanon would later refer to as "epidermalization"—were fundamentally bound up with planetary processes. This meant that the ideological work of anticolonialism, even when it took as its referent the individual, could be achieved only on the scale of the world. And, by the same token, the assault on the anticolonial project began here, ranged against its imagined worlds.[17]

World can mean many things. My usage is primarily literal: the *whole* world and its encompassing scale, which Lefebvre called *"l'échelle mondiale.*"[18] I use both *global* and *planetary* while recognizing that a distinction is often made between the two, in which the global—a knowable, rational, Apollonian sphere—is contrasted with the planetary: "an unfamiliar place riddled with eerie, destructive, and menacing forces."[19] In light of the inexorable rise of the concept of the planetary and its associated climate-related crises, some theorists have gone as far as suggesting that "the age of the global as such is ending."[20] Yet our current planetary predicament is precisely what should draw our attention to countercurrents of global thought. In an era of limited hope, the history of alternative globalities offers a route towards rethinking the problem of human agency on the scale of the world.

As a product of the interwar era, the anticolonial thought I examine saw the space of the world in ways concordant with the rationalist optimism of the global. Yet as a critique of the dominant trends of that era, it also hinted at a conception of the planetary lying beyond the control of that vision. Katherine McKittrick has shown that, despite the richness of articulations of space in cultures of the Black Atlantic, Blackness itself has typically been represented in scholarship as "ungeographic"— somewhere that space *acts*, but which is not itself able to produce and theorize space.[21] In response, McKittrick proposes a "black sense of place," rightly insisting that Black subjects are not only captured by space but also participate in its production.[22] Black interwar writing shows that a "black sense of place" included a sense of the whole world: a body of global thought that was articulated by journalists, politicians, writers, poets, novelists, travelers, anticolonial militants, historians, and scholars, living and moving across the Black Atlantic, and constituting a vibrant "thought zone" of the late colonial world.[23]

No single approach to the question of space was evinced by Black anticolonial intellectuals. But the body of writing they produced shows that, like others in colonized territories, they were intensely preoccupied with the question of understanding politics on the scale of the world.[24] This archive challenges some of the periodizations with which we have become familiar. Contrary to what has become common wisdom, for example, structuralist thinking on the scale of the world was not imported to Africa from Latin America during the late 1960s, but was already a feature of political discourse in West Africa during the 1920s and 1930s.[25] Similarly, the idea of a "world-system" may derive from scholarship produced during the late 1960s by scholars grappling with the way exploitation took place on a world scale—Samir Amin, Andre Gunder Frank, Giovanni Arrighi, and, especially, Immanuel Wallerstein. But that writing did not emerge in a vacuum and did not simply exist in relation to a narrowly defined Marxist tradition. Anticolonial writing, including that which was produced across the Black Atlantic, represents part of the submerged history of such thought—submerged, in part, because it was rarely compiled or systematized and has since languished in the colonial archives.

Voluminous and sophisticated theorizations of scale have been produced by geographers since the mid-1980s, when the concept was wrested from its cartographic fixity and transformed into a movable object. Peter Taylor's pioneering work placed scales into a hierarchy based on Wallerstein's world-systems analysis.[26] But in myriad challenges to Taylor's schema, scale became a "troubling and even chaotic concept", increasingly difficult to systematize, and construed variously as nested, flexible, irresolvable, or discursive.[27] Some theoreticians went as far as suggesting that we "expurgate scale" from our vocabulary.[28]

Though I cannot do justice in this book to the abundance and complexity of these debates, I seek to intervene in the theorization of scale in two particular ways. First, by developing an understanding of scale via texts in the history of Black anticolonial thought, my aim is to add texture to a conceptual tableau that has often been flatly abstract. Theories of scale have been largely disconnected from the history of scalar thinking—especially from "below," in understudied texts and traditions. Second, by drawing on this tradition of what we might call underground scalar thought, I challenge a binary division that has counterposed the scale of the global to the scale of the body. In this view, the insistently wide-angle and stratospheric focus of a global analysis is a "conceit in which only some can luxuriate": a perspective that devalues the positional and embodied forms of scalar knowledge of nonprivileged actors.[29] This retreat from the global has taken different forms—Foucauldian, postcolonial, feminist, posthuman—but usually has at its root an epistemological suspicion of the perspective of the observer who claims to be able see at once the whole world. "Where are you when you are looking at a globe, when you look at the world as a sphere?" asks Bruno Latour. "Do you believe in God or something?"[30]

I offer in this book a set of scalar perspectives at once embodied and global, thus questioning the notion that positioned critique is antithetical to the planetary. By extension, I also confront another idea that has become common in geographic writing: that scales can never be prioritized. "The theoretical and political priority therefore resides never in a particular geographical scale," writes Swyngedouw paradigmatically, "but rather in the process through which particular scales become constituted and subsequently transformed."[31] This jettisoning of the very possibility of the prioritization of scale rests, I contend, on a theoretical perspective that pays insufficient attention to the history of scalar thought. Black Atlantic anticolonial thought often prioritized the scale of the world—not at the expense or exclusion of other scales, but in the face of the relentlessly provincializing discourses of colonial rule.

By recognizing scale as the basis of anticolonial thought, we can reconsider the close but apparently paradoxical relationship between nationalism and internationalism. Rigid models of political thought have found it difficult to appreciate this interrelationship. Seeing nationalism narrowly as a doctrine or ideology, they have failed to account for what Perry Anderson calls "the overpowering dimension of collective *meaning*" involved in nationalisms of various types.[32] And instrumentalist accounts of decolonization, which focus on the struggle between colonial authorities and local elites for state capture, evacuate anticolonialism of its global aspirations. In fact, both imperial and anticolonial nationalisms were animated by large-scale visions that extended far beyond any single nation. European nationalisms had long been concomitant with pan-national projects seeking world transformation.[33] And Black Atlantic nationalisms were also, as Adom Getachew has recently argued, world-encompassing projects.[34] Proponents of pan-African unity were often vague on the institutional configurations that would achieve their goals. This would become a prominent criticism in the postcolonial era.[35] Yet Black writing of the interwar period reveals that ambivalence about the nation was usually derived from an unwillingness to posit too firmly a set of political boundaries, given the unstable, protean, and mobile threat of racialization.[36]

Those writing about the African diaspora have rightly, in recent decades, stressed process over ontology. Diaspora, they have argued, is articulated with other projects, identities, aesthetics, and desires; it is constantly in production rather than a fixed reality; and it is best understood not as rooted in specific territories, but as "diaspora-in-the-making" that takes place against an inescapably global backdrop.[37] Yet typically, both sides of the equation have not received equal treatment: diaspora has overshadowed the world in which it is produced. My suggestion in this book is that we consider how diaspora produces globality and not only how globality produces diaspora.

THE NON-APOLLONIAN GAZE: ANTICOLONIAL VISIONS OF THE WORLD

In his genealogy of the earth in the Western imagination, the geographer Denis Cosgrove identifies globality with the "Apollonian gaze": a mastering vision that imagines itself above and beyond the planet. At these heights it is able to map the world's surface using attributes it believes itself uniquely to possess—universality, rationality, objectivity. In its political form, the Apollonian gaze claims divine authority for the spread of a universal empire across the surface of the earth. It was already implicit in the imperialism of ancient Greece, when Alexander's conquests were associated with a cartographic understanding of the globe. And in Augustinian Rome it expanded into the notion of *urbs et orbis terrarium,* "city and earthly globe." The earthly order of the emperor became inseparable from the celestial order of Apollo. The globe, which now appeared on Roman coins, forged a link between divine and terrestrial realms.[38] For imperial ambition it offered a limitless and legitimating cartography.

Historians of sixteenth-century Europe have shown how the "discovery" of continents to the west provoked a new understanding of the earth's extent and habitability. Formerly perceived barriers were dissolved.[39] But in the tradition of the Apollonian gaze, an expanded view of the globe came with unprecedented colonial violence. The military victories of Western powers in Asia, Africa, the Americas, Australasia, and the Pacific islands depended for their success on "a global knowledge of the world in its entirety," which contrasted with the relative isolation of non-Western cultures.[40] Scholars of international relations have seen these victories as culminating in the creation of the first truly global international system, able to actualize in scope what previous societies had only imagined.[41] Conceptions of global governance and the "global state" articulated during the nineteenth and twentieth centuries reflected a novel capacity to exert control over the world, even if this power was never as total as was claimed.[42]

A historian describes this process of mapping the globe and exerting power over it as "nothing less than the human taking possession of the planet."[43] But we must immediately recognize that the possessing "human" here is partial, or what Sylvia Wynter pertinently calls an "ethnoclass" that "overrepresents itself as if it were the human itself."[44] For those who were not included in its vision of the "human," globality's controlling gaze could be disastrous. In one of his last essays, Foucault insisted that we turn away "from all projects that claim to be global or radical," because the optimism lying beneath such projects had shown itself to be the basis of yet more dangerous forms of power.[45] Others have pointed to the clear association between prevailing imperial visions of the world and the idea of race, which stratifies the diverse populations of a knowable world the better to subject them to colonial rule. The global becomes, in this reading, primarily a category of racial domination. It is an "onto-epistemological horizon instituted by raciality."[46] It is the space produced by imperial difference. It gives rise to "globalcentrism," a deterritorialized idea of world politics that masks the endurance of Western power.[47] And it is loaded with a panoply of oppressions, which can be undone only through the reinscription of alternative systems of thought, particularly those that were violently subdued—but not wholly defeated—during the period of colonial rule.[48]

There is no denying the strength of these critiques of globality. By excavating its genealogy and exposing its concomitance with the imperial vision, they destabilize the commonsense idea that the global can be understood as a neutral space. Like other scales, they show, the global is *produced*, in specific ways and alongside the exercise of certain forms of power. In this way, they recall Lefebvre's defamiliarization of space in general:

> If space has an air of neutrality and indifference with regard to its contents and thus seems to be "purely" formal, the essence of rational abstraction, it is precisely because this space has already been occupied and planned, already the focus of past strategies, of which we cannot always find traces.[49]

But there is no automatic route from a recognition of globality's uneven production to a position that the editors of one volume aptly call a "horrified recoil from any hint of panopticism."[50] In this book, I try to show why Black anticolonial thinkers did not generally undertake the stark gestures of worldly rejection that have since become common in critical writing. Neither did they seek escape routes from the Apollonian gaze in precolonial cultural formations. These intellectuals certainly looked to epistemologies that had been attacked and undervalued by European imperialism. Yet their opposition to a dominating globality was not built on the straightforward recuperation of these alternative ways of thinking. In a manner reminiscent of Césaire's later dismissal of reactionary anticolonialism in *Discourse on Colonialism*, they did not seek "to make a utopian and sterile attempt to repeat the past, but to go beyond."[51] To this aim, they conceptualized the planet in relation to the omniscient globality of imperial discourse. Anticolonial worlds were subversively adapted from the grammar of domination.[52]

A narrative of the world can embody a distinctive theoretical outlook at the same time as it borrows creatively from other sources. Dominant globalities can, as Bruce Robbins suggests, be "manhandled or refunctioned."[53] To appreciate this, we need to pay close attention to form and process. Not only do the multiplicity of "visions of globality across time and space" demand our attention, but so do the unequal relationships *between* these visions.[54] This means moving away from the idea of seemingly separate intellectual lineages and towards what Edward Said called a "surreptitious counter-narrative"—a product of the violent and unequal encounter between the spatial imagination of European imperialism and its subject peoples.[55] Writing about the ubiquity of racism in the contemporary world, Achille Mbembe insists that, regardless of the desire to erect new walls and borders, Europe will never again be "monocolored":

> In other words, never again will there be (if it ever was the case) a unique centre of the world. From now on, the world will be conjugated in the plural. It will be lived in the plural, and absolutely nothing can be done to reverse this condition, which is as irreversible as it is irrevocable.[56]

We are familiar with the grammatical rule that verbs are conjugated and nouns are declined. In a literal sense, the idea of conjugating the world is simply incorrect. But looked at closely, Mbembe's formulation is suggestive. It blurs the distinction between *world* as a noun and *world-ing* as a verb, reminding us of the "world" in traditions of post-Kantian philosophy—the environment that a spirit-possessing being is able to transform.[57] To "conjugate" is also to make a verb agree with the other components of a sentence: to find the correct form of the verb for a grammatical phrase. The sense, then, is not one of complete invention but one of contextualization and adaptation. At the same time, "conjugate" carries the sense of joining two separate things together in a union without combining them ("conjugal," for example), which is very close to the meaning of "articulate" as linking or joining. Like the concept of articulation, conjugation focuses our attention on the conditions under which discursive unities are temporarily achieved.[58] Finally, going back to the Latin *congiurare*—to band together, to swear an oath—also gives us the English "conjure": to summon, imagine, or make something appear, as if by magic or apparition.

In Black interwar political writing, the world was conjugated in the multiple senses of the term: it was the product of an encounter; it helped to configure transient unities of purpose and identity; and it was *adapted*, neither derivative nor singular. To think about anticolonial worlds in this way is to consider their tensely productive relationship with dominant forms. Interwar cultures of the Black Atlantic engaged critically and formatively with the discourses of the White Atlantic.[59] This process of counterreading and juxtaposition was not an incidental methodology, irrelevant to the final theoretical product. It was manifested in the theory itself. Conjugation allows us to think of this process as itself a form of political theory and practice: a way of seizing and subverting powerful discourses without simply reproducing them. Contestatory models of the world could thus be constructed partly *through* a reading of dominant visions.

As an example of conjugation, consider Hubert Harrison, the Caribbean-born militant, who lived in New York from 1900 until his death in

1927. Just after the First World War, Harrison argued that Black people in the United States should seize the opportunities afforded by technologies of imperial communication and the propitious wartime "meeting and mingling of the darker peoples on the plains of France."[60] Harrison did not believe in the supremacy of Western thought. He was a champion of his African intellectual contemporaries, whom, he insisted, African Americans should read rather than "ignorantly aspire to lead"; he contended that Black colleges in the United States should drop Greek and Latin in favor of Hausa and Arabic.[61] Yet his conception of the world's injustices and potentially liberatory futures was not derived from a straightforward recuperation of non-Western alternatives. An intellectual bricoleur, Harrison was also attentive to the novel possibilities of political thought opened up by a post-First World War conjuncture. To this aim, he emphasized the role of print technology and journalism in the service of constructing a radically alternative worldview. In an editorial statement for the magazine *New Negro*, published in September 1919, he insisted that African Americans needed a publication that would both "chronicle" and "interpret" "events of world-importance," thus helping to create an "international consciousness of the darker races."[62] Harrison's idea of the world was of a space burdened with violence, yet weighted with possibility.

Such worlds were conjugated through gendered relations of intellectual production. The distinction between home and the world, the masculine assertiveness of scope, unequal access to travel and print—all are features of this writing, as they are of a broader archive of patriarchal anticolonialism. At the same time, the image of the world in Black anticolonialism constitutes a significant intervention in the theorization of gender, if we consider such theory as seeking to understand how the matter of the body is constituted by power beyond it. In an archive riven by gender, anticolonialists across the Black Atlantic provocatively explored the registration of colonial power on the racialized body.[63]

PRINT CIRCUITS, INTELLECTUAL CORRESPONDENCES: THE BLACK ATLANTIC'S WORLDLY AMBITIONS

Well before the twentieth century, pan-Africanists had invoked the world in order to make comparisons between different experiences of subjugation, to highlight the majoritarian power of colonized peoples vis-à-vis their imperial overlords, and to argue for the potential of pan-African association in a rapidly transforming world.[64] These ideas acquired institutional weight in the 1880s, when, as part of a blossoming of pan-movements, the first official pan-African organizations sprouted. But pan-Africanism's worldly ambitions were held back during the nineteenth century by manifold impediments: the difficulty of travel across the Black Atlantic, the endurance of enslavement in the Americas, a lack of access to literacy and print. Only after the First World War was the pan-African idea matched with a capacity to traverse, in both a physical and ideational sense, the vast geographical distances separating the movement's constituencies. Pan-African globalism expanded fulsomely during the 1920s, 1930s, and 1940s, undergoing a qualitative shift in complexity and traction and drawing on adjacent globalisms—communist, liberal, anticolonial, surrealist.

This was the period of "the emergence of globalism": the elaboration of grand schemes and blueprints for the rational management of what H. G. Wells called in 1940 "the new world order."[65] These interwar worlds did not overwrite what had become before. Cosmological and cultural assumptions that had emerged over centuries in Western Europe—including notions of north and south, torridness and temperateness, heaven and earth—left a lasting imprint on such apparently novel projects for global order.[66] Centuries of legal reasoning aiming to reconcile universalism with colonialism were embedded into the structure of the League of Nations.[67] The League's covenant, which outlawed international aggression, was the basis for its most well-known function, soothing territorial conflict and encouraging disarmament.

But the League also incorporated many technical projects, from air traffic control to epidemic monitoring, and worked to both stabilize and adjudicate the lines of sovereignty that had emerged out of the postwar settlement. In the process, it became—as its critics pointed out—both an enforcer and legitimator of a world order that remained fundamentally imperial.[68]

Beyond the League's globalism lay a host of competing worlds. While some Black intellectuals specialized as academics in the emerging field of international relations, others, attracted by a rigorous anti-colonialism and a marked interest in "the Negro Question," gravitated towards the Comintern.[69] Some also became closely associated with surrealism.[70] Locating writers of the interwar Black Atlantic within and in relation to these many worlds should not, however, mean understanding their work as derivative. In addition to shaping the direction of movements like surrealism and communism, Black critics also articulated visions of the world that aimed to address what was specific to the condition of African, Black, "colored," and non-White peoples.[71] And in dialectical fashion, such racial and regional identities (and their boundaries) were themselves frequently contingent upon this idea of the world and its formative divisions. It is this distinctive narrative, which focused on populations of African descent but was not limited to them, that forms the main subject of this book.

Narratives and counternarratives of the world did not arrive fully formed into West Africa and the Caribbean, or among Black populations in Europe and the United States. They had to be constructed using the available tools of communication. Colonial routes of shipping and telegraph lines—conduits for the dissemination of printed materials and the spread of ideas—had expanded the imperial imagination. Technologies of communication and travel had enabled people to think of themselves as White, to imagine projects of planetary (even interstellar) colonialism, and to maintain connections with their metropolitan fatherlands when, at the enthusiastic entreaty of booster literatures, they sought their fortunes in distant colonies.[72] The same technologies could, however, be seized upon for different purposes.

Newspapers imagined new forms of political community for colonized peoples, spreading ideas across continents. The memoirs of African independence leaders commonly mention the formative childhood experience of leafing through a Black newspaper, produced overseas and transported, often surreptitiously, to the African continent.[73] West African editors admired the African American press for revealing the "calm, calculated expression of the innermost thoughts of a people."[74] "With drops of ink," declared the African American *Chicago Defender* on its masthead, "we make millions think."[75]

Accessing the scale of the world was, for many Black writers in the 1920s and 1930s, rooted in a desire to understand Africa's violent incorporation into global order. At the end of the First Word War, enslavement was not distant history but a living memory, which had been directly experienced by many people still only in their forties and fifties.[76] Political regimes across the Americas and the Caribbean continued, with legal and extrajudicial means, to enforce racialized social control. In Africa, zones of European colonial authority were consolidated and expanded while colonial economies were entrenched, often squeezing out African traders against the backdrop of a series of economic crises. Conscripted—often coercively—into the belligerent armies of the First World War, many Black soldiers were led to believe that they would soon have greater access to rights as subjects or citizens of the United States, France, or Britain. It soon became clear that these hopes would not be realized.[77]

A keen sense of precarity is therefore evident across the publications of the interwar Black Atlantic, despite the elite status of many of their writers and editors. Take the *Sierra Leone Weekly News*. The newspaper was founded in 1884 by a Sierra Leonean, Joseph Claudius May, and the Caribbean-born pan-Africanist E. W. Blyden. Joseph Claudius May came from an elite family. But like many other such families in colonial

West Africa, its fortunes rested on unstable foundations. May's father had been enslaved as a child by a Brazilian ship, the *Dois Amigos*, in Yoruba-speaking Nigeria, before being "recaptured" by a British vessel and resettled in Sierra Leone, where he became a Methodist missionary. He still bore the branding marks inflicted by the Brazilian enslavers when he died in 1888.[78]

By 1919, the newspaper's editor was Cornelius May, the brother of Joseph Claudius. Cornelius May was a figure with considerable power: a prominent businessman, the mayor of Freetown, a member of the colony's legislative council. Yet even he could not protect himself from the backlash against urban elites that took place in colonial West Africa as the British authorities turned towards "indirect rule." In 1926, when he was sixty-nine, a dubious legal process concluded in his conviction for the embezzlement of 160 sheets of corrugated iron. He was sentenced to nine months' imprisonment with hard labor. He died soon after his release, his last months spent disconsolately trying to obtain a royal pardon.[79] The story of these two generations of the May family adds depth to the urgency and restlessness of the *Sierra Leone Weekly News*'s writing in 1919. It gives us a sense of why the newspaper was so determined to look outwards to the world, where, it suggested, the future of West Africa would be determined:

> As a Community and a Colony of people . . . we of Sierra Leone and its Protectorate are citizens of the world. . . . As the papers come into our hands from day to day and week to week we are enabled to follow the doings of the restless human family in Germany, in Japan, in China, in America, Egypt—everywhere; and in our armchair we seem to be partakers of the Joys and Sorrows of people we shall never know and of places we shall never see.[80]

A few years after May's death, a young man who would later be Nigeria's first president, Nnamdi Azikiwe, decided to become a newspaper editor. He was reminded, as he later wrote in his memoirs, "that in West Africa an editor had only one foot in his office; his other foot was always in prison."[81]

Cornelius May and Nnamdi Azikiwe represent the two generations of editors who spearheaded the creation and rapid efflorescence of newspapers across the cities of the Black Atlantic—in West Africa, the Caribbean, the United States, and Europe—from the late nineteenth century to the end of the Second World War.[82] Those who created these publications did so while living under colonial rule, as disenfranchised minorities, or, in the case of Haiti, under direct military occupation. But they typically did not accept that a lack of political power should restrict their compasses or limit their worldly ambitions. "Ours may be a voice crying aloud in the wilds of the African Bush," wrote a journalist for the Lagos-based *Comet* in 1935. "But in the African Bush, away from the turmoil of a super-civilization, one has time for mature reflection."[83]

RACE, NATION, EMPIRE: POLITICAL COMMUNITY IN WORLDLY PERSPECTIVE

By thinking on the scale of the world, Black writers identified race as a form of global hierarchy rather than a natural division of humanity. This understanding of race as a structure that organized and stratified the world, with devastating effects for colonized peoples, had far-reaching consequences: reshaping self-definition and identity, setting out the bounds of solidarity, nourishing projects of federalism and nationalism. In the process, Black anticolonial thinkers prefigured a "hierarchical turn" in international theory, which, in recent decades, has pointed to the forms of stratification that structure the international system.[84]

Anticolonialists challenged the idea that colonial hierarchies had been willingly agreed upon or that empires were equitable polities. But their complex articulations of global inequality are rarely granted the status of theory today. Anticolonialism is still usually seen in evidentiary, rather than theoretical, terms.[85] Contemporary theories of international hierarchy rarely acknowledge this aspect of their own intellectual history: a body of writing that identified and analyzed such hierarchies as part of a political commitment to overturn them.[86] If anticolonial political thought theorized hierarchy on a global scale, international relations theory demarcates its intellectual world from our own.

Expressed ephemerally in newspapers and periodicals, the scattered interventions explored in this book have also been absent from many prominent works of history. Historians, and those writing about the history of political thought, have excavated the racial ideas that underwrote a global "color line" and shaped Western policies on citizenship and migration. They have examined the imaginative basis for projects to "replenish the earth" with setters, construct "cultural economies" with rigged markets, form coalitions between imperial projects, and imagine racial-political formations like "Greater England."[87] But across these studies showing how settlers, administrators, imperialists, and business elites imagined themselves as connected to a tectonic competition between peoples and "races," historical conceptions of racial, imperial, and global hierarchy from "below"—what the African American novelist Richard Wright, adapting Nietzsche, dryly called a "frog's perspective"—have received less attention.[88] Black Atlantic interwar archives have usually been read as literary (rather than political or economic) texts. Yet the boundary been literature and politics—always questionable—is especially ambiguous across an archive which includes literary periodicals founded with explicitly political intent, denunciations of colonialism attached to novels, poetry written to protest occupations, and works of history that bring documentary forms into contact with oral traditions.[89] There is an unavoidable literary-political complicity across this writing.[90]

MY APPROACH IN THIS BOOK is to consider forms of both nationalism and internationalism as political strategies for worldly reconfiguration.[91]

Thinking in this way means moving beyond a standard view in which nationalism is typically understood as "a theory of political legitimacy" one that is concerned with the "singular pursuit of nationhood" possesses strong and weak variants, can be broken down into a list of associated beliefs and principles, and is therefore counterposed to a doctrinally opposite internationalism.[92] These trim definitions, I suggest, do not reflect the protean nature of nationalism and its willingness to be recruited into the service of transnational political projects. From Greater Britain to pan-Latinism, European nations were, from at least the eighteenth century, imagined on grand scales. They were to be the inaugurators of new worlds. No less vast were the claims made for European-settled nations in the Americas. Herman Melville's novel *Redburn* (1849) thus declared that the United States was "not a nation, so much as a world," such that "you can not spill a drop of American blood without spilling the blood of the whole world." The blood of Americans was "as the flood of the Amazon, made up of a thousand noble currents all pouring into one."[93]

Like their hegemonic counterparts, anticolonial nationalisms imagined themselves as the carriers of new worlds.[94] Decolonization, Fanon contended, "sets out to change the order of the world."[95] That global project could incorporate many different—even apparently contradictory—approaches to the "nation."[96] Few of those who were committed to a vision of pan-African liberation during the twentieth century can be categorized simply as either nationalists *or* internationalists. Nor does a third option of *pan*-nationalism, as it is described in the conceptual literature, adequately express their politics.[97] In interwar Black politics, as has long been recognized by scholars, "ethnic nationalism and internationalism were not mutually exclusive."[98] This book explains that apparent contradiction by arguing that Black nationalisms and Black internationalisms of the interwar period both operated in relation to the scale of the world. Neither forms of Black politics typically aimed for hermetic, sealed, and bordered polities. Instead, the overriding ambition of both was to rectify an inequality at once global and racial: what one pan-African activist in 1940s London called the "problem of the relations between the lighter and darker races of mankind."[99] While newspapers like the *Negro World* in New York, *La Race Nègre* in Paris, and the *Gold Coast Leader* in Cape Coast often adopted the terminology of nationalism, the communities they imagined were by no means only "national"; neither were they neatly or definitively bounded.[100]

RECTIFYING A LACUNA ALWAYS RISKS opening others. Instead of trying to provide a comprehensive overview of Black Atlantic interwar writing, in this book I present a selection that reflects, across two key imperial languages (English and French), three different forms of political status for Black writers: citizens of the United States, subjects or citizens of France and its empire, and colonial subjects of the British Empire.[101] In the final chapter, I also explore the more complex statuses of those who lived in the three technically sovereign "Black states" of the period— Haiti, Liberia, and Ethiopia—but I do so primarily from the perspective of the aforementioned parts of the Black Atlantic. Any analysis of this archive must be attentive to the ways it reflects a set of material constraints and possibilities: most obviously in terms of access to literacy and print, but also in relation to different colonial and political economies, levels of state repression, the scope of technologies of publishing and travel, and gendered divisions of labor. Black interwar intellectuals wrote and thought about the international, but not in conditions of their own choosing. Yet their determination nevertheless to confront the world as a whole is striking. They sought not to escape or destroy the world but to seize and transform it.

1

THE NATION AND
THE WORLD

A FRONT-PAGE EDITORIAL BY MARCUS GARVEY in the United
Negro Improvement Association (UNIA) newspaper *Negro
World* in 1923 intervened in a debate about race and the occu-
pation of Germany.[1] The presence of African troops in the
French occupation of the Rhineland from 1918 had fed an
organized international panic, with lurid stories proliferat-
ing about the so-called "black horror on the Rhine."[2] The
Negro World editorial—titled "Are Moroccans and Algerians
Negroes?"—responded to a particular moment in this supposed scandal, when the French government had sought to
declassify some of its troops from the category of Blackness.
It had done so by by asserting "that the Moroccan troops
they are using in the invasion of Germany are not to be classified as Negroes because they are not of that race," remarked
Garvey, quoting an article that had been published a few
days earlier in the *New York World* newspaper. In the same
article, Garvey added, the differential racial status of North

Africans had been confirmed by the anthropologists Clark Wissler and Franz Boaz.

For Garvey, such assertions about the difference between North Africans and "Negroes" showed not something essential about the category of Blackness, but rather the ways in which "Negro" was a flexible category. This meant that

> whenever a black man, whether he be Moroccan, Algerian or Senegalese or what not accomplishes anything of importance, he is no longer a Negro. The question therefore suggests itself, "Who, and what is a Negro?" The answer is: "A Negro, is a person of dark complexion or race, who has not accomplished anything and to whom others are not obligated for any useful service." If the Moroccans and Algerians were not needed by France at this time to augment their occupation in Germany or to save the French nation from extinction they would have been Negroes as usual, but now that they have rendered themselves useful to the higher appreciation of France they are no longer members of the Negro race, but can be classified in a higher type as made out by these two professors above mentioned.[3]

All this simply confirmed, he concluded, the position of UNIA, "that the prejudice against us as Negroes is not because of our color but because of our condition." Propaganda to the contrary had failed to attack the solidarity this prejudice had engendered: North Africans knew "that their destiny is linked up with all other men of color throughout the world." Addressing the Moroccan and Algerian troops involved in the occupation in Germany directly, he hoped that they would "realize their first duty and their interest are linked up with the four hundred million Negroes of the world."[4]

This remarkably supple understanding of the category "Negro" might be read as merely rhetorical, but my suggestion in this chapter is that it signals something deeper: a method by which a conception of the world saturated a nationalism that might initially appear hermetic and exclusionary. The historian Wilson Moses has pointed out that

"Garveyites were not mere racialists; *Negro World,* despite its bombast and its unquestionable ethnocentrism, often displayed surprisingly cosmopolitan content."[5] The type of cosmopolitanism being referred to here is specifically what Nico Slate has called "colored cosmopolitanism" in his study of African American and South Asian solidarity.[6] And my suggestion is that it was the newspaper's planetary imaginary—the "world" of *Negro World*—that explains these moments of unexpected capaciousness. To comprehend these moments, we need to accept that Garveyism was not singular but multiple: under its banner were expressed different and sometimes contradictory political views, and Garvey's own pronouncements were susceptible to strategic as well as simply ideological considerations.[7]

In what follows, I focus specifically on the texture of Garveyism's globality—its seizing and subversion of the Apollonian eye. I want to make a case for understanding how Garveyism, with all its apparent restrictiveness and hermeticism, could at the same time become the basis for a radical openness to the outside world and a vertiginous questioning of purity and identity. I access Garveyism's discourse through a close reading of the UNIA newspaper, *Negro World*. My overarching question is, What particular articulation of the world was carried in the newspaper as it was transmitted from the UNIA's headquarters to millions of "Africans at home and abroad"? And what about that vision was so powerfully generative for so many of those people?

My reading of Garveyism through its own discourse is, in some ways, a departure from a wave of recent scholarship—including work by Claudrena Harold, Mary G. Rolinson, Robert Trent Vinson, Adam Ewing, Ula Y. Taylor, and Jarod Roll—that has explored the lived experience of Garveyism, often showing that the organization's discourse was adapted by surprisingly diverse groups for markedly divergent ends.[8] By studying grassroots Garveyism, especially involving women, and in places other than major urban centers in the United States, these studies have shown that Garveyism was—as Ewing states—"a fundamentally global project" with an "expansive and oversized ambition," which set down roots in the rural United States, among labor activists in the Caribbean, and in independent churches and incipient nationalist organizations in Central, Southern, and East Africa.[9]

These historical re-evaluations have shown that Garveyism had a wider and more manifold appeal than its popular image as a short-lived emigrationist movement might suggest. They have also revealed a contradictory and surprising relationship to gender—Garveyism was at once heavily patriarchal *and* a space for Black women to acquire leadership roles. As a movement, it laid the foundation, as Keisha N. Blain has pointed out, for several decades of Black nationalist organizing led by women.[10] Yet despite this flourishing understanding of the expansive nature of actually-existing Garveyism, there has been little analysis of the specific *content* and *scope* of its global visions.[11] What, exactly, was the "world" conjured by the newspaper title *Negro World?*

GARVEYISM BETWEEN NATION AND WORLD

There is simply no way of coming to terms with Black Atlantic anticolonialism without an analysis of Garveyism. But the divisive nature of Garveyism since its very inception—its hostility to other forms of internationalism and especially Communism, its patriarchal internal structure and language, its appeals to middle-class respectability, its later recuperation by elites, Garvey's own controversial personality—have complicated later appeals to its discursive universe. Garveyism has been criticized as a simple inversion of dominant racism, a form of "racial chauvinism" with "strong Eurocentric ideological currents."[12]

Any claims about Garveyism's openness must grapple with its simultaneous retrenchments. Garvey indisputably promoted forms of racial essentialism. He attacked lighter-skinned Black people for their insufficient African blood; he expressed antisemitic views (while lauding the Zionist movement); he famously met Edward Young Clarke of the Ku

Klux Klan in 1922.[13] There were profoundly conservative tendencies here, as Paul Gilroy has pointed out.[14] Yet if there is no question that Garveyist discourse represented in important ways an embrace of race-thinking, even a tightening of its grip, the forms of essentialism it promoted could also exist alongside an opposite tendency: a radically *non*essentialist interpretation of race.

What is especially striking—and, from the perspective of a reading of the UNIA's racial ideology as "conservative," surprising—is Garvey's refusal, in the editorial "Are Moroccans and Algerians Negroes?" to advance a definition of "Negro" that can escape that category's interpellated nature. Asking "Who, and what is a Negro?," Garvey immediately responds by sarcastically ventriloquizing the voice of domination. By refusing to offer his own definition, Garvey suggests that North African should be seen as "Negroes" *not* because of any essential qualities inhering in their biological makeup, but precisely *because* White supremacist states would prefer them not to be admitted into Blackness. By invoking the operation of global colonial hierarchies and affirming their constitutive bearing on the category of "Negro"—which is seen as a flexible label when used for the purposes of *both* oppression and liberation—this argument undermines the whole notion of biologism. It does so by expanding the category of Blackness without recourse to phenotype, arguing for the primacy of "condition" over "color."

In the process, Garvey seems to reject an ontological foundation for resolving what Brent Hayes Edwards has termed "the ambiguities of diaspora."[15] He emphasizes resistance to a particular world order as fundamental to his own conception of Blackness. Without a critical response to that world and its hierarchies, he suggests, the idea of Blackness cannot be fully comprehended. This argument is radically nonconservative and antifoundationalist in nature. In this sense, it seems to evade Paul Gilroy's later criticism of "raciology," that is, the ideology of race-thinking itself, and "a variety of essentializing and reductionist ways of thinking that are both biological and cultural in character."[16] My suggestion, then, is that we might think about locating a powerful, *anti*culturalist, deeply political strand of critical thinking about race *within* the shell of an apparent embrace of racial ideology. This alternative approach to race is bound up with the scale of the world.

In moments like this *Negro World* editorial, we see the bold outlines of an expansive definition of Blackness that is contingent upon a global understanding of race.[17] The editorial indicates how the "colored cosmopolitanism" of the *Negro World* could destabilize its racial essentialism, and push at (even dissolve) its boundaries. It is the global aspect of Garveyism that helps to explain both its malleability and its enormous appeal. At the same time, Garveyism's globality is what imbued it—at least in some of its manifestations and expressions—with a certain critical distance from the idea of race and its inscription onto human bodies. Instead of encouraging us to search for a definitionally correct or coherent Garveyism (or any other response to race, understood as "ideology" rather than practice), this pushes us in another direction. It encourages us to ask, How did the "world" of *Negro World* function as a portal to *another* way of thinking about race? How did this "world" undermine, in some ways, the closings-off—the "myths of essential innocence"—that, Gilroy rightly suggests, were decidedly present in other parts of the UNIA's discourse?[18]

Adding texture to the world of Garveyism is important for two reasons. Most obviously, it helps us to reconcile the contradictions of Garveyism itself, which seemed to oscillate between the narrow and expansive, the particular and universal. By pointing to the imagined world that lay behind these apparent contradictions, a global view helps to reframe them. In the process, it helps us to address the strange divergence that has seen some scholars call Garvey an "anti-colonial champion," and others state that he was simply "not an anti-imperialist."[19] And secondly, the *Negro World*'s globality also helps us to consider the productiveness of the dialectic between nationalism and internationalism across the interwar Black Atlantic. Instead of seeing nationalism in terms of its definitional fidelity to a particular set of principles, this would be to center the zone of ambivalence—defined by an essentially scalar, planetary ambition—between nationalism and its apparent definitional opposites.

Planetary Imaginaries, Otherworldly Visions: The Early *Negro World* and Its Predecessors

In his classic study *The Golden Age of Black Nationalism*, Wilson J. Moses placed Garveyism at the end of a tradition of Black American nationalism beginning in 1850. He pointed out its many continuities with elements of that tradition: the "pseudomilitarism" of Hampton and Tuskegee; the long history of Black fraternal institutions; the hopeful capitalist ethos of the National Negro Business League; the Ethiopianist religious discourse of Crummell, Turner, and Walters; the popularity of middle-brow literary magazines; the promotion of stocks in a Black-owned migration company. Garvey was, then, "the fulfillment of nineteenth century tradition, rather than its negation."[20] In a related vein, Robert A. Hill and Barbara Bair trace a number of Garveyite beliefs across the popular culture of the 1920s—from the doctrine of success and the idea of the self-made man to the New Thought promulgated in the mental healing movement, the boosterism of newspaper advertising, and the Victorian sensibilities embodied in rosters of "great men."[21]

This way of seeing Garveyism's intellectual landscape enriches our understanding of its continuities with earlier forms of Black American political thought and with doctrines of self-help and capitalist uplift. But none of these traditions can fully explain Garveyism's spatial scope. Garveyism's globality transcended, in radical ways, the insular politics of some of its component parts. Influenced by Black-led efforts in the

United States and Britain to articulate notions of pan-"colored" alliance—particularly African-Asian solidarity—against a White world order, it is in these predecessors and contemporaries of the UNIA that we find the most significant and formative influences on Garveyism's early anticolonialism.

To understand the importance of this broader worldview to Garveyism, we need to read more closely the UNIA's newspaper. The *Negro World*, founded by Garvey in August 1918, quickly became a leading Black weekly in the United States. It was sold in poolrooms and dance halls, convenience stores and beauty shops; its circulation had reached seventy-five thousand by 1921.[22] Readership was significantly higher than this figure, since single editions of the newspaper were often passed from person to person—especially within UNIA divisions—and read aloud to groups.[23] Being a vendor of the newspaper could be dangerous, especially in the South. Malcolm X would "talk often," according to a friend, "about how his father used to get brutalized and beat up on the corner selling Marcus Garvey's paper."[24] Even so, the *Negro World* had significant reach. It "enjoyed comprehensive circulation and discussion in almost every urban and rural southern black community."[25] Carried secretly by Black sailors to overseas ports, whence it was distributed across informal networks, it reached many in Africa and the Caribbean despite being frequently banned in British and French colonies.[26]

Copies of the *Negro World* from its initiatory and most radical period (1918–21) are now rare. Several such editions exist in the National Archives of the United Kingdom, collected by colonial police forces and sent to the Colonial Office in London for evaluation. Two of them are prefaced by a note from the colonial governor of Nassau, who has forwarded them to London with his view that the newspaper contains "matter of a highly undesirable and inflammatory nature."[27] His concern is not unmerited. Each of the enclosed *Negro World* issues is characterized by incendiary and mocking rhetoric identifying White supremacy as the enemy of Black people, calling for the unification of Black and African peoples all over the world, predicting imminent revolutionary change, reporting on assorted anticolonial struggles, and presenting lengthy transcripts of Garvey's speeches as well as front-page editorial addresses by Garvey.

Yet such itemization does not fully convey the planetary imagination of the *Negro World*, which was more than the sum of its parts. Imbued with a sense of movement and, through its many transcriptions of speeches, a feeling of orality and direct address, it constantly impressed upon its readers the urgency of its message and the boundless breadth of its scope. The "Negro world" it evoked was simultaneously one that already existed, one that was at risk of being destroyed, and one that loomed prophetically over the horizon—for which, as a huge banner headline proclaimed in the October 11 issue, "Negroes Should Prepare." Writing from Virginia, Garvey declared that a transformation was taking place in that region, in which African Americans were becoming politically organized. He represented this as a kind of opening up to the globe: "the Southern Negro now feels that he too has a part to play in the affairs of the world."[28]

What Theodore G. Vincent has characterized as the "South-North axis" of Garvey's thought emanates from these early issues.[29] Black and African peoples are presented as being in movement alongside people of color across the colonized world, against a common imperial enemy.[30] Going into the 1920s, this world of revolt is invoked through a constant stream of reports: on the Rif War ("Riffian Tribesmen in Gallant Struggle for Independence"); the threat to Liberia's independence posed by Firestone Rubber; the departure of Sir Hugh Clifford, the British governor of the West Coast of Africa ("Natives Rejoice as the Tyrant Leaves Nigeria"); the rise of pan-Arabism ("Great Uprising Planned to Drive Europeans from Asia and Africa").[31] Articles were reprinted from the African press, especially the *Gold Coast Leader;* sometimes these were furnished with new, stronger headlines. One article from the *Gold Coast Leader*, for example, reprinted in the *Negro World* on May 14, 1927, was retitled, "Long, Long Ago Should Africa Have Hacked at the Coils of the Hydra-Headed Englishman."

The world that we encounter in these issues of the *Negro World* had been prefigured. Before founding his own newspaper, Garvey was steeped in another transnational and solidaristic world of "darker races": one envisioned by *The African Times and Orient Review (ATOR)* a journal founded in London in 1912 by Dusé Mohamed Ali—an actor, playwright, activist, and editor of mixed Egyptian and Sudanese background who, according to a secret British War Office report, "dabbles in any sort of mischievous agitation which comes to hand."[32] Garvey was employed as a young man in London to work on *ATOR;* the magazine strongly influenced his developing worldview.[33]

Reading over issues of *ATOR,* which ran until 1918, shows how Ali's utopian (and patriarchal) world of color fed directly into Garvey's own vision. *ATOR's* first issue explained that it had come into existence because there was "ample need for a Pan-Oriental Pan-African journal at the seat of the British Empire which would lay the aims, desires, and intentions of the Black, Brown, and Yellow races—within and without the Empire—at the throne of Caesar . . . herein will be found the views of the coloured man."[34] An appeal for writers invoked a roster of great men of color, from Blyden to Mustapha Kamil, and argued that for too long the darker peoples had allowed themselves to be represented by Europeans. Now, "we are anxious that Europeans should know us as we are, appreciating us at our own valuation." Samuel Coleridge Taylor, the Black British composer, agreed that it was "imperative this venture be heartily supported by the coloured people themselves, so that it shall be absolutely independent of the whites as regards circulation."[35] During its six-year run, *ATOR* evoked a "coloured world" of striking diversity.[36] It boasted of its reach: "We are READ in those corners of the earth where no other periodical circulates."[37] UNIA slogans—like "Africa for the Africans"—found earlier expression in *ATOR,* which also valorized a vision of diasporic return. In an article that Garvey himself wrote for *ATOR* in 1912, the magazine predicted that "West Indians" would be key to uniting the African race, "who before the close of many centuries will found an Empire."[38]

Garvey's global vision also drew on the thinking of another Caribbean migrant in New York. Hubert Harrison had founded the Liberty League in 1917 and a corresponding newspaper, *The Voice*, with the intention of carrying out "an international as well as a national duty to the seventeen hundred millions [who] are colored—black and brown and yellow." For "the 250 millions of our brethren in Africa," Harrison's League felt "a special sympathy."[39] Harrison "pioneered the tradition of militant street corner oratory in Harlem"; Garvey, an early member of the Liberty League, was inspired by his encounter with Harrison to stay in the United States rather than return to Jamaica.[40] Harrison became editor of *Negro World* in 1920 and wrote for it until 1922. He carried his vision of a rising world of color into early editions of the newspaper (and—like Ali—he would soon acrimoniously break with Garvey.)

Like Ali, Harrison envisioned political action as requiring solidarities of color; he, too, celebrated the alternative internationalisms that promised to connect projects of anticolonial nationalism. "We must . . . learn a lesson from those others who suffer elsewhere from evils similar to ours," wrote Harrison in a 1921 *Negro World* article. "Whether it be Sinn Fein or Swadesha [*sic*]," he wrote, referring to Irish and Indian nationalist movements, "their experiences should be serviceable for us." A congress of "darker races" would counterpose a "stark internationalism of clear vision" against the "pseudo-internationalism" of global capitalism:

> Today the great world majority, made up of black, brown and yellow peoples, are stretching out their hands to each other and developing a "consciousness of kind." They are seeking to establish their own centres of diffusion of their own internationalism, and this fact is giving nightmares to Downing Street, the Quai d'Orsay and the other centres of white capitalist internationalism.[41]

These strains of colored cosmopolitanism were embedded within the UNIA's nationalism. They are detectable across its aesthetic of nationhood. The organization's red, black, and green flag was especially popular with many members. When the *Negro World* ran a "Why I am a Garveyite" competition in 1927, multiple winning entries referenced the organization's flag. Readers explained that "when the flags of the various nations are being unfurled I shall see the banner of the Red, Black and Green, the flag that had been given to us by our leader, Marcus Garvey." This was "the only flag representing the Negro peoples of the world"; it helped one to imagine "four hundred million Negroes marching under the banner of the Red, Black and Green."[42] One large UNIA meeting was told in 1919 that the organization "has secret service men all over the world now," and that its flag would "some day . . . be raised on the hilltops of Africa."[43] When UNIA members were asked "by a white man" about their red, black, and green badges in 1919 they replied: "Why, that is a secret order we are connected with."[44] These assertions point to the multiple valences of the flag: a harbinger of future military victory, but also an indication of ongoing, secretive activity in the service of an African revolution.

While the creation of a Black flag may seem to be an instance of insular and nationalist boundary-drawing, a closer look at the UNIA's red, black, and green tricolor points to the solidarities that a flag was intended to facilitate. Before Garvey, in June 1917, Hubert Harrison's Liberty League had adopted a tricolor. This flag, which was black, brown, and yellow, was intended to be symbolic of the various shades of Black people in the United States. Crucially, it was also meant to symbolize their community with the other "colored races" of the world.[45] It seems likely, as Harrison insisted, that Garvey's flag was derived from that of the Liberty League.[46] The precursor to Garvey's flag had been envisioned as uniting Black Americans with other colonized peoples. The UNIA's conception of Black nationhood was also tied to a vision of the revolt of the colonized world. Interpretations of the flag's colors vary, but in at least one interview Garvey contended that "red showed their sympathy with the 'Reds' of the world, and the Green their sympathy for the Irish in their fight for freedom, and the Black—the negro."[47] As Hubert Harrison's earlier attempt had made plain, the use of a flag evoked a global uprising of colonized nations. Since the flag was explicitly *not* that of the United States, it also performatively distanced African Americans from their putative citizenship within the imperial nation in which they lived.

Like its other nationalist accoutrements, a flag helped to constitute the UNIA "as an embryonic form of the new African nation itself, a government in exile."[48] Henrietta Vinton Davis, a UNIA leader, put this plainly on August 25, 1919:

> After this great World War, in this period of reconstruction, the negro has come into the idea of his own solidity, the ideal of his own unity, no matter what country he may have been born in, no matter what flag may have floated over him, the negro, although patriotic and loyal and faithful to all the flags under which he has served, yet he feels the time has come when he must stand forth among the other races of the world, among the other darker skinned people of the world; he must stand forth and ask, in fact he must demand his rights in this reconstructive period.[49]

This aspect of Garveyism was what most worried governmental authorities. "Garvey's office on 135th Str. is a sort of clearing house for all international radical agitators," reported one informant for the US government in August 1919, "including Mexicans, South Americans, Spaniards, in fact blacks and yellows from all parts of the world who radiate around Garvey, leave for their destinations, agitate for a time, and eventually return to Garvey's headquarters."[50] The same year, a US military intelligence note found that

> this agitation goes far beyond the redress of the alleged grievances of our negro population. It aims at Pan-Negroism and a combination of the other colored races of the world. As a colored movement it looks to Japan for

leadership; as a radical movement it follows Bolshevism and has intimate relations with various socialistic groups throughout the United States. With this latter connection it naturally sympathizes with and has relations with the Irish, the Jews and Hindus. In fact all of the alleged oppressed nationalities. The program is Liberty, Justice and Equality . . .[51]

Another report emphasized that "correspondence and exchange of views between American Negroes and prominent colored men in other countries such as Africa, India, China, Japan and the West Indies, will no doubt have its effect in due time in establishing a closer relationship between the colored races of the world."[52]

These intelligence reports doubtless contained exaggerations, but they were not wholly inaccurate. Developments in Asia, especially the rise of Japan, formed a crucial element of Garvey's global vision during the First World War and early postwar years. In 1918, a spy at a UNIA meeting recorded Garvey as saying that "Japan is catering to the senti-ment of the darker peoples of the world."[53] A year later, Garvey pro-claimed that

at last the darker peoples of the world have started out to make their united demands on Occidental civilization. The world war will not have been waged in vain if the principal peace aim of Japan, representing the interests of the races who are discriminated against in the world, is upheld.[54]

This interest was not one-way. Ho Chi Minh, who said he had seen Garvey speak in Harlem, published articles at this time about the oppression of Black Americans.[55]

The nationhood aesthetic, then, captured an idea of global reposi-tioning. The possession of a flag located members of the African diaspora among the ranks of nations recovering their statehood from colonial authority. The red, black, and green flag can be seen, in this sense, as a pictorial instantiation of the worldliness of the UNIA's Black nationalism. The nation thus envisaged was one that did not seek to isolate a community through boundary-drawing, but to connect that community to others—using the nation as a tool of alliance, not separation.

Nationalism as Power: Militarism, Race Equality, and Anticolonial Community

Behind the adoption of a flag and other trappings of nationhood lay a principle: that nationalism was a legitimate goal for Africans and those in the African diaspora, as it was for colonized peoples in general. In early issues of the *Negro World*, Garvey repeatedly associated Blackness and Africa with the power and accoutrements of nationalism. In a speech printed in the *Negro World* in February 1923, for example, he explained that he spoke "in the language of building a government: of building political power and all that goes with it," including "big guns and cannons":

> Systems of government come with political independence. . . . We are talking about a system of government that will give to Africa and the Negro race the same kind of utilities that the other races and nations use in their government for the protection of their people. We are talking about battleships; we are talking about hundreds of dreadnoughts and hundreds of cruisers; we are talking in terms of thousands of aeroplanes. . . . [We will be] coming up the Hudson Bay with a flotilla of battleships (applause), dreadnoughts and cruisers to land our first ambassador. . . . We will be entertained in the White House as the first ambassadors from the great African republic. (Renewed applause.) And let me tell you, they will hear us then. . . . Why does the white man act today as he does towards you and me? It is not because there is a difference between us in religion or in color, but because there is a difference between us in power.[56]

Speeches like these were infused with a sense of nationhood's vertiginous possibilities. With independence, an African government would not simply wait for recognition: it would be able to force that recognition through the exercise of military power, going as far as an invasion of the Hudson Bay. The naval images—"hundreds of dreadnoughts and hundreds of cruisers"—invoked the vast mobilizations of the recent war but inverted the agency behind them, gesturing to the possibility of the Black Atlantic as a site of Black militaristic power.

This sense of nationalist and militaristic salvation was often mocked, as in Richard Wright's novel *Lawd Today!*, written in the 1930s but only published in 1963.[57] Yet these later satirizations do not always convey the extent to which the UNIA's claims to sovereignty were not simply understood as rhetorical by members, but as the actual instantiation of political power, especially in the early postwar years. UNIA members were encouraged to think of themselves as prepared for imminent war. The primary vehicle of this war was to be the Black Star Line shipping company—the ill-fated flagship project of the UNIA whose striking advertisements dominated the newspaper. In 1919, readers were warned that the "white man . . . is going to make an attempt to cut off communication," at which point the Black Star Line would be a key means of maintaining independent communication—"because four hundred millions of us have declared that we are going to float it even if we have to float it in an ocean of human blood."[58] Articles, speeches and letters in the *Negro World* insisted that violence was on the horizon in the struggle for Black liberation: "You have to spill blood in Africa before you get what is belonging to you."[59] Garvey depicted Black nationalism as a project that aimed at the prestige of the European, who "comes before you in his imperial and majestic pomp and tries to impress upon you the idea that he is your superior."[60] "If government is good for the Englishmen, if it is good for the Frenchmen, Germans and Italians, it is also good for the Negro."[61] And there was "absolutely no reason why the four hundred million Negroes of the world should not make a desperate effort to reconquer Africa from the white man."[62]

What did it mean to insist on the possibility of militarized Black sovereign power in this way? Clearly, this language contributed to what one historian calls "the intensity of the UNIA's masculinist cast."[63] At the same time, the claimed ability to perform Black state power was an assertion of geopolitical realignment—with anticolonial uprisings, and with besieged sites of Black sovereignty like Haiti, Liberia, and Ethiopia (see chapter 5). By making a direct claim to sovereign national power, the UNIA challenged the association of sovereign nationhood with what Barnor Hesse has called "Europeanness."[64] As international theorists have shown, sovereignty is a globally rooted concept, which, from its origins, depended on the bifurcation between planetary zones imbued with sovereignty and those denied it. Such a racialized division is what gave rise to the "impossibility" of Black sovereignty.[65] If the basis of sovereignty was a planetary racial disequilibrium, it was precisely against that disequilibrium that Garveyite nationalism pitched its provocative claims to imminent state power and actual sovereign capacity. Robbie Shilliam has provocatively argued that the UNIA's success in achieving a transient form of sovereignty destabilizes standard narratives about the evolution of sovereignty and its relationship to territoriality.[66]

A vision of competing racial blocs and an advocacy of racial chauvinism clearly replicated some dominant modes of race-thinking. Yet Garveyism also challenged a key aspect of that thinking: the idea of a naturalized racial hierarchy. Since the world color line was founded on economic exploitation, Garveyites claimed, it could, through a form of collectivist capitalism, be resisted. "Prestige and standing in the commercial and economic worlds is a potent weapon with which to buck the color line," said W. H. Ferris in an address in 1919 that was printed in the *Negro World*.[67] "The thing that counts in this world is money, it is material wealth," read a transcription of a speech by Garvey in the paper the same month. "Today we are determined to get our portion of the material wealth in this world, and when we get it to the extent that we want it, we know there will be no more color line." After all, the "white man has his millions, but he protects it with his gun." Similarly, "we can only protect" our own wealth "when we have behind us a strong government."[68] The suggestion that Garveyite thought was "anti-materialist" does not withstand a reading of these texts.[69] Garvey—a former timekeeper on a United Fruit Company banana plantation in Costa Rica—repeatedly described racial oppression as a product of economic exploitation. A similar view of race had been elaborated at length by some of Garvey's predecessors, like Hubert Harrison, who had refused to accept that racism had any "innate" basis, and maintained instead that it was a product of exploitation.[70] This argument found renewed expression in the *Negro World*.

The discursive nationalism of the *Negro World* cannot be understood apart from its planetary imaginary. The newspaper's claims to imminent Black and African sovereignty were not simply premised on the replication of dominant modes of racialization. Instead, and without wholly escaping race-thinking, they decisively rejected the idea of naturalized international hierarchy. Nationalism as a tool of "race equality" meant two forms of global alignment: first, a "colored cosmopolitanism" that placed Black and African revolution alongside anticolonial uprisings; and second, a claim about the legitimacy of Black sovereignty that attacked the presumed convergence of sovereignty and Europe. Garvey's nationalism was born, in this sense, from a vision of anticolonial community in relation to a project of global reconfiguration.

A White World, A Black Planet: Between Nation and Extinction

Garvey's ideas about race are sometimes situated in the context of a broader reckoning with assimilationism and colorism among Black Americans during the 1920s. Du Bois's jab at Garvey for being "ugly" sparked a bitter response from Garvey: it was Du Bois, he wrote, who was a mixed "monstrosity" typifying the light-skinned Black elite, who were "nearly all Octoroons or Quadroons."[71] Garvey's hostility to "mixedness" and his attack on what came to be known as colorism were themselves castigated by Du Bois, who argued that they represented a misapplication of Jamaica's specific racial stratification to the United States.[72]

But these disputes can be read differently. If a focus on Garvey and Du Bois's divergent understanding of Blackness at this moment highlights the gulf between two different ways of thinking about race, skin tone, and elitism, a focus on their shared desire to comprehend and theorize Whiteness suggests a zone of striking similarity. Their acid disagreements about color and Blackness took place in the context of a dubious discourse suggesting that African Americans were either becoming a "new race" or merging into the (White) body politic.[73] Both Du Bois and Garvey rejected this idea; both refused the dissolution of Blackness through the promotion of gradations—or proximities—towards Whiteness. Their jointly critical approach to Whiteness was based, I want to suggest, on a deeper convergence with respect to the spatial location of race at the scale of the world. In its vehement attacks on Whiteness as a world order that would lead to Black extinction, the *Negro World* aligned its vision of race along a North/South global axis: Blackness was imbued not only with its own inherent value, but with the value of planetary realignment. This spatial view is the necessary correlative to Achille Mbembe's claim that Garveyism was based on a "promise of a reversal of history."[74] In its identification of planetary Whiteness as its primary enemy, Garveyism was also based on the promise of a reconfiguration of space.

Du Bois's writings show a similar and sustained dual engagement—with both what he called "the religion of whiteness" and, running alongside that critique, his own version of colored cosmopolitanism: a keystone of his thinking, and the subject of his novel *Dark Princess*, a meditation on African-Asian solidarity.[75] In the next chapter, I examine more closely writing about Whiteness across various texts of the period. But while I leave aside a lengthy excursion on Whiteness for that chapter, the *Negro World's* approach to Whiteness deserves some treatment here. We have already seen that Garvey's North/South global axis drew on the solidaristic imaginaries of *ATOR* and the Liberty League, which saw African Americans as participating in a global anticolonial revolution. As it did for Du Bois, this conception of the world came with a vision of what Garvey called in a book-length poem "The Tragedy of White Injustice."[76]

In its provocative challenges to White power, the *Negro World* offers a case study of what I have called the *conjugation* of political theory, in which resistant forms of thinking can exist in a tensely productive relationship with dominant forms. The *Negro World* drew on representations of transnational White power in diverse bodies of writing—those which championed that power, and those which subjected it to harsh critique. This articulation of global Whiteness took place in a broader context. During and after the First World War, Black writers and militants, using technologies of print, were already making such arguments. A leaflet distributed by a Black physician during the First World War, for example, explained that White imperialism had "gobbled up practically the entire earth's surface, exterminated or subjugated the natives, seized, exploited their land and resources, and denied all colored races rights and citizenship." Now, "dark-skinned people the world over" sought "a re-apportionment—a redistribution of the earth's surface."[77] The same argument could be found on the pages of the *Negro World*. "It is a blot on justice and humanity," ran one article in November 1919, "that the whites, who constitute less than one-third of the world's population, assume to control the world."[78]

Consider two speeches by Garvey, the transcriptions of which were published in the *Negro World*. In the first, published in October 1919, Garvey deftly moved between different frames of Whiteness— declaring the end of White supremacy, emphasizing its material basis, and proclaiming an anticolonial revolution in Africa:

They said the white man was the superior being and the black man was the inferior being. That is the old time notion, but today the world knows that all men were created equal. We were created equal and were put into this world to possess equal rights and equal privileges, and the time has come for the black man to get his share. The white man has got his share and more than his share for thousands of years, and we are calling upon him now to give up that which is not his, so that we can have ours.

[...] the United Negro Improvement Association is sweeping the world. Last night one of our African members in New York, a prominent African, came to me and said he had just got news from Sierra Leone that a few weeks ago the natives cleaned out every white man they found in Sierra Leone. (Cheers.) The "Negro World" has done the job.[79]

In the second speech, pushed in March 1923, Garvey described White supremacy as a threat to the very survival of Black peoples:

On every side we hear the cry of white supremacy—in America, Canada, Australia, Europe, and even South Africa. The whole world of white men are becoming nervous as touching their own future and that of other races. With the desire of self-preservation, which naturally is the first law of Nature, they raise the hue and cry that the white race must be first in government and in control. What must the Negro do in the face of such a universal attitude but to align all his forces in the direction of protecting himself from the threatened disaster of race domination and ultimate extinction.[80]

Alongside these two speeches, we might usefully read another transcription of a speech—this one not by Garvey, but by a US lawmaker. In 1925, Congressman Horace Henry Powers was quoted in the *Negro World* as arguing that "the weak, the ignorant, and the slothful races cannot expect to remain undisturbed in their habitat," since "we cannot leave them to their indolent siesta if they hold in accidental and unconscious keeping the energies needed for advancing civilization. . . . Will the world wait for child-peoples to grow to the measure of these requirements when it can displace them with better stock?" To this advocation of genocide, the *Negro World* added: "the white race certainly is well protected by its racial thinkers and prophets, who warn their people continuously of the dangers ahead."[81]

In these three speeches, presented in the pages of the *Negro World*, Whiteness was depicted as a dynamic, reflective, world-shaping force.[82] Counterposing the UNIA's vision of a future of African-descended peoples was a White world (see chapter 4): a potential future of the subjugation and extirpation of Black peoples. In this sense, the *Negro World* performed a counterreading of what Patrick Brantlinger has called "extinction discourse"—the long-standing idea in European thinking that "savagery" was "self-extinguishing," producing a "fantasy of auto-genocide or racial suicide" that "has helped to rationalize or occlude the genocidal aspects of European conquest and colonization."[83] The *act* of counterreading was frequently emphasized by Garvey.[84]

An analysis of White power—both "the worst enemy that the Negro has ever had" and "the Keynote of Western Civilization"—was at the core of the *Negro World*'s sense of planetary injustice.[85] Represented as a structure of oppression that had shaped the history and would threaten the future existence of Africans, it was rooted in the ordering of the world and the concomitant inequality between the "white" imperial powers and the colonized, "colored races."[86] At the same time, it had been weakened by the First World War and would soon be supplanted by a victorious series of revolutions.[87] The Black nation was therefore imbued with a sense of emergency. Its opposite was not simply stasis but the threat of racial extermination. One historian correctly points out that this "was as serious an ideological weapon as the 1886 Haymarket bomb."[88] In an emotive critique that contradicted its portrayal of Social Darwinism as a natural feature of human existence, the *Negro World* reiteratively argued that colonized peoples had a moral claim to a reordered world.[89]

I HAVE BEEN SUGGESTING THAT, far from the nativism that it became known for, much of the *Negro World*'s "nationalist" language can be read as a series of claims that were global in ambition, designed to undermine the precepts of the world's racial ordering. Addressed to "Africans at home and abroad," the newspaper sometimes evoked a sense of diaspora rooted in the ontological certainties of biological "race." Yet it also pushed at the boundaries of that ontology. Querying the boundaries of Blackness and emphasizing the common "enemy" of Whiteness—both understood as worldly categories—Garveyism's deterritorial solidarities were premised on a planetary vision.[90] Garvey's racial self-help doctrine may be critiqued as "bigoted," but it cannot be understood apart from the scale of the world on which it was imagined.[91]

A study of Garvey's texts shows us how Black anticolonialists grappled with nationalism while remaining conscient of race's globally structuring power. Representations of the nation in their writing, particularly during the early 1920s, do not neatly fit with the bounded and territorial polities that are posited in most theories of nationalism. Instead, appreciations of the world and its stratification helped to interrogate the scope of categories like Blackness and African identity. They illuminated the worldly ambitions that lay behind expressions of nation and state. There was something productive about this unsureness, which resists later attempts to comprehend Black nationalism in terms of ideological purity. The nation was not simply an end in itself but a route towards another world, and there were particular acts of spatial imagination involved in these resistant forms of national imaginary.

The outcomes of Garveyism were protean, its trajectories diffuse. As I will show in chapter 5, engagements with the three sites of Black sovereignty during the interwar years—Haiti, Liberia, and Ethiopia—grappled with a tragic structuralism. This outlook saw these states as at once in need of defense and at the same time doomed to failure. Garvey's nationalism might be seen as a precursor to the states that came to exist across Africa and the Caribbean. But the relationship of those states to the *Negro World*'s vision is complicated. The later adoption of Garvey by the Jamaican state has, for example, taken place "with discernible ambivalence and nervousness," as Charles Carnegie points out, given Jamaica's enduring and "unresolved contradictions of class and colour" and the disconcerting claim of the UNIA to a transnational form of sovereignty.[92]

The political formation that came to be understood as Black "cultural nationalism" in the United States during the 1970s, with its associated aesthetic strictures and economic programs, represented only one possible outcome of this earlier moment.[93] While conservative elements of Garvey's philosophy may be detected in later forms of nativist thinking, as Paul Gilroy has rightly suggested, other elements of the same philosophy can be located in the internationalism of the Black Panther Party, whose theory of "intercommunalism" drew on a spatially radical form of Black nationalism.[94] There were, then, no inevitable outcomes of Garveyism. What has often distinguished diverse formulations of Black nationalism in the supervening century has been their underlying scalar presumptions—the extent to which they conceptualize Black politics on the scale of the world.

2

THE STRUCTURE OF
THE WORLD

‖‖

TWO YEARS AFTER THE END of the First World War, an article was published in the *Gold Coast Leader* suggesting that "the future of the black man's status in the British Empire" could be understood by looking carefully at "the white man's views." Titled "The Back of the White Man's Mind," the article performatively eavesdropped on imperial power. Its main evidence for "the white man's views" was an article in the *Illustrated Sunday Herald*—a middlebrow, right-wing British newspaper— that had argued frankly for "the colour-bar" to be observed in order for "the white races of the earth" to retain "their white supremacy." Reading this *Herald* article against the grain, the West African *Leader* derived a lengthy and critical commentary on the nature of British imperialism:

> We have often observed in these columns that the Englishman is on the Coast primarily to promote British trade and thereby to add to the wealth of Britain, and that although there has been a change in name the present Government is the lineal

descendant of the administration under the "Committee of Merchants" whose principles still dictate its policy. When the British Government in Africa talks of "development," though it must be conceded that the "development" in its incidence benefits the aboriginal Natives, such "developments" aim chiefly at augmenting British trade. That is the reason why we hear so much of railways and roads and so less of such purely social reforms . . . .

Now the maintenance of the supremacy of one race connotes the keeping down simultaneously of a servant race in a position to minister to the wants of the supreme race, and here we have in true perspective the key to British policy in Africa on the authority of a representative Englishman. We wish our readers to mark this observation carefully and to study it in connection with the conditions of all the coloured races within Empire . . . .

If you study British Colonial constitutions you will observe that whereas all the Dependencies peopled by white races have local autonomy, and are for all practical purposes independent states, the Dependencies inhabited by coloured races, including even India with her ancient civilisation, are placed under a system of autocratic rule having all the inherent qualities of despotism. This disparity is based on the policy of the maintenance of the supremacy of the white races. In Canada or Australia, for instance . . . there is no danger of the supremacy of the white man being disturbed. Hence they are allowed to govern themselves in their own way. But in West Africa, where black and white alike hold offices under the Crown, it is recognised by the English that unless a system of Government is enforced under which even a Blyden or a Booker Washington must have to hold a subordinate position under a white man, the supremacy of the white race would be seriously disturbed. Hence the repressive Crown Colony system.[1]

The world was not directly invoked by the *Leader*. But its scale implicitly made the whole argument possible. In rising above West Africa to the British Empire, the *Leader* identified a global project— "the supremacy of the white race"—as the ultimate ambition of the imperial system. A comparison of Africa, Asia, and the Caribbean with the "Dependencies peopled by white races" revealed a disparity in levels of political autonomy that was not coincidental, but fundamental to the imperial order.

Such readings of the metropolitan press were not unusual.[2] West African newspaper offices during the 1920s and 1930s were commonly filled with newspapers, journals, and magazines published outside the region. Through what Stephanie Newell has labeled a "chain of imperial articulations," articles cited from the international press traveled from one West African newspaper to another, in each case attracting a novel commentary.[3] The region's intellectuals spent time making selections from their personal press archives, reprinting excerpts not only in newspapers but also in books—a practice one scholar of West African historiography has described as "literary montage."[4] This citational practice was central to the way in which the scale of the global was approached. Citations acted as self-conscious referents to the process of discovery and interpretation ("We were reading the other day an interesting article" is, for example, how the *Leader* introduced its *Illustrated Sunday Herald* quotation.)[5] The disparity between the source of the original quotation—usually a European or American politician or race theorist—and the African writer thus found formal representation within the West African text.

Conceptions of the planet and the cosmos did not arrive in West Africa in 1919. Indigenous worldviews and histories of travel, migration, and return had for centuries underwritten a repository of worldly understanding.[6] What was new, in the wake of the First World War, was a sense in British-occupied West Africa that the region's present condition and possible future depended not only on the cultural and economic resources it could muster internally, but also on its place in the machinery of global order. For a politics of liberation, that place had to be understood so that it could be transformed. West African journalists and editors developed their critiques of the imperial system by performatively reading, relaying, and analyzing snippets from the outside world, making adept use of the techniques that Derek R. Peterson and Emma Hunter have identified in their study of colonial-era African editors: "cutting-and-pasting, summarization, citation, excision, juxtaposition."[7]

The idea of Africa's planetary exploitation became central to an alternative topography of the imperial order. Through glimpses into metropolitan discourse, West African newspapers claimed to reveal the inner workings of the imperial mind. These arguments were rarely formalized into lengthy monographs on politics or economics. Yet that should not prevent us from seeing them as political and economic interventions. As historians have shown, economic and political claims in anticolonial writing often sought novel textual forms appropriate to their critiques of imperial discourse.[8]

West African political writers recruited, manipulated, and transformed a vision of the world from the imperial metropole. Methods of citation, commentary, bricolage, recontextualization, and repurposing— taken together, these represent a theoretical grammar through which worlds could be grasped and turned against themselves. What some literary critics have described as a "planetary system" of literary production is implicated in the meeting between non-Western traditions and forms like the newspaper, novel, and play—an encounter that took place under the shadow of a Western-dominated colonial order.[9] Innovations in West African writing represent, these scholars have shown, moments of meeting and confrontation between differently positioned forms.[10] I suggest that we think about West African political and economic writing, published mostly in newspapers but also in some monographs and pamphlets, as part of the same encounter.[11] From the region's history to its colonial economy, West African political writers depicted the region as occupying an exploited position within a world system. Surreptitiously adopting the Apollonian vision emanating from London, they hypothesized the anticolonial liberation of the region as a project of planetary scope.

West African intellectuals had been systematically writing works of history in English since the 1870s. Several books and many newspaper accounts of the region's history—written by urban, English-speaking, Christian, male intellectuals—had been published before the First World War.[12] This historical writing was inherently political in the sense that it contested the supposed nonhistoricity of the continent. It also helped a class of West Africans to rediscover tradition in the face of colonial dislocation. Except for E. W. Blyden's work, however, West African history-writing had been scholastic in focus and its political remit had remained implicit. While "apolitical" histories of West Africa continued to be written in the interwar period, the genre opened up to the world in a new way during these years.[13]

Two books published in the 1920s—Ladipo Solanke's *United West Africa (or Africa) at the Bar of the Family of Nations* (1927) and J. W. de Graft-Johnson's *Towards Nationhood in West Africa: Thoughts of Young Africa Addressed to Young Britain* (1928)—merged analyses of West African history and culture with explicit political arguments for West African autonomy and independence.[14] Similarly, Nnamdi Azikiwe's *Liberia in World Politics* (1934) was presented as an explicit defense of Liberian sovereignty while his *Renascent Africa* (1937) was a vision for revolution on a continental scale. Taken together, these works—all published by West Africans who had spent politically formative years as students in the United States or Britain—indicate a shift towards a new type of writing that combined historical analysis with contemporary global politics. As the title of Azikiwe's first book suggests, this new approach was fundamentally worldly. No longer was it concerned exclusively with the history that would reveal the venerability of African political organization. It now scrutinized the global order within which West African autonomy had been sapped.

De Graft-Johnson was born to a prominent Cape Coast family in 1893. His father was a founding member of the Gold Coast Aborigines

Rights Protection Society (ARPS). De Graft-Johnson studied law in Britain after graduating from mission schools, was an active member of the West African Students' Union (WASU), and would later be part of the group that organized the United Gold Coast Convention (UGCC) in 1947.[15] In *Towards Nationhood in West Africa,* he wrote about the rise in British racism, particularly that which was directed towards so-called "educated Africans" (a term he abhorred). This racism was detectable in the "scathing diatribes" being published "to discredit the educated African in the eyes of the world."[16] He defended African traditions in moral, social, and institutional terms. Though his book was directed at the youth of Britain—"Africa stands bleeding from wounds inflicted by your grandsires"—his criticisms reached beyond any single imperial power.[17] He quoted with approval the German military governor of Kamerun (now Cameroon), Jesko von Puttkamer, who had contended that the "entire colonial policy" was based on "Europeans depriving the inferior natives in foreign lands" by force.[18] Citing a defeated British enemy in Africa, de Graft-Johnson implicitly condemned Europe as a whole by allowing the German official to speak for the continent.[19]

Later in the book, de Graft-Johnson realighted on the theme of anti-African racism. He explained that it was part of a trend, "a crusade against coloured ascendency," which had recently been rearticulated in the writing of White supremacist intellectuals in the United States and Europe.[20]

> The clash of colour appears to a number of the Caucasian element as a menace to the peace of the world. Rightly or wrongly they are apprehensive that with the awakening of coloured peoples from the position of subject races to national consciousness, white domination is everywhere to be assailed in the future. Some have started preaching that civilisation is threatened, that the permanent stability of white institutions is undermined, and that white peoples should undertake a crusade. . . . To the seers among them this era in world history is the twilight of their race and they have sounded a warning to their people. . . . It is in order to preserve

this disequilibrium in human destinies that the white race is faced with the tremendous problem and difficulty of the rising racial awareness of coloured peoples. . . . they opine that the way to stem the tide of Coloured ingress is to plead for inter-racial harmony and peace. But how can peace result in a world dizzied in the whirlpool of selfishness, hypocrisy and cant . . . ? Can this tilted balance be held in place by force of arms and oppression?[21]

De Graft-Johnson's use of American and European presagers of "white decline"—his footnotes referenced both Lothrop Stoddard and Maurice Muret—allowed him to "jump scales" by identifying a force that rose above West Africa, the British Empire and even European imperialism *tout court*. This was nothing less than the structuring force of global inequality: a "disequilibrium in human destinies."[22] No longer was West African nationalism simply a matter of historical investigation into ritual, custom, and politics. It had now become contingent upon an analysis of the world as a whole, gleaned in part from the self-confessed opponents of African liberation. De Graft-Johnson's discussion of global inequality meant that his work surpassed in scale the West African political writing that had come before, such as Bandele Omoniyi's *A Defence of the Ethiopian Movement* (1908).[23]

Citation was used to similar effect in the contemporaneous writing of Ladipo Solanke, a political activist of Yoruba background. Born in southwest Nigeria, Solanke had been educated at Fourah Bay College in Sierra Leone and at the University of London, where he cofounded WASU and its associated journal, *Wasu*.[24] While he was living in London, Solanke began critically reading the British press and objecting to its attacks on African peoples and customs.[25] The press cuttings he collected soon found their way into his political writing. In an article published in the *Gold Coast Leader* in 1925 titled "Open Letter to the Negroes of the World," he deftly employed citations from two London newspapers—the *Evening Standard* and the *Daily News*—to suggest that British commercial interests were keen to acquire land in West Africa on a significant scale. "It is of course a nuisance that there are Negroes in Africa at all," the *Daily News* had remarked, complaining about the obstacles to gaining control of African land, "though they have their uses as labourers for the whites."[26] Solanke presented a dystopia for West Africans: the seizure of their lands and their extermination, banishment, or servitude. Drawing, like de Graft-Johnson, on metropolitan sources, Solanki contended that, despite official British discourse, there was no way of firmly separating the different types of colonization taking place in Africa. There was no rigid division between the rapacious brutality of the Congo, the settler-led dispossession of large areas of eastern and southern Africa, and the supposedly milder system of colonialism operating in West Africa.

In his book *United West Africa (or Africa) at the Bar of the Family of Nations*, published in 1927, Solanke developed these themes in a composite work, at once anticolonial, pro-self-help and implicitly Garveyist. Solanke divided the book into three parts. Two of these parts were historical, examining the region's "ancient" and "medieval" history in a manner which drew on traditions of West African historiography. But the third part of the book, titled "West Africa in the Future," contained stern warnings to European commercial interests about their plans for land acquisition in the region. These would fail, Solanke insisted. The European merchant "should know that we [in West Africa] are quite aware of his activities in this matter for the past three or more years. We keenly and closely follow him in his propaganda work relating to this matter everywhere in this and other countries." West Africans should meanwhile look to Japan as an example of what could be achieved. Japan was an appropriate source of inspiration since "West Africa is an Oriental country by history and tradition."[27]

If Solanke's positioning of West Africa alongside Japan was partly about a shared non-Western cultural heritage, his pro-Japanese sentiment also embodied an idea of their mutual oppression by the colonial order.[28] Japan represented the success of self-help outside the European order. Solanke presented this in dynamic, Garveyist language: it meant "being ever pushful, ever persevering, and ever daring, nothing discouraging, nothing daunted, and ever to look forward to ultimate victory in all noble undertakings."[29] But self-help was also tied to the ability to follow and analyze the machinations of commercial interests seeking to exploit colonized territories. The opposite of this forward movement was ossification under a dispossessing colonialism. For de Graft-Johnson and Solanke, attention to the world order as it currently existed was a necessary correlative to an exploration of West African history.[30]

Writing history against racism was not new to West African intellectuals. Casely Hayford had insisted in 1902 that "on the Gold Coast, you are not dealing with a savage people without a past." And John Mensah Sarbah had written *The Fanti National Constitution* in 1906 as a direct response to an article in the British *Spectator* that had asked why Africans had never developed any form of government.[31] But during the 1920s, West African intellectuals recognized more clearly than before that the possession of a past was insufficient for the actualization of freedom. The world in which that freedom was to be obtained also had to be confronted.

WEST AFRICA IN THE WORLD ECONOMY

Interwar West Africa did not produce works that have been canonized within the history of economic thought. But while it might be assumed that economic thinking was either nonexistent or derivative in West Africa, this is far from the truth. In books and especially newspapers, a distinctive economic understanding of the world took shape. Africa was seen in terms of enforced immobility: it suffered from the akinetic position it had been assigned in the world economy. Seeing imperialism as an extractive component of a planetary economy was a radical way of thinking about the colonial relationship. It was based on an image of the world as connected by hierarchical exploitation, structurally underprivileging Africa. Like its political equivalents, this economic image—the product of adjustment and refitting—was open to outside ideas without being simply derived from them.

A vision of the world as structured by exploitation had existed long before the interwar period. Herder recognized in 1764 that "the delicacies of our tables" are a product of "the pillage of distant worlds."[32] And Marx's concept of primitive accumulation famously linked the birth of capitalism in Europe to the violence of enslavement and genocide in Africa and the Americas. But an undue emphasis on formalized theory—and a restrictive view of the Marxist tradition—has left us with a radically incomplete picture of conceptions of global exploitation in anticolonial thought. Surveys of dependency and world-systems theory as applied to Africa have presented ideas about unequal exchange and dependency as being transported to Africa from Latin America by scholars during the late 1960s and 1970s. They do not mention that traditions of understanding African economies in world perspective already existed on the continent before the Second World War.[33] Histories of economic thought omit Africa and the Black Atlantic entirely, while studies of West African nationalism are overwhelmingly concerned with political (as opposed to economic) thinking.[34]

The image of an exploitative world in West African interwar writing has been obscured by two interpretive obstacles. First, the class position of the region's intellectual elite means that the economic writing they produced is sometimes seen reductively as the attempt to overcome obstacles to capital accumulation among a commercial and medial class, with scarce wider relevance.[35] Second, West African thought is overshadowed by the Third International. Theories of global exploitation and hierarchy are often missed if they are not legible to a narrowly defined Comintern tradition. The concept of exploitation on a specifically global scale is seen as the guarded province of narrowly defined Marxist theories, which theorized capitalism's production of spatial and temporal unevenness as uneven and combined development. A subsequent body of structuralist economic thought is identified closely with a group of Latin American economists who, from the 1950s, tried to explain the difficulties of industrialization in formerly colonized territories.[36]

But thinking about West Africa as a simple receptor of economic thought—and seeing its intellectuals as a mere comprador class—fails to grasp the dynamism of the region's economic expression between the wars. Across the region's print cultures, economic pessimism helped to shape a critique of the colonial order. This recognized that commodity-export-oriented economies were being established across the region, linking West Africa to the world-system in a process that Marxist analysts would later describe as the articulation of modes of production. It also took into account the role of the political system—indirect rule—that was being expanded across West Africa, from its testing-ground in Northern Nigeria, as a way of dissimulating the direction of colonial authority. In a fragmentary way and without systematic compilation, West Africa's interwar economic writing traced the contours of a global system.

J. E. Casely Hayford and "The Bedrock of the Whole Matter"

J. E. Casely Hayford, a lawyer by profession, was the editor of the *Gold Coast Leader* between 1919 and 1930 and a luminary of West African politics, active in organizations like APRS and the National Congress of British West Africa (NCBWA).[37] The timing of his political career means that he is often understood in terms of a kind of nationalist teleology: an important figure, but someone who was superseded, after his death in 1930, by the "properly" nationalist politicians of the 1940s and 1950s. In one historical survey he is described as a "nativist," profound elitist, and devoted follower of Blyden—based chiefly on a reading of his 1911 experimental book, *Ethiopia Unbound*.[38] Another highly critical study locates him within the "coastal petty bourgeoisie."[39] Such appraisals emphasize the elite status of Casely Hayford, his romantic, Blyden-influenced Ethiopianism and his antediluvian, quasi-aristocratic pan-Africanism. Yet missing from these accounts is the collection of articles that Casely Hayford curated as editor of the *Gold Coast Leader* during the 1920s: an archive comprising richly varied descriptions of colonialism's exploitative nature. Without necessarily contradicting other readings of Casely Hayford's politics, an analysis of writing about race and the economy in the *Gold Coast Leader* casts a different light on his thought and that of his milieu. It points to a body of writing far more attuned to race as *structure* than the "nativist" label implies.

The roots of the *Leader*'s economic critique extended back to the 1880s and 1890s. Historians of imperialism in Africa have described the shift at this time from commercial imperialism to formal colonialism, stretching into the continent's hinterlands, which left many African coastal elites—previously a vitally important medial class—in precarious positions.[40] By the early twentieth century, economic discontent with colonialism was finding expression in West African writing. To Casely Hayford, writing in 1903, it seemed that "time and again the Native does the hard work, and the European draws the hard cash."[41] Five years later, E. W. Blyden identified Africans' inability to generate wealth under colonialism as a *systemic* property of the colonial order. There was a categorical and even tragic sense to Blyden's argument, a suggestion that the very possibility of African wealth accumulation under colonialism was inimical to the operation of the system:

> Not one civilized native, who fifty years ago was, for this country, independently rich in the European sense, has left any descendant who is not to-day living from hand to mouth. . . . All their wealth, sooner or later, goes back to the European, in spite of the most stringent provisions of Wills and Codicils. Men may doubt this, object to it, hate it, and think that their case will be an exception to the rule, but the law goes on all the same. It is not a rule but a law—the law of disintegration under the European competitive order.[42]

At this early moment, the tracks of an upward conjectural progression were already visible. Though the British Empire remained the main object of analysis in relation to West Africa, Blyden and Casely Hayford here wrote in generalizing theoretical terms—as if they were theorizing the relationship between European and Native *tout court*, and not only its West African manifestation.

A comparative analysis was essential because colonialism in West Africa threatened to replicate patterns that had been seen elsewhere. British attempts to transform West African land tenure, for example, sparked widespread fears that land alienation in West Africa could take place on the vast and dispossessing scale which had been seen in eastern and southern Africa.[43] In 1913, Casely Hayford argued against the proposed Forest Bill of 1911 by writing that the bill could reduce West Africans to "mere squatters, depending, in effect, upon the foreign capitalist for a daily wage as hewers of wood and drawers of water."[44] The Biblical reference invoked notions of enslavement and ancient forms of domination and conquest.

Citations from metropolitan newspapers assisted this move—away from the specific and singular, towards the broad and theoretical. The *Leader* used snippets and quotations from London newspapers to expose the raison d'être of the colonial relationship. Evidence of an exploitative attitude was, for example, found in *Reynold's Newspaper*, London, in which a 1918 article had suggested that "Europeans have been chiefly interested in the black races in regard to their potentialities as wealth producers for the benefit of the European peoples."[45] A similarly unadorned view of colonialism was expressed by the *Leader* columnist writing under the name "Africanus": "The material interest of the exotic rulers is first and last the supreme objective" of colonialism, "and any benefit which might have accrued to us by the connection is only secondary and incidental."[46] Another editorial imaginatively ventriloquized the leaders of the United States and Britain: "The blackman may become a rival power some day, but let us postpone that day till we get all the palm oil, palm kernels, rubber, gold, diamond, ivory, timber and other raw materials denied to Europe by nature, from Africa."[47]

Understanding colonialism as exploitative meant seeing it as a process of unequal exchange that steadily diminished the economic position of the colonized. Two features of this relationship were stressed in the *Leader* during the 1920s. The first was the importance of racial ideology. West Africa's economic troubles were compared to its suffering under enslavement during the previous two centuries.[48] A resurgence of European race-thinking during the Belle Époque was connected to the intensified exploitation of the region.[49] "At every turn the black man is reminded of his supposed role," the editorialist "Ahinnana" wrote exasperatedly in 1923, "and every attempt to rise about a certain stage is marked with sneers and jeers." This was because "the dominant powers of this world are interested in keeping the African in his place." But "why should some be perpetual rulers and others perpetual burden bearers?"[50]

Second, colonialism's exploitation was analyzed with reference to internal divisions *within* the British Empire. A critical analysis of the doctrine of indirect rule—against which Casely Hayford vociferously and unsuccessfully fought—underlined the consequential differences between those defined as natives and as nonnatives in the British Empire. Writers in the *Leader* remarked on the distinctions in treatment for different territories of the British Empire.[51] The "white man" is "free to roam wherever he pleases, and is expected to be received with open arms wherever he roams. But he denies the same right to the yellow, the brown, and the black man."[52] The Black man was even "barred from free entry and intercourse, as though he were a pariah and an outcast."[53] A column by "Scrutineer" put the matter in candid terms:

> The bedrock of the whole matter is that the white races within the British Empire are regarded as the "children" who must have all that they ask for,

while the coloured races are merely regarded as—well, I had almost said—the under-dogs who must be satisfied with the crumbs and such other trifles that fall from the table. These are not palatable truths, but they will out.[54]

Responding to an article in the colonial journal *West Africa* suggesting that different British imperial polities were intended for different "stocks," a 1926 editorial in the *Leader* protested the domination of "the European Empire-stock" which sought to "monopolise the economical and industrial position in the Dominions and also in the Dependencies," and thus threatened to transform "the owners of the soil to mere wage-earners."[55]

These two angles of attack on the economics of British colonialism both depended on a broader conception of the world and its animating structures. By pointing to the undergirding power of race, they emphasized its terrible fixity. This was what the *Sierra Leone Weekly News* identified as the "pagan and unrighteous idea that Africans exist for the purpose of wealth production . . . for the white man": an idea which referred not to a single imperial system, but to the operation of a global racial order.[56] A binary division at the heart of empire—between citizen and subject, as Mahmoud Mamdani would later influentially argue—showed that the expansion of supposed customary forms of imperial rule was actually built upon a racial distinction.[57] The same process that permitted African participation only at demarcated levels of government also destroyed the economic viability of West Africa, understood in terms of the kind of wealth accumulation under a colonial order that was possible in the White dominions.[58] Intra-imperial differentiation not only was evidence of racism within the British Empire, but also pointed to racial stratification on a global scale.

Often these observations were allied to demands for British imperial reform. Yet even in cases where the British Empire technically constituted the scale of the analysis, a reading of the distinction in imperial treatment as *racial* pushed beyond the boundaries of that scale. The enforced rootedness of the African vis-à-vis the kinetic movement of the European carried within it a sense of the world. The *Leader* defined "white exploitation" as that which was "exhibited in an undying desire and determination to keep the black man in his place," prefiguring Fanon's later image of the "native" as "a being hemmed in," taught always to "stay in his place" (see chapter 4 for more about this bodily language).[59] As in other West African newspapers, these representations of the colonial economy operated on the scale of the planetary division between the European and non-European. Surpassing distinctions between empires, they created a sense of alliance and shared interest with colonized peoples outside the Black Atlantic—especially in Asia—through a global conception of "pan-colored" affinity.[60]

The worldliness of the *Leader's* anticolonialism underlines the importance of the scalar leap by which Casely Hayford—along with other West African figures of the period—identified the obstacles to the region's progression on the level of the world. This global scale, encapsulated in the distinction between Europeans and Natives, manifested itself in West Africa in myriad ways, argued the *Leader:* in the differential treatment of indirect rule; in the tragic impossibility of economic accumulation under a rigged system; in the racist doctrines propounded in Europe and implemented in Africa. A vision of the world as divided by race helped to achieve what the geographer Neil Smith calls "the abrogation of boundaries."[61] It allowed West African analysts of imperialism in the *Gold Coast Leader* to refuse the imaginative political boundaries imposed by the British imperial system. It also helped them to identify divisions *within* that system between White and Black, citizen and subject. In many respects, their analysis was prescient. Historians have since shown that, for example, levels of imperial economic investment radically diverged between the "black empire" and the "white empire"—a racial division within, and constitutive of, the British imperial system.[62]

Towards the end of his life, Casely Hayford distanced himself from radical politics and became a municipal representative—a traitorous decision, according to former allies like Kobina Sekyi.[63] He reconciled with the now-knighted Nana Ofori Atta, the major beneficiary of indirect rule.[64] But the *Leader's* expressions of pessimism about the economics of colonialism were not dependent on Casely Hayford as an individual. Despite the apparently successful imposition of indirect rule, the decline of regional organizations like the NCBWA, and Casely Hayford's death in 1930, the West African press did not retreat into provincialism over the following decade.

Cocoa, Communism, and Colonialism

Alfred John Ocansey, a wealthy merchant and newspaperman, traded cars and trucks and built entertainment venues like Accra's first music hall, the Palladium. But he was also under British surveillance because he was a regular correspondent of the Comintern militant George Padmore and a known admirer of Marcus Garvey, as well as a recipient of Garvey's newspaper *Negro World*.[65] Ocansey was not himself a writer and did not carry the intellectual heft of a figure like Casely Hayford. He was, however, a major benefactor of West African anticolonial expression during the 1930s—in particular through his newspapers the *African Morning Post* and the *Gold Coast Spectator*—as well as an organizer of cocoa farmers in a dispute with the colonial government that took on a strongly anticolonial tenor.

The permeability between Ocansey's worldview and that of both the Comintern and Marcus Garvey points to the ways in which West African writing kept alive the economic critique of the colonial order and held the world firmly in view, despite the provincializing ambitions of indirect rule. Nnamdi Azikiwe—recently returned from the United States—was hired as editor of Ocansey's *African Morning Post* in 1934. Like Azikiwe's own *West African Pilot,* founded in 1937, the *Post* became known for its populism and anticolonial audacity. Nowhere was this clearer than in its castigations of the colonial economy. As the columnist writing as "Gump" memorably put it in the newspaper in 1935: "the white man came for our goods and not for our good."[66] Other regional publications concurred. "No colonial acquisition has ever been attempted solely in the interest of the people," wrote Dusé Mohamed Ali, the Sudanese-Egyptian immigrant to Lagos, in *The Comet* the same year. "Such acquisition has always been undertaken in the economic interests of the Colonizers. There have been no moral considerations whatever."[67]

Colonial authorities often insisted that the region's agitation was Communist-instigated.[68] But their refusal to take seriously West African conceptions of the world meant that they did not see the ways in which the perspectives of the Comintern adjoined ways of thinking about colonialism that already existed in the region. No West African interwar newspaper can be called Communist, but the influence of George Padmore—a Comintern official until 1934, pan-African militant and professional anticolonial revolutionary—is evident in the region's newspapers starting at least in 1931. In that year, R. Benjamin Wuta-Ofei, the editor of the *Gold Coast Spectator*, established contact with Padmore, who was then head of the Moscow-backed International Trade Union Committee of Negro Workers.[69] Padmore would write hundreds of articles for West African and Caribbean newspapers over the 1930s, 1940s and 1950s.[70] Others affiliated with international Communist networks included Kweku Bankole Awoonor-Renner, who had spent time in the Soviet Union before returning to West Africa in 1928, and I. T. A. Wallace-Johnson, the Sierra Leonean militant who became closely involved in the region's newspapers and anticolonial politics during the 1930s.[71] These individuals existed in the context of a broader engagement signified by figures like Kobina Sekyi and Ocansey, who were in regular contact with Padmore.[72]

Communist traditions offered ways of thinking about the world as structured through exploitation. But part of the importance of the analysis offered by figures like Padmore and Wallace-Johnson was that it could be adapted to the already-existing body of structuralist economic thought in the region. Since Blyden, this had sought to analyze the persistently diminishing material position of the colonized African vis-à-vis the colonizing European. Profoundly structuralist in approach, what distinguished this West African economic writing was its emphasis on the *affinities* that lay behind exploitation—the anticompetitive chauvinism of imperialism—rather than its self-propelling nature. What Kobina Sekyi had called in 1922 "the spirit of group morality" that was "now rampant in Englishmen" had, in this view, created a *cultural* economy of intra-European solidarity.[73]

European merchants were not "commercially moral," explained the *West African Pilot* in 1938. They sold goods to Africans at artificially inflated prices. Though they depended on African produce, they "insist on skinning us to the bone in order to declare dividends for their heartless shareholders," assisted by the unfair lending practices of banks. Africans, "the owners of our land, their hosts" were ruthlessly exploited.[74] This view located West Africa's economic crisis within a global economy that had made Africans, as Kofi Pekiyi put it in 1938, "solely contingent," with no independent systemic authority.[75]

The context for these assertions was an economic crisis that was part of global trends, but whose particular form in West Africa was tied to the region's export-oriented economy, which suffered cruelly during the Depression. When prices for West African crops plummeted 60 to 70 percent, new taxes were instituted and new austerity measures implemented by the colonial administration, transferring costs back onto the population. African critics argued that these measures shielded the metropole from responsibility for West Africa's economic woes in a way that contrasted with the favorable treatment received by the White dominions. Strikes, demonstrations, riots, and protests spread across West Africa.[76] What made the price declines even worse were two concurrent developments. First, European cocoa-buying firms—Cadbury's, the United Africa Company, and Holts in particular—colluded in a price-fixing scheme, supported by the Colonial Office, to depress the price of cocoa. Second, African international shippers of cocoa were permanently excluded from the industry in favor of large expatriate firms. Organizing against the price-fixing, farmers' organizations such as the Gold Coast Farmers' Association orchestrated cocoa hold-ups in 1930–31 and 1937–38—effectively sellers' strikes, during which they refused to sell cocoa at the artificially lowered prices.[77]

In West African newspapers, the economic crises of the 1930s and their radiating effects were not represented simply as an outcome of the operation of the natural laws of capitalism. Instead, and notwithstanding the vociferous denials of the colonial government, they were described as an outgrowth of the global racial order. In a subversive counterreading of colonialism, the relationship between the cocoa-buying companies and African farmers was described as one of explicitly racist exploitation. The collusion between the companies was repeatedly compared to the enslavement of Africans.[78] The "whiteness" of the exploiting companies and the racist contempt with which they treated Africans were emphasized.[79] In this way, the cocoa crisis became a case study of a global pattern of exploitation targeting non-Europeans, and especially Africa and its diaspora. For W. E. B. Du Bois, writing a decade later, it was an excellent example of the ways in which "African colonial governments are virtually ruled by investors in England."[80] And though its former editor Cornelius May had been silenced, the *Sierra Leone Weekly News* used the 1930s crisis to protest against the injustices of the colonial economy, in which collusion and monopoly had depressed prices for the region's raw materials and created "terrific poverty among the millions in West Africa." West Africans were not asking for special treatment, the newspaper insisted: only "a fair deal in return for their products" and "a place in the economic relationships of the peoples of the world."[81]

In words which echoed de Graft-Johnson's evocation of the "disequilibrium of human destinies," J. A. Wachuku explained in the *West Afri-*

can Pilot in 1938 that the dangerous rearmament taking place among Western powers had a planetary origin, economically grounded in "the unequal distribution of material resources" between supposedly "'civilised' nations" and "backward countries." This relationship of base exploitation was disguised by "the claim of superiority of the white nations over other nations, and their unscientific and misleading support by their scientists."[82] Articles like Wachuku's pointed to a global system of inequality and distribution whose beneficiaries were assembled under the banner of Whiteness. Emphasizing the pseudoscience that bound together the "white nations," they drew attention to the powerful discursive legitimation for worldwide inequality.

West African political figures were sometimes criticized for their incomplete Marxism, but these attacks failed to recognize the distinctive outlines of the idea of worldwide exploitation in West African writing. Diverging from official theories, West African analysis saw race as embedded in the very texture of Africa's exploitation. At the Second World Congress of the League Against Imperialism in 1929, the African American Communist James W. Ford criticized Ladipo Solanke's book *United West Africa* for its suggestion that European powers might assist financially in the development of Africa. "Is he so naïve to think that capitalists from these countries have any other design but the subjugation of the African people?"[83] Ford did not, however, specify that he had been in contact with Ladipo Solanke earlier the same year and had sent him copies of the Communist periodical *Negro Worker,* which Solanke had described as "a great eye-opener."[84] If Solanke did not subscribe wholly to Ford's analysis, neither was he uninfluenced by it.

Similarly, while West African newspapers during the 1930s invoked global hierarchies of production in ways that sometimes recalled the language of the Comintern, they virtually always stressed the importance of race in the overall system of exploitation. Comparing the Gold Coast and Jamaica, the *African Morning Post* wrote in 1938 that "huge profits have been extracted from the very life blood of hunger bitten negro workmen" in Jamaica's sugar industry, suggesting that "all over the world the fate of the negro race is identical." The African was "helpless . . . before hydra-headed, inexorable and self-centred capitalism."[85]

This notion of enforced and racialized dependency was prevalent in analyses of crisis in the region during the 1930s. These insisted on seeing imperial capitalism through the lens of Whiteness. Thus the *African Morning Post* argued that the "white commercial firms," whose links with the metropole gave them preponderance, were a key instrument of economic domination. The African was now "perpetually dependent upon help from outside sources," dependent "upon the foreign supplier for almost every article of food and drink" and thus deprived of "the most effective barrier against foreign intrigues—INDEPENDENCE and SELF-RELIANCE."[86] The 1937–38 cocoa crisis had "shattered to pieces the hopes and ambitions of every individual African, literate or illiterate."[87] Before the arrival of the colonizer, the African "was the supplier of his own salt, cloths, fishing nets, cutlasses, soap and many other things necessary to fit him in life." Yet now he had "become parasite on the white man's commodities."[88]

Elsewhere, West African commentators articulated their own perspective on primitive accumulation—what Marx described as the "prehistory of capital"—by pointing to the historical relationship that had enriched Europe through the impoverishment of Africa and Africans.[89] By making this argument, they combatted the idea that Africa was a net recipient of charitable aid from Europe. Again, this was a structuralist reading of the metropole-periphery relation, but one which stressed race over the operation of abstract capital. Hence the "Rambler," who wrote a regular column in the *Sierra Leone Weekly News*, fulminated in 1938 against the idea that Sierra Leoneans should be "grateful" to the British for founding the colony:

> It was the sweat of the black man's brow which laid the foundation for the present day opulence of Britain and White America. What has England

done for Sierra Leone in 150 years in comparison with what the Sierra Leone slaves did for England during their 400 years of forced labour in British plantations? Talk of gratitude? It is the other way about. . . . You cheated me of 400 years' income, traded with it, made a million percent profit and then flung a paltry 150 years' income back to me and expected me to put my hands behind my back and say "many, many thanks!" Can anything be more ridiculous? Who is to be grateful to the other? The cheat—or his victim? Not until the former makes full and complete reparation will there be any reasonable expectation of gratitude from the latter.[90]

By underscoring race in the operation of the colonial order, West African writers drew attention to the corporeality of exploitation. To experience colonialism in Africa was to feel a sense of being crowded, forcibly confined in one place, denied movement and progression. During these "troublous times" in which "the indication of the horizon of world politics in inter-racial and inter-national relations do not say well," explained the *West African Pilot* in 1938, "now, West Africa is in the hands of the capitalists. It is the same story everywhere. The black man, the black woman and their children are being crowded out."[91] One now found "harsh laws being passed against them to cripple them both economically and politically," including censorship and immigration controls.[92] And as rearmament sped up and another war began to look likely, the newspaper saw Europe's self-destruction as a product of this competition to dominate a globally bifurcated system, erected on the exploitation of colonized peoples. "White men all over the word have armed themselves on a colossal scale in order, they say, that other powers may not prevent them from governing the non-white races from whose country they get all that they require to satisfy their domestic want."[93]

A WHOLE WORLD—CHARACTERIZED BY EXPLOITATION, illuminated through citation—became visible in West African writing before the Second World War. But its landscapes have been obscure to subsequent analysis, overshadowed by the Comintern on one side and imperial globality on the other. The economic worlds conjured by West African interwar figures have been too easily cast aside by later analysts, read as incompletely or insufficiently Marxist. Thus arrives the notion that structuralist thought on a world scale was imported to Africa during the late 1960s.

The world that surfaced in West African interwar writing required careful balancing to remain in view. A sensitive accounting of the interrelationship between the region's internal dynamics and the wider world was not automatic: there was nothing permanent about this dialectical way of thinking. Forms of nativism, provincialism, and retrenchment always threatened to erupt. Even before the end of the Second World War, there were signs of a retreat from the racial lens through which the world had formerly come into view.[94] After the war, the capaciousness of West African understandings of political community narrowed.[95] But to represent the post-1945 period solely in terms of contraction would be inaccurate. From March 1957 until 1963, a political project tried vigorously to dissolve continental state boundaries with a view to pan-African unification. The United States of Africa, led by Nkrumah's Ghana, was a project whose intellectual roots (though they stretched across the Black Atlantic) were embedded in West Africa's intellectual culture under British colonialism. In ways later unrecognized, that culture operated on a radically expansive scale, seeking not only regional but also planetary reconfiguration.[96]

3

THE WHITENESS OF
THE WORLD

||||||||||||||||||||||||||||||||||||||||||||||||||||||||||||||||||||||||||||||||||||||||||||||||||||||||||||||||||||||||||||||||||||||||||||||||||||||||||||||

AT THE THIRTEENTH ANNUAL CONGRESS of the Société de médécine publique, which took place at the Institut Pasteur in
Paris in October 1926, the keynote report was written jointly
by two officials who worked for the French government:
Georges Dequidt, from the Ministry of Interior, and Georges
Forestier, a departmental health inspector. Together, they
warned the assembled delegates of "the advanced indices of
the twilight of our Western Civilization and the decline of
the white race." They cited the American eugenicist Madison
Grant's book *The Passing of the Great Race*—originally published in 1916, but only translated into French earlier that
year. Its French edition had been prefaced by the influential
anthropologist, eugenicist, and socialist Count Georges
Vacher de Lapouge (with Marx's son-in-law, he had cofounded
the French Workers' Party). Dequidt and Forestier relayed
the advice of Vacher de Lapouge to the members of the
Société. It was vital that they not "forget that the first waves

of Orientals and Slavs that are breaking on France presage the invading flood which threatens to submerge that which is left of our civilization and the health of our race."[1]

When Dequidt and Forestier were delivering this address, France had become the most important destination for immigrants in the industrialized world, surpassing even the United States. Over the course of twenty years, its foreign-born population almost tripled—a demographic shift unknown to other European nations until after the Second World War.[2] The sociologist René Maunier warned in 1932 that France faced "penetration" by "thousands, hundreds of thousands of natives" arriving as immigrants.[3] In response, France developed the "largest, most sophisticated immigration service anywhere in the world," an intricate system of identification, segregation, and enforcement directed at the workers, dissidents, refugees, and colonial expatriates who had arrived in France since 1914.[4] Between 1919 and 1933, over ninety-three thousand foreigners were expelled from France by order of the French Interior Ministry.[5] At the same time that it found new ways to order and regulate its subject populations, interwar France also systematically produced representations of them. From films and avant-garde art to human displays at colonial exhibitions, African, Asian, and Arab peoples were envisaged as distant, dangerous, and criminal, yet also holding the promise of exotic replenishment for a country wracked by war.[6]

Dequidt and Forestier were not the only government officials who saw interwar immigration as threatening France's claim to be among the "civilized" nations of the world. As the first country to recognize the pattern of a declining birthrate, interwar France saw the rise of powerful pro-natalist, neo-Malthusian, eugenicist, "social hygiene," and immigration restriction movements, each of which, influenced by widespread neo-Lamarckian beliefs in the hereditary qualities of populations, claimed to hold the keys to the biological regeneration of the French population.[7] Some of their efforts culminated in the 1939 law known as the *Code de la famille*, which, among other measures, restricted the sale of contraceptives.[8]

At the same time as French officials were anxiously deliberating the "assimilability" of migrants and colonized peoples, Black writers in interwar Paris were publishing their own analyses of French imperialism and republicanism. Both "nationalist" and "assimilationist" newspapers were preoccupied with the world-spanning power of race, and they covertly or directly referred to Whiteness as a way of capturing the global power of race and its reverberation or refraction into France. Through acts of imaginative travel and comparison, newspapers attached to African and Antillean organizations in Paris reassessed the French colonial system and the range of possibilities it offered to its Black citizens and subjects. In so doing, they commonly adopted a view whose scale operated at a level above that of the French empire-state. For Black writers as well as for officials like Dequidt and Forestier, "declinist" writing—which cast doubt over the racial future of the world, and, especially, over the security of White dominance—spoke not only to the disequilibrium of the international system as a whole, but also to the racial inequality found in French national and imperial policy.

In British-occupied West Africa during the same period, newspapers and books were full of analyses of Whiteness and "White prestige"— "the most damnable doctrine in the Empire" and an idea premised on delusion, like "a fetish, blind idol with clay feet."[9] Racial boundaries hardened across British colonial policy during these years. There were clear signs of a color bar in the expansion of indirect rule, the spread of "scientific" racism and doctrines of separation, and the racially differential treatment of the British Empire's populations. Disturbed by this situation, West African intellectuals often returned to the concept of Whiteness. For them, Whiteness helped to explain why, despite the hopes of colonial subjects, racism had not been extirpated from British colonial policy but had actually intensified, despite all that African,

Asian, and Caribbean soldiers had done for the victorious powers during the First World War. If race was inescapably global, that meant the operation of Whiteness within both the French and British imperial contexts was an instantiation of a planetary structure. It was "but a local phase of a world problem," as W. E. B. Du Bois wrote of the African American condition.[10] In this way, a critical account of Whiteness helped Black intellectuals in both West Africa and France to destabilize boundaries between imperial systems and the global order in which those empires were embedded.

This chapter examines how Whiteness became a world-gesturing category in France and anglophone West Africa. At both of these vectors of the Black Atlantic, writers sought to capture the global power of Whiteness. As a form of imperial identification constituted on the scale of the world, Whiteness disoriented the spatial and temporal underpinnings of assimilationist hopes. For some Black critics of colonialism, Whiteness fatally undermined the idea that imperial structures and polities could possibly evolve to include their racialized populations on equal terms. For others, less pessimistic about the prospect of imperial reform, the Whiteness of the world nevertheless leavened optimism with suspicion. In both cases, it acted as a reminder that the spatial limits of colonialism—the scalar bounds at which its constitutive affinities operated—could not be restricted to individual imperial systems, despite the claims made by proponents of colonial evolutionism.

As an investigation into Black readings of Whiteness, the following pages can be read as an intellectual history of Whiteness from "below" in the period before the Second World War. They offer a counterpoint to the many studies of White political identification from "above" that have been published in recent decades.[11] The intellectual origins of Whiteness studies, a field of scholarship founded in the United States during the 1990s, are typically traced to twentieth-century African American intellectuals—especially W. E. B. Du Bois and James Baldwin.[12] This chapter expands that prehistory by showing that the origins of the critical analysis of Whiteness were global. Sylvia Wynter remarked about Negritude that it drew attention to "that implicit cultural *blanchitude*" which was "central to the social machine of the world system": a cultural norm "in relation to which all other cultures had been made subservient."[13] During the 1920s and 1930s, drawing attention to the *"blanchitude"* of the world was, for anticolonialists, an act of both explicit and implicit comparison. Seized through the eavesdropped words of its devotees, Whiteness became an object of Black study. Transformed from paean into critique, it helped bring into view the lineaments of a world defined by race.

WHITENESS AND ASSIMILATION IN FRANCE

Two and a half years after the Société de médécine publique warned about the "flood" of immigration threatening France, the Black newspaper *La Race Nègre,* based in Paris, published an article titled "Parliamentary Representation or a Chimeric Panacea?"[14] The article began by observing that, one hundred years after the French colonial conquest, the parliamentary representation offered to Algeria's majority population was still very limited. The question of Algeria's status was being investigated by an interministerial committee. Yet the problem was not technical; it was political *("il est d'ordre politique").*

To demonstrate this point, the article compared the treatment of the Antilles and Réunion—which had been "assimilated" into France in 1848 and their populations thus permitted to elect representatives to the French Parliament—to the treatment of Algeria, where a "hypocritical" assimilation strategy continued to disenfranchise the majority of the Indigenous population. In Algeria, the "political hypocrisy of assimilation" had immediately dissolved in the face of "the burning need to protect the European population against the indigenous 'flood.'" Why should the Algerian case be so different from that of the Antilles and Réunion? Since the assimilation of those small islands in

1848, explained the article, successive conquests had seen the French Empire expand to Tunisia, Indochina, West and Equatorial Africa, and Madagascar:

> A great empire has been established, covering millions of square kilometres and peopled by around 70 million inhabitants, a figure which, by virtue of the vitality of the indigenous races, could be doubled, or even tripled, in the near future.
>
> Here, the politics of assimilation have been brought to a halt; eyes have been opened to their dangers. The colonial population being superior in number to that of the metropole, what will be the politics of France with regard to its immense "possessions"? It can no longer be *assimilatrice;* the politics of association properly understood would lead us to independence; colonialism being only a form of "tutelage."
>
> Inevitably, assimilation will pose the question of political representation in French legislative assemblies: either its full consequences will be accepted or attempts will be made to attenuate them, leading to injustice. Indeed, based on the demographics, the majority of the two chambers would eventually pass onto colonial representatives. *This would lead to a "rising tide of color."* Revenge of the descendants of Ham and Shem! Good people of France, do not worry! I know your "honorables" are unwilling to merrily pave the way for their own political obsolescence.

It was, then, "the menace of a proportional representation"—an empire that no longer assured White dominance—that prevented true colonial reform and accounted for the difference in treatment between Algeria and the Antilles. The article concluded that parliamentary representation, unless it were genuinely proportional, was mere hypocrisy, intended to disguise the fact that colonialism represented "perpetual theft, the violation of the right of peoples to self-determination, the tyranny of the strong against the weak." Hence the opposition of *La Race Nègre* to "assimilationist" demands.[15]

The prominence given in this *La Race Nègre* article to an (unattributed) citation from a contemporary White supremacist writer is striking. "The rising tide of color" is italicized for emphasis, invoked at the apex of the argument against assimilationism, and, unusually, given first in English before being translated into French ("la marée montante des humanités de couleur"). La Race Nègre, with political positions absolutely opposed to those of the Société de médicine publique, nevertheless also found in Lothrop Stoddard's The Rising Tide of Color a convincing argument for understanding the debate over political assimilation in France. The newspaper suggested that Stoddard's preoccupation with preserving White dominance was reflective of Western imperialism, which made it impossible that a French empire with a large non-White majority could be truly democratized. By drawing attention to intra-imperial, racialized solidarity on the scale of the world, La Race Nègre challenged hopeful liberal claims about the "assimilability" of non-White populations into France.

La Race Nègre's insistence on Whiteness also challenged official Communist discourse. Anticolonial politics in interwar Paris are often discussed in terms of the close but fraught relationship of expatriates from Africa, Asia, and the Caribbean with the French Communist Party (PCF). After the First World War, many African and Antillean activists had been drawn to the PCF, which, in striking contrast to the European socialist parties, foregrounded the issue of colonial liberation.[16] A shift away from the Comintern was long in the making—Lamine Senghor took the decision to form a new and specifically Black organization in late 1925.[17] When, starting in May 1934, Moscow ordered the muting of colonial criticism during the Comintern's Popular Front period, the gulf widened. The Communists were "shrewd agents of imperialism," thundered La Race Nègre later that year.[18] Behind this changing language lay a series of organizational splits, often seen as a divide between Communist and Black nationalist factions, with the Ligue de Défense de la Race Nègre (LDRN)—which published La Race Nègre—pushing further into Black nationalism. But this characterization, while not inaccurate, does not capture the content of the LDRN's arguments during this time. The LDRN did not simply retreat into an abstract and hermetic valorization of Blackness. It derived its skepticism of collaboration and critique of assimilation from an analysis of Whiteness, which was understood as underwriting global order and as refracting that order into France.

The increasing skepticism about the possibility of solidarity between Black and White workers expressed in *La Race Nègre* drew accordingly not on essentialist ideas of race, but on the idea of a *generalized basis* for colonial exploitation, by which European workers—and not only their bosses—had been drawn materially into the colonial project. In late 1934, now under Emile Faure's editorship, the newspaper denounced the White "bourgeois parvenu"—"even the communist"—who, "imbued with a sense of his racial superiority," saw travel to the colonies as a way of hauling himself up the class ladder at home.[19] It was often said that colonialism was only in the interests of major capitalist companies, the newspaper stated, while European *populations* were themselves innocent. If this were true, overthrowing the colonial system would be a relatively simple matter, given the trend for "Anglo-Saxon capitalism" to accommodate itself to the granting of formal independence—as evidenced by the United States in Haiti and the Philippines, and the United Kingdom in its dominions. But on the contrary:

> resistance will be strong because the true beneficiary of colonization is a supremely selfish and comfortable being. He is someone who believes that everything is due to him, and who admits no sacrifice except from other people. He is the one who pitilessly destroyed the Redskins of the American continent, the Caribs of the Caribbean, the Kanaks of Australia.
> *The beneficiary* [profiteur] *of colonialism is the European population itself.*
> . . . . The peoples of Europe, too, profit from colonialism. It is to defend the French worker, whose job involves transforming exotic products, that governors combat, whether openly or surreptitiously, all local industries. The housewife is happy to have her oil and chocolate on the cheap. Small households fit themselves out with decent and inexpensive furniture

thanks to the wood of our forests. Those who really believe that the dictatorship of the proletariat would put an end to the voracity of these classes are very naïve indeed.[20]

These late 1934 articles in *La Race Nègre* represent the furthest extent of disillusionment in the European Left across the whole range of Black francophone writing of this period.[21] W. E. B. Du Bois had famously taken a different direction than Lenin in his analysis of imperialism during the First World War. Both saw imperialism as a result of the class conflict that gripped Western powers. But Du Bois emphasized the role of race—and especially Whiteness—in resolving (or at least proroguing) this conflict, by incorporating workers identified as White into the imperialist project. This was why, Du Bois had argued, an increase in the structural power of labor had *not* weakened imperialism, despite Marxist predictions.

Under Emile Faure, *La Race Nègre* took this argument to its fullest extent. Because the "beneficiary of colonialism" was "the European population itself," it was foolish, they argued, to propose a commonality of interests between Europeans—even European workers—and colonized peoples in Africa and the Caribbean. They emphasized in particular the ways in which the colonial service provided a means of class mobility for workers in imperialist countries, an instantiation of the broader sense in which such workers had come to see in the colonies prospects for their own advancement. Images of the destruction of Indigenous populations by European settlers reminded the readers of *La Race Nègre* that European settler colonialism had mobilized Europe's exploited classes for the purposes of colonial rapacity. Underlying national prosperity was an international division of labor.

La Race Nègre's position drew on the Comintern's own analysis, yet extended and reforged it. Lenin had, after all, accepted that "*to a certain degree* the workers of the oppressor nations are partners of *their own* bourgeoisie in plundering the workers (and the mass of the population) of the oppressed nations."[22] And this theme had been taken up in *Le*

Paria, the official newspaper of the Comintern-affiliated Union Intercoloniale. An article published by "Ali Baba" in December 1923 had
explained that while modern imperialism was a result of late-stage
monopoly capitalism, "the European proletariat, before the beginning
of this century, remained impassive in the face of the predatory policy
that was colonial imperialism: the oppression of millions of natives in
exotic countries had maintained a decent standard of living for the
European worker."[23]

For the Comintern, though, this observation did not lead to a theorization of Whiteness as a major obstacle to solidarity between workers
across the imperial divide. By contrast, during the 1930s *La Race Nègre*
found itself radically skeptical of the possibility of such solidarity.
Drawing on the conceptual language of Whiteness, the newspaper
suggested that race underwrote forms of global exploitation to which
even Communists were not immune. A current of this skepticism
endured in anticolonial thinking. Fanon, writing in 1957, would give it
unequivocal expression: "In a colonial country, it used to be said, there
is a community of interests between the colonized people and the
working class of the colonialist country. The history of the wars of
national liberation waged by the colonized peoples is the history of the
non-verification of this thesis."[24]

La Dépêche Africaine and the "White Aristocracy"

With political positions ranging from assimilationist to Communist,
none of the other newspapers published by Africans and Antilleans in
interwar Paris arrived at the same critique of Whiteness as *La Race
Nègre* in 1934. The more regulated and repressed press in French West
Africa was even further from that position. In July 1919, the Dakar-
based newspaper *A.O.F.*—a European-dominated publication whose
editor was the French lawyer Paul Defferre and whose political
director was the Senegalese politician Lamine Guèye—went as far as

denouncing activists who had, for vexatious purposes, made "the question of color" so prominent in the colony.[25]

But if these other newspapers did not agree with La Race Nègre's stark anti-assimilationism, they nevertheless often grappled with Whiteness in ways that have been little noticed in subsequent scholarship. Among the most interesting examples of this engagement comes from La Dépêche Africaine. Founded by the Guadeloupean political activist Maurice Satineau, La Dépêche Africaine was a major Black newspaper in interwar Paris, with a print run of twelve to fifteen thousand—perhaps five times larger than that of La Race Nègre.[26] Its editorial line was reformist rather than radical. T. Denean Sharpley-Whiting emphasizes the role of internal divisions, as well as the official attacks on its early Garveyism, in pushing it in a moderate direction, and Brent Hayes Edwards calls it "without a doubt the most conservative of the interwar Francophone journals in the metropole," though he adds that there was no consistent party line and that Satineau's procolonial editorializing was balanced by other content.[27]

La Dépêche Africaine confronted the question of Whiteness in a way that was less direct than La Race Nègre, but no less significant in its implications. In July 1928, the newspaper published an article titled "L'Aristocratie Blanche Contre les Peuples de Couleur" (The White Aristocracy against the Peoples of Color). The article consisted of a series of extracts from the writing of Paul Morand, the leading French novelist and travel writer whose popularity soared during the interwar period.[28] Morand's work had already been criticized for its exoticist representations of Africa and Blackness by Paulette Nardal in the first issue of La Dépêche Africaine and by Tiemoko Garan Kouyaté in La Race Nègre.[29] But a brief preface to these extracts of his work in La Dépêche Africaine did not reference those critiques. It explained instead that the "esteemed" Morand had been "to the Caribbean, to Louisiana and to the African heartlands, where he studied the living conditions, customs and mores of the blacks, which he accurately described in his new book

La Magie Noire. The brilliant novelist resumed in *Le Journal* his impressions of the journey in the following article, where he demonstrates the lamentable situation in which the great majority of populations of color find themselves."

Next came the extracts from Morand. He began by "affirm[ing] that, compared to the peoples of color, whites—all the whites, including the most miserable—form a privileged aristocracy." Yet he did not proceed to reflect upon this observation in terms of its injustice, as one might have assumed from the prefacing editorial remarks. Instead, he reflected upon its dangerous implications for France as a "white" country:

> For France, everyone knows, is a palace. In front of so many frozen or burning deserts, torrents without water, deadly climates, these crowded [*surpeuplés*] continents where the real proletarian forces are recruited, are our people of the extreme left naive enough to believe that they will be left to live in peace, in their fat Norman lands, on the banks of their rivers full of studs, under their soft southern sun (O greengrocers, "Var Rouge" millionaires!), that they would be allowed to keep these French lands, with barely seventy-eight inhabitants per square kilometer? Do our French Communists know what terrible and relentless brothers they are about to acquire?
>
> Which police force could stop the entry of millions of Blacks [*Noirs*] into a country whose borders have disappeared? What labor regulations will prohibit these overloaded ships of Chinese agricultural laborers coming to exploit every inch of the Cote d'Azur, to enjoy the sweet smell of its sap, to impoverish the soil with their insect-like toil that knows neither night nor day . . . ?
>
> Hardly will our committees of peasants and soldiers have prized power from our bourgeois hands than at their newly rich door will come knocking the famished and terrible Asian migrations of the real poor, the real beggars, for whom communism is not a word or a fad but an eternal, organic state; hordes of aggressively thrust hands and bared teeth, with outstretched arms and gaping jaws.

By reproducing Morand's vision of a "white aristocracy" confronting a deluge of Africans and Asians, *La Dépêche Africaine*—an "assimilationist" newspaper that supported a multiracial vision of French citizenship—showed that it was more attentive to the power of Whiteness to inflect French political discourse than has sometimes been assumed.[30]

Meanwhile, *Le Cri des Nègres*, the newspaper of a Communist splinter group that emerged from the Ligue de Défense de la Race Nègre, explicitly rejected a blanket anti-White hostility. It pointed to Communist defense of the Scottsboro boys in the United States as an example of intraracial solidarity.[31] But when condemning the US occupation of Haiti in 1934, it printed a denunciation of such "colonial fascism"— which earned a comparison to Hitler—as "white imperialism."[32] The short-lived *Le Colonisé*, another "assimilationist" newspaper, found in November 1936 that the line between Nazism and colonial racism was becoming blurred: "In the same way as the Jews, the races of color feel themselves in effect threatened by the storm of racism which sweeps across Germany with so much violence. They fear that tomorrow, other nations—colonizers—will be carried into this odious whirlwind."[33] And Kouyaté's journal *Africa*, which came to represent the view of the "neo-assimilationist" left after Kouyaté had rejected the politics of *La Race Nègre*, nevertheless argued that "the colonial regime was born of war. It is by force that the whites imposed their domination on the men of other races."[34]

Whiteness was cause for reflection in all these newspapers. For some, like the group around the Nardal sisters, it was not understood in a wholly negative light: T. Denean Sharpley-Whiting points out that Paulette Nardal explicitly rejected an outright assault on what she called "the white world in general."[35] But Whiteness nevertheless came increasingly to be contrasted with alternative values and cultures emerging from the African heritage of *assimilés*. "We are fully aware of what we owe to white culture," wrote Paulette Nardal in 1932 in *La*

Revue du Monde Noir, "but we intend to go beyond the framework of this culture . . . to try to give back to our fellows the pride of belonging to a race whose civilization is perhaps the most ancient in the world."[36] Similarly, Aimé Césaire, writing in *L'Étudiant Noir*, mocked the *"Nègre"* who "put himself into the school of the Whites: he wanted to become 'other': he wanted to be 'assimilated.'"[37]

For *La Race Nègre*, political developments during the 1930s—not least the sidelining of anticolonial demands by the Comintern—showed that promises of anti-imperial solidarity from Europe were hollow. Populations of the imperial core, including workers, collaborated in the plunder of African colonies. The consequences for assimilationist politics were clear: "There can be no assimilation between a colonized people and a colonizing people, even less so between an oppressed race, treated as inferior, and the so-called 'superior' race oppressing it."[38] Other newspapers, like *La Dépêche Africaine*, which did not join *La Race Nègre* in this radical stance, nevertheless invoked Whiteness as an idea, a structure of power, and a cultural field. Carrying citational traces from the wider world, Whiteness threatened to destabilize the rigid barriers between *"la plus grande France"* and a more capacious system that lay beyond the country and yet was expressed within its organizing structures and institutions.

Assimilation and Federation: The Scalar Leap of Whiteness

The writing on Whiteness that we find in *La Race Nègre*, among other Black newspapers published in Paris during the 1920s and 1930s, was indicative of a global outlook. It was the *world*, and not only France, that was envisaged as White. This reaching outward was, in part, a response to the transnationality of Whiteness itself. As a view of the world, a conception of the world's hierarchies, a vision of the world's future, and a notion of freedom, Whiteness influenced attempts to define the French nation and its people.[39] One scholar points out perceptively that the racial policies of interwar France cannot simply be read as domestic phenomena, since "racial ideologies were constructed and concretized in a world-system rather than confined to the boundaries of one nation."[40] But the world-system that so preoccupied Africans and Antilleans in interwar Paris is strangely absent from most contemporary studies of African and Caribbean political thought under French colonialism. If scholars in this field sometimes claim to reject methodological nationalism by going beyond the French metropole, their scope typically remains locked onto the French imperial system. Attempts to deprovincialize French history have seldom traversed the borders of the French empire. Absent the scale of the global, the French empire or empire-state is treated as a more or less sui generis polity, generating its own dynamics of race and citizenship that function according to an essentially internal logic. The invisibility of the scale of the world is striking in this work.[41]

La Race Nègre's stark rejection of assimilation brings to mind another body of subsequent research, one which has explored visions of federation between France and its African and Caribbean colonies between 1946 and the collapse of the Fourth Republic in 1958.[42] By exploring the archives of the political negotiations between political leaders— especially Léopold Sédar Senghor from Senegal, and Aimé Césaire from Martinique—and France, these scholars have shown accurately that independent states were not always seen by these politicians as the inevitable or even desirable outcome of decolonization. At various points, leaders like Senghor and Césaire argued for closer association with France as a means of achieving their political ends. Other historians have criticized elements of this argument. They have, for example, suggested that a claimed desire for federation on the part of African and Caribbean politicians can be understood as representing "tactical goals, plausible objectives within a tightly constrained political space," rather than any optimism about French republicanism.[43]

My aim here is not to adjudicate between these positions. It is instead to suggest that some of the arguments about Whiteness we find in

Black newspapers of interwar Paris—especially in *La Race Nègre*—offer an alternative view of imperialism and its possibilities. They do so primarily through a series of starkly different scalar assumptions. Directly challenging the spatiality on which federalist hopes were premised in subsequent decades, they posit that the spatial limits of a racial and colonial order are impossible to contain within any individual imperial system. Contrary to the claims made by proponents of colonial evolutionism, this is a view of empire that centers transnational affinities between empires. These take priority over the putative solidarism that exists within any imperial system.

Conceptualizing France on the scale of the world meant thinking about its interwar ordering and range of possible futures as conditioned and constrained by the transnational affinity of Whiteness. There are interesting concordances between this view and recent reevaluations of race and interwar French colonial policy. Historians have shown how the control, policing, and regulation of immigration in the metropole was matched by a heightened consciousness of race expressed by French colonial officials in Africa, Asia, and the Caribbean. Both tendencies were subtended by the same preoccupation with "assimilability," which placed groups of people in a hierarchy according to their supposed ability to become French. At home and abroad, the French body politic was classified, sorted, and defined. As Elisa Camiscioli has demonstrated, interwar French immigration policy was simultaneously sexualized and racialized. Immigrant labor power—a key imperative of interwar policy—was "evaluated and hierarchized with persistent reference to racial origins" and with a special focus on "a color-based racism."[44] Racial hierarchies and their attendant reproductive practices led to the "proliferation of racialized embodiments," in which intimate bodily practices were projected onto the grand categories of race and nation.[45] An analysis of debates over mixed-race ("*métis*") children in the French empire by Emmanuelle Saada similarly indicates the central role played by race in the definition of French nationality from the 1890s to the 1930s, pointing to the desire for *some* French bodies over others.[46]

The work of these scholars shows how French imperial and citizenship policy, preoccupied with France's place in the world, privileged particular embodiments of Frenchness over others. The central elements of population management in interwar France—immigration control, natalism, citizenship policy—were suffused with the imaginative ordering of populations in terms of race. Assimilation in the French empire had always been sharply attenuated, and metropolitan ambivalence about it long predated the First World War.[47] Raymond Betts has shown how, during the two decades immediately preceding the war, the doctrine of "association" emphasized the need for variation in colonial practice. This argument found powerful expression in works like Jules Harmand's Nietzsche-influenced *Domination et colonization*, published in 1910—a book described by its author as "the systematic repudiation of assimilation."[48] But it was the First World War that provoked a heightened consciousness of race in French colonial policy and discourse. Alice Conklin explains that the key turning point took place during the war itself, when widespread resistance against conscription in the region during 1915–16 coincided with the spread of pan-African and anticolonial ideologies in port cities like Dakar. Colonial officials increasingly came to see race difference as the explanation and separation as the solution. Sexual relations between French and African people—once encouraged—were now condemned; discourse in France on topics like immigrant labor became more overtly racist; and the National Assembly shifted rightwards in the context of the rapid growth of the eugenics, social hygiene, and pro-natalist movements. "In West Africa as in France," writes Conklin, "an intensifying respect for hierarchy in all its forms—social, sexual, and racial—represented the Third Republic's true face in the 1920's." Such beliefs penetrated colonial government in West Africa, as indicated by the systematic use of forced labor.[49]

We have seen, with Dequidt and Forestier's speech at the Institut Pasteur, how race theory from the United States could support anti-immigration arguments in interwar France. The citation of Madison Grant by French government officials during the 1920s may seem distant from the hopes for a post-Second World War federation between France and the territories it occupied in Africa or the Caribbean. But if there were always debates, schisms, and sharp differences in French politics when it came to the future of France's imperial projects and the populations implicated in this history of conquest and expansion, the scale of the world—conceptualizing France's population in relation to global racial lineaments and divisions—did not simply disappear during the 1940s and 1950s.

La Race Nègre was prescient about the ultimate failure of hopes for the transformation of the French republic through imperial democratization. In particular, by emphasizing Whiteness as a reason for the "hypocritical" and partial assimilation that was being debated in 1929, *La Race Nègre* suggested that attempts to understand French colonial policy needed to look outwards, to the global racial order that bounded the possibilities of individual states and imperial systems. Whiteness was always global *and* national—"at once transnational in its inspiration and identifications but nationalist in its methods and goals."[50] And this meant that any attempt to consider the future of a national unit within Europe had to reckon with the global political system in relation to which that nation existed.

WHITE PRESTIGE AND THE LORDS OF THE LOWER WORLD

In British-occupied West Africa, journalists, editors, and intellectuals drew on the concept of Whiteness to destabilize boundaries between the British empire and a global racial order. West African anticolonialists devoted critical attention to racial affinities among Europeans and between Western states and empires. They contended that White solidarities were a hindrance to African progression. A variety of West African writers made reference to "White prestige," a theoretical construct that referred to the idea of White racial supremacy and its consequences in imperial policy.[51] White prestige allowed West African anticolonialists to refer to the ideology underpinning the global racial order. That planetary unevenness was, they argued, the basis for inequalities *within* empires and states. By drawing attention to the forms of intra-imperial affinity that had accompanied the colonization of Africa, Asia, Latin America, and the Caribbean, White prestige showed how the racial bifurcation of the world fastened bodies to the roles they were expected to perform in a planetary division of labor.

Prestige is, according to one scholar of international relations, "the reputation for power."[52] The concept was part of the imperial vocabulary. British colonial officials in West Africa recognized, as one wrote to his wife in 1916, that "the position of every white man, sometimes his life, depends on his caste, his prestige. . . . After all it's only our prestige that keeps these millions of black men in order at all."[53] West African writers used the same concept to describe the alchemy of consent and coercion involved in the exercise of imperial power. White prestige referred to the ideology that legitimized a global disequilibrium in power. It did this by valorizing a planetary aristocracy, both to its beneficiaries and to its victims. White prestige allowed "White folk . . . to imagine they are the only folk who really count in this world" and "to treat the rest of mankind with contempt and arrogance and, on occasion[,] with heartless cruelty."[54]

As a product of imperial self-legitimation and a powerful sedative for the subordinated, the potency of White prestige was, these writers emphasized, fast diminishing in the wake of the First World War. "The great majority of the blacks no longer admire some of the ways of and actions of the white man," explained the *Sierra Leone Weekly News*. "Governors though they are; dominant as a race; and priding themselves as being depositories of great ideas . . . these lords of the lower world might, if they chose to see, [realize] that they are no longer trusted, no longer believed in, no longer loved as before."[55]

White prestige also referred to the determination to retain unjust privileges for a global minority. Operating through forms of psychological subjugation in addition to brute material force, it replaced physical slavery with "mental slavery" in order to impose "a colour bar or race disability"—"a most flagrant injustice" enacted by "Europeans as a race" in order "to keep the black man down" with "artificial barriers."[56] For White settlers in Africa, "the apprehension of the end of the existence of what has become known as white prestige" was "the fear that if the Africans are granted equal political rights and privileges, they will far outnumber the Europeans, and will in time, rule them."[57]

Britain was, explained the *Sierra Leone Weekly News,* "obsessed with the idea of white prestige," and had "based her principle of government" on the suppression of the rights of Black people. Joseph Chamberlain "with his imperialistic notion of colonizing the 'vast open spaces' of Africa and exploiting their great resources for the sole benefit of the white man" had become "the chief apostle of this dangerous school of thought." White prestige meant, in short, that the "white peoples of the Empire were, in effect, to show a united front in an endeavor to make a hewer of wood and a drawer of water of the black man and keep him in his place."[58] This terrible idea of "Prestige" had "been responsible for many strokes of mis-rule and flagitious conduct":

> The deeds of wrong and injustice perpetrated in such centres where treasures lie buried of the earth . . . [and where] Europeans or, to use a more comprehensive word, the white man, [are brought] in contact with the black, particularly that section required in the performance of unskilled labour, may never be fully known; but there is no doubt that very often such ghastly deeds are perpetrated which would shame the very name Civilisation, under whose banner such monsters claim the right to the exercise of control they have so infamously been misused.[59]

Such examinations of White prestige were multifaceted. They connected the material and psychic aspects of White prestige to colonialism, prefiguring anticolonial theory in the post-Second World War period. They assumed the operation of racialized power on a scale beyond any one empire in a manner that helped to explain specific aspects of British imperial policy in West Africa. As "every African student of world events" could see, "the trend" of those events was "to make the world safe, not 'for democracy,' as they used to say during the War, but for white prestige."[60] If White prestige was dominant, it was also fragile, dependent on a kind of mysticism that was fading among Africans.[61] Yet its retreat did not necessarily signal victory for colonized peoples. A vociferous revanchism could be expected. White prestige continued to underpin the world's economic machinery. Born of the shameful and unjust social relations forged in places "where treasures lie buried," it operated as an essential justificatory principle for the endurance of a global aristocracy whose continued wealth required Africans and others to be kept in an underprivileged position in order to secure both their land and labor.

The most systematic examination of White prestige came in a series of articles titled "Our White Friends," published by Kobina Seyki in the *Gold Coast Leader* in 1921–23. A writer, lawyer, and politician born in 1892 in Cape Coast in colonial Ghana, Sekyi is best remembered for his emphasis on the revival of African culture in response to colonialism (he famously vowed never to wear European clothing again); his play *The Blinkards*, which in English and Fante satirized the mimicry of European culture among Africans, remains a seminal work.[62] In "Our White Friends," Sekyi—who was widely read across anglophone West Africa—systematically explored relations between Britain and West Africa. He introduced the series with an extended citation from the metropole: an article in the colonial journal *African World* by J. Withers-Gill, which had criticized the National Congress of British West Africa and defended British imperial policy, particularly in relation to indirect rule.[63] Sekyi subjected the article to a methodical and withering critique. "I am writing about our white friends who are whiter than they are human, the men whose humanity is not even 'sicklied o'er with the pale cast' of colour prejudice, but deeply ravaged by the latter to such an extent that their humanity is very much in danger of being, if it has not already become, exclusively *white*."[64] It was obvious that cause of the hostility of the average White official to the National Congress of British West Africa was "his *amour propre,* graced by him with the name of *prestige*."[65]

Sekyi attacked the expansion of indirect rule, the supercilious attitudes of the British authorities toward Africans ("our white, patronising friends"), and the pompous language used to justify colonial decisions that were, in truth, based simply on profit. Why, after eighty years of the "systematic demoralisation of indigenous institutions," did the British now take these institutions in their "emaciated and moribund condition" and give them "a spurious sort of life" through the Native Jurisdiction Amendment Ordinance of 1910? And why, if the British had been interested in strengthening African institutions, had they historically deported so many West African leaders who had stood in their way? European rule had, he argued, relied principally and ultimately on repression, setting aside reams of florid rhetoric. African institutions had been permitted to exist only to the extent that they could service European needs. The arrival of "half-educated and bigoted" missionaries had led to the disintegration of African institutions and social forces, the suppression of African religions, and the creation of "half-breeds." And colonialism had led to the fetishization of European culture and the ludicrous spectacle of the African imitation of Europeans. All this could be understood in terms of the restriction of the natural course of African development, a process whose outcomes could only be disastrous in the long term.[66]

For Sekyi, White prestige was a superstructure rooted in the economic exploitation of Africa through colonialism. It constituted a whole set of attitudes and beliefs about Africans whose prevalence in England was such that they could not easily be escaped even by those who might not have been personally hostile to Black people:

> There are white men who have the best intentions towards us—that I grant: I met several when I was a student in England; but that does not blind me to the fact that for a very long time to come even these good white men will be, to some extent, subject to the influence of all the undigested thoughts that have been spewed forth by prejudiced or careless writers about the Negro race.[67]

Prestige did not exist only in the colonizing society. It had been diffused among the colonized themselves, manifesting in the imitative behaviors one witnessed among Africans. In that sense it was a form of "credit, that white men have acquired in the minds of most of our own people, for the material development of the Western World." It allowed for the imposition of "badly thought out or malicious schemes, ostensibly for our advancement, but really for our easier exploitation," which had swept a tide of political, cultural, and institutional destruction over West Africa.[68]

West African writers used the idea of White prestige to show how the lineaments of a planetary system of extraction, accumulation, and dispossession were refracted in and through British colonial policy. By referring to colonial officials as White, these writers underlined the racial basis for colonialism. Sekyi's term "our white friends" spread across West Africa as an ironic way of referring to the colonial authorities.[69] More than simply drawing attention to the role of race and racism in imperialism, White prestige emphasized the organizing and commanding role of Whiteness in global order. As with Paris-based anticolonialists, those in interwar West Africa adopted Whiteness as a tool of scalar expansion. Whiteness pointed beyond official colonial discourse—with its emphasis on the "community" of empire and its elision of intra-imperial affinities—towards another, sinister and powerful realm of world politics, in which the structuring order of race was organized around the keystone of White supremacy.

Beyond ontological critique, White prestige also identified a target of anticolonial praxis: the forms of "race science" that argued for the "objective" hierarchization of the world's peoples and promoted scandalous academic theories about Black and African peoples. The Lagos-based *Comet*, edited by Dusé Mohamed Ali, mocked "That Aryan Bogey," ridiculed the average anthropologist as "a highly amusing personage" whose "extraordinary ideas . . . bear no relation whatever to fact," and singled out for attack the "racial superiority mongers."[70] Quoting a racist section of Gustave Ducoudray's *Histoire Sommaire de la Civilisation*, the *Sierra Leone Weekly News* remarked that "when our people read statements of this kind they should remember that they are down at the very sources where the relationship between white and black is being regulated by the white man." The next war, they predicted, would be "for the emancipation of the Negro race: from European philosophizings about the Negro, and from the determination to poison Negro consciousness at the source."[71]

THE WHITE WORLD

In the seventieth stanza of his poem *Cahier d'un retour au pays natal* (Notebook of a Return to My Native Land), originally published in 1939, Aimé Césaire presents a teetering and sclerotic "white world" whose exhaustion is barely concealed by its *amour-propre:*

> Listen to the white world
> horribly weary from its immense efforts
> its rebellious joints cracking under the hard stars
> its blue steel rigidities piercing the mystic flesh
> listen to its proditorious victories touting its defeats
> listen to the grandiose alibis for its pitiful stumblings[72]

Though he was responsible for one of its most arresting formulations, Césaire did not invent the White world. Black writers had long before gleaned the concept from a dominant tradition. For them, the image of a White world drew attention to the intimate relationship between globality and Whiteness. The White world implied not only the brute fact of the color line, but also a deeper and vaster, yet harder to articulate, hierarchy of concepts and ideas underwriting the global racial order. The White world was both a fact—a world-spanning hierarchy based on race—and a collection of principles, ideas, and behaviors that made that world seem natural and inevitable. In a reading of Fanon's later use of the White world, Keguro Macharia insightfully explains that the image refers to both "the world conquered by Europe" and "the systems of being, knowledge, and feeling . . . that subtend that world."[73]

Connecting globality with Whiteness, Black writers exposed at once the vertiginous ambition of race-thinking and its surprising fragility. Advising their audiences to eavesdrop on dominant discourses, they pointed to the demise of a globality defined by Whiteness. By parodying anxious forecasts about the collapse of the White world through mockery, satirical elegy, and overblown declamation, they ironized the literature of decline. Taken together, these references became a tradition—what the African American journalist William Gardner Smith, referring to the poetry of Chester Himes, identified as an "undercurrent of contempt for the white world."[74]

In English and French, the "white world"—a centuries-old literary device for evoking snow-blanketed landscapes—had acquired this secondary meaning, as a planetary racial system defined by Whiteness, at some point in the late nineteenth century.[75] The essay "The Color Line" (1881) by Frederick Douglass was a very early (perhaps the first) example of the White world being invoked in a critical argument about race. Remonstrating against the idea that people are "naturally" offended by the mere sight of dark skin, Douglass asked his readers to imagine a colorless and *literally* white world. "In such a white world," he wrote, "the entrance of a black man would be hailed with joy by the inhabitants. Anybody or anything would be welcome that would break the oppressive and tormenting monotony of the all-prevailing white."[76]

For those with radically opposed political views to Douglass, the White world was not the subject of mockery but of impassioned defense. In 1889, the French journalist Edouard Drumont—a vociferous anti-Dreyfusard, and the author of an ominously popular antisemitic tract, *La France juive* (1886)—published a book titled *La fin d'un monde:* a 556-page prophesy of the end of Western civilization (not excepting France, *"cette nation, si cruellement humiliée"*) at the hands of a Jewish-bourgeois alliance. *La fin d'un monde* presaged a genre of "declinist" literature that warned of the possible collapse of racial order on a specifically global scale.[77] Over the following decades and especially in the wake the First World War, the malaise of the White world was a central and recurring image in works including Madison Grant's *The Passing of the Great Race* (1916), Oswald Spengler's *The Decline of the West* (1918–22) and *The Hour of Decision* (1933), and Lothrop Stoddard's *The Rising Tide of Color* (1920). Stoddard lamented "the frightful weakening of the white World during the war."[78] Spengler asked, in light of the "Coloured Revolution over the whole earth," what "resources of spiritual and material power . . . the white world [could] really muster against this menace."[79] For these writers, the image of a collapsing White world captured a sense of globality as a tectonic racial struggle. This was a politically influential view. In the United States, it helped to justify tightening racial restrictions on citizenship; in France—overseeing an expanded empire and an influx of immigrants—it helped to define who could and who could not become French.[80] Declinism traveled between these empires; its distinctly francophone genre comprised both translations of American texts and those originally written in French.[81] Into the 1930s, *"le monde blanc"* persisted in French political writing.[82]

Yet from its very inception as a political image, the White world was also resonant in Black writing. W. E. B. Du Bois, who was in constant and conflictual dialogue with declinist writing, invoked the "white world" four times in *Souls of Black Folk* (1903), as well as in his essay "The Souls of White Folk" (1910; revised and republished in *Darkwater* in 1920.) In his 1940 autobiography, *Dusk of Dawn*, he would title a whole chapter "The White World."[83] At first, Du Bois used the "white world" to refer to the dominant culture of the United States: it was the society that surrounded but excluded Black Americans, separating itself from them with a "Veil."[84] This was also the sense in which the idea appeared in the work of others, such as in Mary Church Terrell's autobiography *A Colored Woman in a White World* (1940).[85] By the time Du Bois wrote *Darkwater*, however, the "white world" had become fundamentally global in nature and material in basis:

> Rubber, ivory, and palm-oil; tea, coffee, and cocoa; bananas, oranges, and other fruit; cotton, gold, and copper—they, and a hundred other things which dark and sweating bodies hand up to the white world from pits of slime, pay and pay well, but of all that the world gets the black world gets only the pittance that the white world throws it disdainfully.[86]

Though it is virtually never placed, by the *Cahier*'s interpreters, in the context of previous Black Atlantic representations of the White world, Césaire's expended but unyielding White world has much in common with that tradition.[87] The *Cahier* draws attention, as other uses of the term did, to the White world's exhaustion and its pitiful attempts at self-legitimation. Like them, it calls for eavesdropping on the White world. And the mocking tenor of the subsequent stanza— "Pity for our omniscient and naïve conquerors!"—echoes a tradition of ironic reference to the white world.[88] Yet we should also be attentive to the ways in which images like the White world have shifted across different kinds of writing. The *Cahier*'s "white world" is not straightforward. Perhaps more than any other representation of the White world, it deliberately resists visualization, as if to complicate the idea that the Whiteness of the world can be logically or sensorily comprehended.[89]

From a White World to a Black Planet

Between the world wars, Black writers, journalists, editors, poets, and political activists in both France and British-occupied West Africa invoked Whiteness as a world-encompassing force that shaped the lives of those involved in the colonial encounter on an intimate scale.[90] The Jamaican poet Claude McKay, running into trouble with the colonial authorities in Morocco, felt that "even in Africa I was confronted by the specter, the white terror always pursuing the black. There was no escape anywhere from the white hound of Civilization."[91] Writing about the "rise of the Black Internationale" in opposition to "the White Internationale," the African American writer George Schuyler depicted the "New Negro" as "the Damoclean sword dangling over the white world," "containing vast potentialities of which the white world is all too painfully cognizant."[92] It is surprising, then, that so little attention has since been paid to this insistent conjoining of Whiteness and the world in Black writing. This is a topos whose articulation has not been limited to European languages, as the Yoruba saying *"Aiye d'aiye Oyinbo"*—the world has become a White man's world—suggestively indicates.[93]

After the Second World War, the White world resurfaced repeatedly in Black writing on colonialism. Frantz Fanon suggested that his *Black Skin, White Masks* (1952) was at bottom about "the problem of the man of colour in the white world."[94] Fanon concluded the book with the forceful assertion that "there is no white world, there is no white ethic, any more than there is a white intelligence."[95] Giving an account of the Congress of Black Writers and Artists, which was held in Paris in 1956, James Baldwin speculated that it was only in relation to "the white world" that a common Black identity existed.[96] But he, too, rejected the existence of the White world. "I attest to this: the world is not white; it never was white, cannot be white," he said in a speech he gave in 1980. "White is a metaphor for power, and that is simply a way of describing Chase Manhattan Bank."[97] As an image conveying the intimate relation between race and globality, the White world has found repeated and insistent articulation in Black Atlantic political writing.[98] But so too has its obverse and alternate horizon. The Black planet, Public Enemy's famous provocation in 1990, has become a way of referencing a different relationship between race and the world: one whose looming realization merely awaits the White world's inevitable destruction, thus finally fulfilling the centuries-old nightmares of declinist writers.[99]

4

THE BODY AND THE WORLD

IN LATE JANUARY 1920, the *Gold Coast Leader* observed with alarm "the great influx of Europeans into our country."[1] West Africa's climate had, only a few years earlier, been considered so ill-suited to European health that it was notorious as "the white man's grave." But today, "by dint of persever-ance and scientific skill on the part of the Europeans the climate is now spoken of in favourable terms and for that reason our country is being flooded by white men of all grades on commercial pursuits and acquisitions." Remind-ing its readers that "very good climates" in Africa had been associated with places where "the Europeans have gone and made themselves masters of the land and thereby put the original inhabitants of the country into the back-ground," the *Gold Coast Leader* concluded with two confronting ques-tions: "WHAT WILL BECOME OF WEST AFRICA IN TIME TO COME? AND AGAIN WHAT WILL BE THE POSITION OF THE INDIGENOUS NATIVE?"[2]

Two years later, the West African newspaper found more evidence for the "the vigorous rush of the white races to Africa" in the British press.[3] It reprinted, "for our readers to mark and digest," long sections from an article about Kenya in the London *Outlook*. In these excerpts, Kenya was presented as an extremely promising frontier for British settlers, boasting a bucolic and hopeful plateau: "very like an English park, and . . . populated by myriads of animals":

> Except for the nomadic savage, it lies empty of mankind, as did the Western prairies of America fifty years ago. It is a virgin land, awaiting the coming of the white man, ready to nurture and breed a great race, to rival in wealth and population the Mississippi Valley. This is our heritage, the refuge of our teeming millions whom it is doubtful whether our industrial system at home can much longer support. It is the "last white-man's country" yet undeveloped and suitable for Englishmen to conquer.

For the London-based *Outlook*, there was no real future for Africans in Kenya. The only question was whether Kenya was "to be white or brown." Either way, the struggle was likely to be violent. For the "rule of a few men of one race over many thousands of another must always, whether we like it or not, depend in the last resort on force. We govern India by force, and we govern the natives of East Africa by force."[4]

The same year that the *Gold Coast Leader* republished these commentaries from London, which imagined African land as feminized and virginal, awaiting the thrusting, masculine, reproductive power of "the white man," the *Sierra Leone Weekly News* reprinted long sections of another metropolitan commentary on Africa. From the British journal *United Empire*, this saw in Africa a salvation for the war-ravaged economies of Europe, especially now that medical advances had pacified the previously inhospitable and recalcitrant territories outside the known temperate zones:

> We can no longer afford to neglect those tropical areas which nature has endowed with lavish hand. Tropical medicine has made vast strides during

the last decade, so that jungle fever no longer possesses the same terrors, and the tropics may yet come to be regarded as a health resort during certain months of the year when they will be within a day or two's aeroplane journey from Europe. Europeans may then possess and manage vast estates in tropical areas, returning at the end of the season to temperate climes to recoup.

Europe could now develop "vast areas of Africa" where limitless land was available. In the process, "unlimited demands will be put upon labour and the *dolce far niente* of the African native is doomed to disappear. Africa must awaken from its torpor and by wise policy and sound counsel."[5]

West African journalists reprinted these articles from the British press to give their readers a sense of the imperial uncertainty regarding the existential future of Africans in their own lands. Hopeful visions of mass English settlement in Nigeria, Ghana, and Sierra Leone—displacing or otherwise dominating the African inhabitants—may have represented only a peripheral section of British elite opinion. But their presentation to West African audiences as what the *Leader* called "the naked truth" was not simply sensationalism. It constituted a profound reckoning with the radically destabilizing potential of colonialism. This sense of existential threat was reflected elsewhere across the Black Atlantic: magazines, newspapers, books, and novels, in different ways, undermined the idea that colonialism might lead to stability for those living as the subjects of imperial rule. Black Atlantic anticolonialists suggested that the future under colonialism for Black peoples was freighted with a radical instability far from progressive development or modernization: "We do not know what coming years may bring."[6]

Many have, in recent decades, turned their attention to what the historian Albert Hurtado called "the intimate frontiers" of empire. They have shown how relations between colonizer and colonized were not restricted to military barracks, police headquarters, courts, prisons, and schools, but included those spaces—"kitchens, bedrooms, and nurseries"—in which colonialism, knotting together gender and race, structured and policed intimacies.[7] The work produced by these scholars illuminates the ways in which colonial authority intersected with the scale of the body. An always-gendered process in which conquest, desire, and sex were enmeshed, the psyche of colonial expansion saw to-be-conquered territory represented as lasciviously female and subject races conceived as sexually deviant, even monstrous.[8] At the same time, the emphasis of this writing tends to be on the history of colonialism rather than on the intellectual history of anticolonialism. Its insights about imperialism's intimate effects are typically not those theorized by the colonized themselves, but those which we can read post-facto *into* the archives of colonial encounter.

In this chapter, I seek to show that colonialism's corporeality can also be thought about with reference the anticolonial archive.[9] Reading texts produced in Paris and anglophone West Africa, I find that, rather than looking at the intimate relations between the colonizer and colonized, Black interwar writing often examined intimacy in another light: that of one's own personhood in relation to the vast and apparently impersonal scale of global order. This writing suggested that the condition of colonization produced—for those interpellated as Native—a radical bodily instability, which contrasted sharply with the corporeal security granted to settlers under a colonial order. Such instability was expressed in this writing with two distinct ideas: first, the idea that colonialism was eliminationist, leading ineluctably to the destruction of Black people; and second, the idea that the Black body was defined at once by its loneliness and its labor. My contention is that these two sets of images produced an understanding of the world by conceptualizing the Black body in relation to that world. If a global racial order made itself visible on the skin and in the sensations of that body, it also threatened that body with ontological uncertainty and decline—even disappearance. It was through this body-world dialectic, then, that Black anticolonialists conceptualized how the world was ordered by race.

In poetry, novels, and newspapers, Black Atlantic writers investigated colonialism's effects on the body. But they did so with what might seem a paradoxical emphasis on the scale of the world. These textual conjoinings of the body and the world have a bearing on much later, and even apparently distinct, questions about the imprint of power on flesh. Predating Fanon's coinage of "epidermalization" to describe racism's sensory inscription and more recent attempts "to reclaim the atrocity of flesh as a pivotal arena" in Black politics, such arguments were not simply proleptic.[10] They derived from a critical reading of imperial debates and the formulation of literary images connecting the colonized body to a hierarchical global order. In different ways, they represented a series of textual *methods* for accessing international political theory, enacting the jumping of scales between the body and the world, and conveying the effects of colonial rule—at once radically destabilizing and powerfully intimate—on the racialized body.

These texts from the 1920s and 1930s indicate some of the ways in which Black writers were preoccupied with the corporeal and existential ramifications of colonialism—what David Lloyd calls the "lapse of the subject into object"—several decades before Fanon's landmark book *Black Skin, White Masks* appeared in 1952. Racism's ability to shape bodily experiences (to make the Black man feel "the weight of his melanin," in Fanon's phrase) extended to the very possibility of that body's ontological existence under a sovereign, and always potentially exterminationist, colonial regime.[11] The politics of the Black subject was therefore tied to intertwined global processes of accumulation, imperialism, dispossession. If the body was a site at which a world-spanning colonialism operated—provoking experiences like confinement, starvation, loneliness—its subjecthood was not wholly reducible to the effects of colonialism. This would have been to sap the colonized subject of interiority.[12] Instead, these writers drew attention to the ways in which the very existence of the Black subject was bound up with the operation of colonialism on a world scale.

The Negritude movement of the 1930s was not the first organized Black intellectual response in Paris to French colonialism. What Christopher Miller called "a fractious vanguard of black intellectuals"—foremost among whom stood Kojo Tovalou Houénou and Lamine Senghor—wrote original political texts confronting the colonial order and Blackness, which preceded the poetry of Aimé Césaire, Léopold Sédar Senghor (no relation to Lamine), and Léon-Gontran Damas.[13] In recent years, these earlier writings have been more comprehensively analyzed and claims made about the novelty of the Negritude pioneers have been thrown into doubt, particularly in light of the unwillingness of those poets to recognize their own precursors.[14] My interest here, though, is a *shared* preoccupation between these generations of Black critics in Paris in delineating colonialism's effects on the body.

Here is *La Race Nègre* making a case, in February 1932, for why anti-colonialism is a struggle for the very existence of Black peoples:

> This struggle for independence and the complete return of our old, well-tested, forms of organizing, is, for black people [*nègres*], a question *of life or death. To be or not to be,* that is the only question that presents itself. For the European, the black countries are above all territories intended for settlement [*repeuplement.*] The native is part of the current, picturesque fauna, destined to rapidly disappear. In the European's evocations of the future of our countries there is no more place for us than for lions, gazelles, or scorpions.
>
> According to a journalist who recently conducted a major investigation of the French possessions in the Pacific, an island where only natives live is, for the European, a *deserted* island. As he explains: "The arrogance of white men is so great that an island peopled exclusively by blacks *cannot* be considered by them to be an inhabited island."
>
> . . . The destruction of the blacks is taking place at an accelerated pace. We won't invoke the astronomical figures revealed by the statistics: each one of us carries the memory of a populous region where today not a

single person remains; some race of which not a single representative has survived; a once-great city today in ruins and uninhabited.

It won't be long, if we persist in our passivity, before Africans become—like the Red-Skins and the Australian Kanaks—a mere memory.

The struggle to save ourselves is only a question of years. It is now that we must react.[15]

Headlined (in English) "To be or not to be," the article thus proclaimed the threat of destruction and replacement to be the greatest danger facing Africans under colonial rule. It argued that European colonialism, by amalgamating colonized peoples and wildlife, established sovereign authority over both human and nonhuman bodies in the territories it seized.[16]

This argument may appear overstated in relation to French imperial policy in Africa. But it is essential to consider the context in which it was made: a period of interwar flux, during which former certainties and previous boundaries were suddenly cast into doubt. As historical reassessments of the interwar period have shown, colonial "settlement remained a crucial part of imperial domination" into the twentieth century.[17] France was no exception. While at the end of the nineteenth century, settler colonies (colonies de peuplement) were considered by French policy-makers undesirable—the French citizenry was too attached to French soil, and most of France's colonies were located in tropical climates "largely unsuited to white populations"—by the interwar period, French settler communities in Africa had nevertheless materialized.[18] Seeking to expand their power in the metropole, they found a voice in right-wing organizations of the interwar period like Action Française. Charles Maurras was just one high-profile intellectual who "praised settler communities as the embodiment of a lost patriotic virtue based on powerful masculinity, ardent Catholicism, and attachment to the soil." By 1939, over 20 percent of the French colonial service was recruited from these settler populations.[19]

The backdrop to La Race Nègre's allusions to colonial genocide in Africa was, then, this changing dynamic of settler power in the interwar French empire. The fact that settler frontiers were never truly closed was a reminder of the totalizing view of European settlers, who saw everything that predated them in the colonized territory as ripe for replenishment: both "Native" and "fauna" were aspects of the same "nature" that had to be dominated or swept away. With this analysis, *La Race Nègre* foreshadowed a much later critical understanding of settler colonialism as grounded in a form of Cartesian dualism. As the theorist Patrick Wolfe explains, the nature/Native relationship underlying colonialism's *longue durée* meant that "colonised peoples could be assimilated to nature, placing them on the receiving end of Cartesian dualism and, accordingly, as in need of control" because they had "failed to disembed themselves from nature."[20] A branch of feminist theory has also been premised on a critique of the Cartesian notion of nature as the basis of an interrelationship between science and patriarchy.[21]

In addition to his articles in *La Race Nègre*, Lamine Senghor—the Senegalese communist and pan-African militant—propagated his radical critique of colonialism's extirpatory potential elsewhere. He published, for example, a didactic allegory about the impact of French colonialism on Africa.[22] *La violation d'un pays* (1927) warned Africans of the example ("What an example!") of "red men . . . destroyed by the whites [*pales*] whose invasion they had resisted until the end, until the last unit of their race."[23] The same year, he was involved in the publication of a series of Joint Resolutions on the Negro Question at the Brussels-based conference of the League Against Imperialism. These resolutions framed the "Negro question" in global perspective, comparing the relentless spread of European colonial power across the African continent to the legally sanctioned racism in the southern United States. Both were seen as structures of potential *elimination*, and not only of subjugation. In Kenya and Sudan, "the expropriation of lands" was tied to "the extermination of people"; in the United States, a host of oppressions—"banishment, servitude, legal injustice, debt and peonage, lynching and savage violence"—worked not only to "degrade" their subjects, but to "annihilate" them.[24]

Senghor died in late 1927. But his sweeping critique of colonialism was apparently vindicated when Mussolini's Italy invaded Ethiopia in 1935. Here was a Fascist European state embarking on a new conquest and settlement project in Africa, extinguishing one of the world's only sites of recognized Black sovereignty. In his newspaper *Africa,* Tiemoko Garan Kouyaté drew attention in 1935 to "the fascist leaders' imperialist wish to hold political power" in East Africa "in order to exterminate at their leisure the Blacks and to substitute them for Italians." As evidence, he pointed to Italian policy in North Africa. "Has not the general Graziani, of sinister reputation, entirely destroyed the inhabitants of the Green Mountain in Libya? Were not 80,000 Arabs of Tripolitana deported in 1931, contrary to their rights to the soil of their ancestors?"[25] Elsewhere, Kouyaté warned of "the extermination of our race" in "a new war, without equal in the annals of human history."[26]

During the 1930s, Fascist Italy and Nazi Germany brought settler frontiers into Europe and expanded them in Africa. Debates over Madagascar as a possible outlet for Jewish emigration pointed to the endurance of Africa as a virgin land in the European imagination. The threat of renewed German control over colonies in Africa was a reminder that its campaigns of genocidal violence in southwest Africa could be resumed.[27] For many, these political developments pointed to the merits of Senghor and Kouyaté's analysis. In 1936, articles in *Le Colonisé* remarked upon the language of appeasement issuing from some quarters in France (including from "erstwhile friends") with a sense of amazement and betrayal, while remarking that an application of Hitler's ideas threatened to reduce all colonized peoples—Jewish and non-Jewish alike—to the rank of slaves.[28]

Achille Mbembe writes about the "desire for extermination," which he calls elimininationism, that animates colonial war and gives it its borderless, lawless nature. Driven in large part by racism, he suggests that this desire can be understood as necropolitical in its wholesale and organized destruction and in the compulsion to loss and the cheapening of human and nonhuman life. If sovereignty's major expression lies in its power to permit and deny life, the function of necropolitical racism gestures to the inverse of sovereignty: the "loss of rights over one's body," especially for "those human bodies deemed either in excess, unwanted, illegal, dispensable, or superfluous."[29] In relating the history of European settlement in the Americas and Australasia to the ongoing seizure of land in eastern and southern Africa, Lamine Senghor and Tiemoko Garan Kouyaté may not have seemed to be writing directly about the body. But their analyses were proleptic of a reading of colonial sovereignty as necropolitical. With others, they argued that the tragedies endured by populations under European settler colonialism were profoundly relevant to Black politics on a global scale. Suffusing this argument was a conception of the world as hierarchical, divided into zones of White life and Black death, and an understanding of colonialism as bringing death to the racialized body under its crushing sovereign power. Colonial subjection, in this view, always carried the threat of elimination for the subject peoples of European imperialism (hence Mbembe's suggestion that it is characterized by an eliminationist drive.) For these subject peoples, colonialism brought an uncertain and fractured relationship with land, space, and the very possibility of a future, threatening to overwrite their spatiotemporal existence with a settler sovereignty.[30]

"We Are Nothing but Bodies to Be Taxed"

Writing in *Légitime Défense*, a Marxist-surrealist intervention published on June 1, 1932 by a group of Martinican students living in Paris, René Ménil condemned what he saw as the imitative style of Black writers in French. In contrast to Black writers in English like Langston Hughes and Claude McKay, he argued, those writing in French had avoided important themes, like "the feeling of the loneliness of the black man all over the world" [*sentiment de solitude du noir à travers le monde*] and the expression of "revolt against the injustices he suffers."[31] Ménil's use of the term "loneliness" is striking. It prefigures a scene in Richard Wright's novel *Lawd Today!*, written three years later in 1935, in which a humiliated man "felt the loneliness of his black skin."[32] It also foreshadows Aimé Césaire's famous description of Toussaint Louverture in *Cahier d'un retour au pays natal* (Notebook of a Return to My Native Land), published in 1939 in which Toussaint's loneliness is emphasized:

> What is mine
> a lonely man [*un homme seul*] imprisoned in
> whiteness
> a lonely man [*un homme seul*] defying the white
> screams of white death
> (TOUSSAINT, TOUSSAINT L'OUVERTURE)[33]

And it is a description which reappears, a few years later, in Léopold Sédar Senghor's 1945 poem "Neige sur Paris," recalling images of racial injustice that include:

> The hands that whipped the slaves, that whipped you
> The powdery white hands that slapped you, the
> painted powdered hands that slapped me
> The sure hands that have delivered me to loneliness
> [*solitude*] to hatred.[34]

The image of the lonely Black body corresponds to a sensory experience in which "the body is at once sequestered and forcefully given space," as Ato Sekyi-Oto writes with reference to Fanon.[35] It also suggests continuities between the political writing of *La Race Nègre* and the literary writing of the figures associated with Negritude (I leave aside here West African newspapers, which also complained of colonialism's desire to "keep the black man by himself").[36] In different ways, both

types of writing were preoccupied with the imprint of the global structure of race on the intimate scale of the body.[37] In contrast to the proponents of Whiteness—who saw utopian future worlds springing from
the European male body—this approach drew attention to the ways in
which race vitiated and obviated the racialized body, turning it into a
machine for work, a vanishing feature of a colonial landscape, or an
isolated object surrounded by hostile blankness.

Theorists of colonialism and race have repeatedly returned to the
body, seeking to show how it is degraded, mechanized, and transformed in the racial vision associated with colonial power, and how it
therefore becomes what Mbembe calls "a worldless and soilless body, a
body of combustible energy, a sort of double of nature that could,
through work, be transformed into an available reserve or stock."[38] For
Patrick Wolfe, the intimate scale of the body and the impersonal scale
of the world are yoked together through race, which "recruits biology
to install the international division of labour at the level of individuals'
own sensory experience."[39] Katherine McKittrick has written about
the "territorialization" of the "racial-sexual" body, which marks it as
"decipherable and knowable—as subordinate, inhuman, rape-able,
deviant, procreative, placeless."[40] A Janus-faced approach to the body
under regimes of colonial rule becomes apparent in this theoretical
writing. At once required for labor and destined for replacement, the
racialized body inhabits a space of deep uncertainty, problematized by
its relationship to the land that empire always seeks ultimately to
possess.[41]

Nowhere are these themes more apparent than in the novel *Batouala,*
which was published in 1921 by the colonial civil servant René Maran.
Maran, who was from Martinique (and whose parents were Guyanese),
worked for the colonial service in French Equatorial Africa (AEF). The
success of *Batouala*—the first novel by a Black person to win the Prix
Goncourt—catapulted Maran out of government employment and into
public life.[42] Breaking with the exoticism of the colonial novel, *Batouala*

portrays Europeans in Africa as violent intruders through the eyes of its eponymous protagonist. For "in the language of the whites," thinks Batouala to himself early in the novel, "work took on a very strange meaning. It meant getting tired without achieving immediate or tangible results, it meant trouble, annoyance, suffering, the squandering of health, the pursuit of imaginary ends."[43] Later in the novel, during a fiery speech, Batouala denounces "the whites," exclaiming:

> We are nothing but bodies to be taxed [des chairs à impôt]. We are nothing but beasts of burden. Beasts? Not even. A dog? They feed dogs, and take care of their horses. Us? We are less than these animals, we are the lowest of the low. They are slowly killing us.[44]

Maran's preface to the novel bitterly ironized the civilizing mission:

> After all, if [the Natives] die of hunger by the thousands, like flies, it is because their country is being developed [met en valeur]. Only those who do not adapt themselves to civilization disappear. Civilization, civilization, pride of Europeans, and their charnel-house of innocents. . . . You build your kingdom on corpses.[45]

Maran was pressured to resign from his post in Chad in April 1923. He became a central figure among the Black intelligentsia of Paris, continuing to write critically about French colonialism in the pages of Les Continents. Batouala became influential for a generation of Black writers, including the proponents of Negritude. Maran was visited regularly at his home by Léopold Sédar Senghor, Damas, and Césaire; Senghor famously identified him as the precursor to the movement.[46] And Maran's characterization of colonialism as transforming Africans into taxable flesh and "beasts of burden" found resonance in the early writings of those figures. In Senghor's poem "Prière de paix," included in his 1945 collection Chants d'ombre, a narrator examines his conflicting feelings towards France. He invokes godly forgiveness for France; at the same time, he is forced to acknowledge that

she too like some northern cattle
rustler raped my children to swell the cane and cotton
fields, for negro sweat is like manure.[47]

In Césaire's *Cahier*, first published in 1939, a series of images confront the reader with the relationship between Blackness and labor. The narrator of the *Cahier* finds "not an inch of this world devoid of my fingerprint / and my calcaneum on the spines of skyscrapers and my filth in the glitter of gems!," invokes "a hundred years of whip / lashes," and ventriloquizes a racist:

the smell of *nègres*, that's-what-makes-cane-grow
remember-the-old-saying:
beat-a-*nègre*, and you feed him.

And—in a section during which "childish fantasies" about Africa are spurned—the narrator exclaims that "the only unquestionable record we broke was that of endurance under the whip."[48] Ancient lineages of African labor are also invoked in the writing of the Haitian poet and Communist Jacques Roumain, such as in these lines from "Bois d'ébène" (Ebony Wood, 1944):

Here for your voice is an echo of flesh and blood
black messenger of hope
           for you know all the songs of the world
ever since those of the Nile's immemorial workpits.

Each word reminds you of the weight of Egyptian stones
and the muscle of your misery erected columns of temples
The way a sob of sap raises the stalks of reeds.[49]

Like Maran's *Batouala*, each of these texts posits a relationship between Black corporeal experience—characterized either as a "body" (*corps*) or as "flesh" (*chair*)—and unfree labor. Senghor and Césaire make use of the same image: the sweat of Black people physically fertilizing crops. Roumain's "sob of sap" erecting "the stalks of reeds," also invokes forced agricultural labor, the stalks suggestive of sugar cane. Césaire's skyscrapers, imprinted with the heel-bone of the narrator, expose the role of that labor in the urban metropolis. Across these texts, the body as a site of meaning transcends the French imperial state: the smallest of political scales, the body brings into view a planetary order and its concomitant hierarchies of labor. The global is produced *through* Black labor; it cannot exist without that labor.[50]

In their images of exploitation, these poems resonate with the reclamation of the word *"nègre"* by Lamine Senghor. By reclaiming the term, he argued that Black militants could make visible the exploitation of Black labor by refusing to see themselves as bourgeois "men of color" who could dissociate themselves from "those who are exploited in the cotton fields of the Niger valley" and "the sugarcane cutters in the plantation fields of Martinique and Guadeloupe."[51] What was evident, he suggested in *La Voix des Nègres,* was that "when we are needed, to get killed or to be put to work, we are French; but when it comes to giving us rights, we are no longer French, we are negroes."[52] Notwithstanding its growing distance from the French Communist Party, *La Race Nègre* continued to stress the labor-based exploitation of colonialism: there was a continuum, it suggested, between the exploitation of and the extinguishing of Black life. "To work black people to death, to make super-profits at our expense, to plunder the riches of our countries—this is what the colonial project comes down to."[53]

The image of the *lonely* Black body underlined the isolation of race, powerfully conveyed in Césaire's depiction of Toussaint Louverture in the vast whiteness of the Jura Mountains. The image of the *laboring* Black body, by contrast, suggested the potentially unifying power of race for those subjected to its exploitation. In each case, references to the body helped to locate and explain race. If the idea of loneliness brings to mind a sense of isolation that is geographically located in space—what McKittrick has described as "a landscape of systemic blacklessness"—shared histories of unfree labor also point to the interrelationship between African dispersal and the grandiose architecture of Western cities.[54] Compare this with Anna Julia Cooper's claim, in an essay written in 1891–92, that "what the dark man wants then is merely to live his own life, in his own world."[55] Loneliness has come to carry connotations of a kind of humiliating emasculation and a sense of the collapse of self-worth. Yet these images—of Black sweat fertilizing crops, and of Black bodies being taxed, worked, and exploited— also reflect another act of the spatial imagination: as with the insistence on identifying Whiteness (chapter 3), they imaginatively traverse the boundaries of the French empire-state, connecting bodily and planetary scales in a manner that transcends the national-imperial unit.

SPECTERS OF SETTLEMENT IN WEST AFRICA: ON THE PROSPECT OF COLONIAL EXTIRPATION

In his book *Native Life in South Africa* (1916), Solomon Plaatje, who cofounded the organization that would become the African National Congress, described how European land acquisition in South Africa carried grave consequences for Native peoples. His book meticulously conveyed the progressive diminishment of rights for Africans in areas of large-scale European settlement. But West Africa did not seem to be one of those areas. Conventional wisdom in Europe had implied that the region was protected from settlement because its climate was disastrous for Europeans. In July 1919, the British colonial journal *West Africa* cautioned the British to "beware of the error of supposing that a policy towards the African races of tropical Africa can safely be based upon what has, so far been found possible in South Africa and Rhodesia, where the European can live and rear his young."[56] Predicting the future of "white settlement" in 1922, the Australian geographer and racial cartographer Griffith Taylor confirmed that "the hot wet regions of the tropics" possessed a "climate [that] is quite unsuited for close white settlement or indeed for any white settlement requiring constant manual labor."[57]

Yet these certainties did not endure. During the interwar period, newspapers and books across British-occupied West Africa were full of concern about the possibility of European settlement in the region. They compared forms of settler colonialism across time and space. They asked if West Africans might one day suffer a fate similar to that of Native peoples in the Americas or Australasia—or, closer to home, the dispossessed peoples of southern or eastern Africa. A profound uncertainty arose about the existential endurance of African peoples in the context of European settlement in Africa. This anticolonial sentiment does not fit easily into the picture that emerges from most histories of nineteenth- and twentieth-century colonialism. Historians have documented the impulse for settlement that accompanied colonialism starting in the sixteenth century, promoted by governments, social reformers, penal administrators, and private business interests. They have identified a "settler revolution": a nineteenth-century "tsunami" that "turned whole continents white."[58] They have pointed to the importance of settler colonialism as a vital ingredient in the racialization of international politics.[59] They have excavated a seam of pro-settlement "Anglo" international thought.[60] And they have demonstrated the protractedness of nineteenth-century settler conquests, the porousness of settler frontiers, and the endurance of settler projects well into the twentieth century.[61] These insights accord with the growing attention that has been paid to "unfinished" settler projects in Africa—Algeria, Kenya, Southern Rhodesia, Mozambique, and Angola—all of which precipitated major twentieth-century decolonizing conflicts.[62]

But these studies of settler colonialism overwhelmingly restrict themselves to territories in which settlement was, on its own terms, successful. Even in revisionist work, which has emphasized the porousness of settler frontiers, both West Africa and the Caribbean are more or less invisible because no significant European settlement took place in those regions.[63] By contrast, West African interwar writing suggests a way of thinking about settler colonialism that is not limited to the strictly empirical reality of settlement, but which invokes the ideological firmament under which settler projects descended on specific territories. In English- and French-language writing, in West Africa and Paris, the ontological security of Black and African peoples was destabilized through the prospect of settler sovereignty.[64] The prospect of settler-led displacement—always inherent to a colonial order—was dissolved into an anticolonial structure of feeling, which found expression in the work of writers, political activists, editors, and journalists across the Black Atlantic during the 1920s, 1930s and 1940s. It shows us how the ideology and practice of earthly repeopling preoccupied anticolonial thought even in territories that seemed distant from the most egregious examples of settler practice. Seeing the Black body in relation to the world was partly a response to the imaginative and propagandistic literatures produced in Europe regarding the prospect of expanding settlement in Africa. It represents, however, more than a simple transfer of pro-settler propaganda into anti-settler anxiety. By considering descriptions of the replaceability of African bodies alongside examples of current and historic European colonial practice, West African writing identified the prospect of extirpation as integral to a colonial order.

"The Visiting White Alien to Tropic Shores"

We have seen that some London-based publications advocated reopening settler frontiers during the 1920s, sometimes specifically pointing to West Africa. Their arguments, pointedly reprinted in the West African press, were premised on developments in tropical medicine and on the essential replaceability of the African "native." Going into the 1930s, the *Sierra Leone Weekly News* continued to find evidence of this discourse in the British press. It presented an argument by the British politician, diplomat, and editor Lord Lothian (originally published in

The Listener, a London-based magazine), against the commonly held belief that "the white race cannot settle in the tropics." Lothian was sure that science would discover "how to temper the rigours of the tropics to the European mind and body." It was therefore "only a question of time for both Europe and Asia to overflow into Africa." Africa, "the largest of all the continents except Asia," was, after all, "extraordinarily thinly populated":

> Nothing, in my opinion, can prevent the ever-increasing settlement of Europeans and Asiatics in Africa. It may come slowly or it may come fast. But it will come. North and South America, Australia and New Zealand have been filled by the overflow of Europe—transported not by political but by economic forces. Exactly the same process will happen in Africa also, as its resources are opened up.[65]

These predictions about a European deluge into Africa came alongside concrete shifts in colonial policy in the region. The spread of indirect rule, the racial narrowing of the colonial service, a ceiling on African participation in government, racial hierarchies in pay and conditions, an increase in British personnel, developments in tropical medicine, the privileging of expatriate capital—all could be interpreted as working to establish a "color bar" in West Africa, such as already existed elsewhere on the continent in territories targeted by European settlers.[66] In 1925, the *Gold Coast Leader* warned that "the only thing that will save Imperial interests in Africa will be the West-Africanisation of Africa East and South rather than a halting policy which leans toward the East-Africanisation of West Africa."[67] Yet "East-Africanisation" remained an ever-present threat, embodied in what *The Comet* called "the visiting White alien to tropic shores."[68]

The *Gold Coast Leader* argued that West Africa might look like South Africa—and its Indigenous peoples would have been similarly dispossessed—if malaria had not made Europeans reluctant to settle in the region. "Even as things are," the newspaper added, "we have to be cir-

cumspect, since we do not know what coming years may bring."[69] In Freetown, the views of "a progressive European" on the perplexing endurance
of Africans were quoted: "We shall exterminate its ravenous beasts, abolish malaria, build houses cooled by electricity and freed from the million
insect pests, but we cannot exterminate the African—he is a vigorous
being and on the increase. Railways, roadways, airways are being made,
and even the Sahara will be conquered. But what are we to do with the
Africans?"[70] The *Sierra Leone Weekly News* suggested sardonically "that an
emblem of a mosquito should be erected in a prominent position in the
Coast towns by the Africans" because "there is no need concealing the
fact that as long as the mosquito was capable of doing its worst and to
make the climate unhealthy for the European, the more opportunity
the African had of receiving his due position."[71] "We do not think," wrote
the newspaper, that "West Africa should be the dumping-ground of the
unemployed of Great Britain."[72] At the same time, Frederick Lugard's policy of indirect rule showed that the hope of maintaining "white supremacy and black servitude" remained alive in British imperialism. After all,
the "whole object of the policy of indirect rule is to keep the black man by
himself, keep him in excluded areas, in order that the white man may
thrive in reserved areas with all modern improvements in sanitation."[73]

These critiques targeted a spatial dynamic in imperialism, in which
White mobility—as in the form of a settler or *colon*, backed by modern
medicine and sanitation—was premised upon a commensurate Black
immobility—the assimilation of the "native" into the category of
nature, to be swept away through modernization. By castigating at
once indirect rule and settler colonialism, West African newspapers
attacked both in terms of the fixity they assigned to Africans. This
writing about settlement in the West African press showed a spatial
orientation, traversing the region's boundaries to bring into consideration contemporaneous processes of settlement elsewhere on the
continent. But it also had important temporal dimensions. Writers in
West African publications analyzed historical case studies of colonial

settlement, asking what lessons the fate of other peoples subject to settler colonialism might hold for Africans. Some, like Theodore Heline in the Lagos-based *Comet*, condemned "the three hundred years war of expulsion and extermination of the red man" in the United States.[74] An Australian traveler wrote in the *West African Pilot* about the "more or less open policy of extermination" that had been carried out against the "Australian native."[75]

Such accounts help to explain why the *Gold Coast Leader*, when it surveyed the history of European colonialism, concluded that "wherever the European gets into contact with weaker peoples in parts of the world where the European can live and thrive, the tendency has been to oust the aboriginal people from their legitimate rights and bring them into servitude." And "the European would seem to have no conscience in the matter. He thinks of his security and his prosperity without the consideration of the rights of those whom he had met on the land." This had taken place "in America with respect to the Red Indians and in South and East Africa as far as our African brethren in those parts are concerned, and that forms one of the nasty problems of the age."[76] Zones of European settlement on the African continent were a central point of comparison and analysis. Processes of African immiseration and land alienation in those areas, alongside the proto-apartheid ideology that buttressed and sustained them, were widely reported in the West African press.[77] It was clear that "relations between black and white in Africa, south of the equator" were "anything but a credit to the local Government." It was "a grievous error to assume that Africans elsewhere view with indifference the wretched conditions under which members of their race live there."[78] The *Leader* cited reflections on "the future destiny of Africa as a white man's home, and it gave warnings to the "South African Boers," who would have to learn that "African Natives cannot be repressed all of the time."[79]

Some in West Africa argued that what was being implemented in South Africa constituted a genocidal policy, comparable to those of the

European fascists. In a *West African Pilot* article titled "Extirpation Policy," published in 1935, the Union of South Africa was seen as enacting "a gradual extermination process worse than the Fascist-Nazi abhorrence":

> The entire Bantu people are living a life of chronic dejection and economic wretchedness, so acute, that their very manhood and racial moral virility are sapped, leaving them just mines and unskilled labour automatons. . . . The domestic life of the Natives is a sheer mire in which they wallow in abject unremitted misery . . . because it has pleased the white parvenu, in search of wealth and power, to suck the life blood out of a race which has no means to rid herself of white vermins.[80]

Three months later, Nnamdi Azikiwe recounted in the same newspaper a visit to South Africa during which he had observed that the "whites look upon the Africans like a dog under their table," giving them "no social or political equality"—a "savage policy" resulting in segregation and discrimination.[81] George Padmore, writing in *The African Morning Post* in 1935, excoriated the South African government for trying to "ruin the economic basis of the Natives" and asked, "Would the Jews of England vote to live under Hitler? Why then should the Africans vote to live under Hertzog?" It would be a "crime," he wrote, if they came under the control of South Africa's rulers, whose brutality was equaled only by that of the Nazis.[82]

A book like S. D. Cudjoe's *Aids to African Autonomy* (1949) encapsulated these themes. Cudjoe, a doctor and musicologist from colonial Ghana, centered settlement territories in his analysis of the obstacles preventing African autonomy under colonial rule. He warned of the "unabating desire of the Boers of South Africa" to absorb African territories, which would "seal the doom of the African Colonial peoples."[83] It was "not so much the backwardness of the Africans which threatens European civilisation in Africa," he wrote, "as the advantage which Europeans take of that backwardness. Racial segregation in Africa does not remove the dreaded contagion, for European civilisation is its own contagion," he added, in words that prefigured those of Césaire in *Discours sur le colonialisme*, which would be published a year later.[84] For Cudjoe, the policies and ambitions of the Boers, the British, and European fascists could not be cleanly separated. "It is not possible for impartial minds to condemn Mussolini or Badoglio in Africa and applaud Cecil Rhodes or Lugard at the same time," he insisted. "German and Italian Fascism drew its notions of the British people not from their political democracy at home, but from the horrible pages of their Imperial history."[85]

This body of West African interwar writing on settlement has not been the subject of scholarly attention, perhaps because European settlement on a mass scale did not finally take place in the region. Yet the significance of this writing lies not in its actual power of prediction. It is rather in the theoretical picture of imperial power that emerges from this work, infused with a critique of the destructive power of European settler colonialism—identified as the destruction of Native existence, the large-scale dispossession of Native land, and the wholesale replacement of Native society—which, it suggested, lay beneath the surface of any structure of European control, ready to erupt at any moment. The extirpatory nature of colonialism thus constituted an ideational foundation of West African anticolonialism and its structures of feeling, with echoes across the Black Atlantic.[86] This was a theory connecting the body and the world, destabilizing the idea that bodily security was possible under a colonialism premised on racial hierarchization. As with the critique of colonialism's extractive nature (chapter 2), this argument was developed through specifically textual mechanisms: drawing upon, citing, repurposing, and recontextualizing imperialist texts. By putting West Africa into the context of a world defined by its colonial hierarchies, West African writers extrapolated from histories and cases of settlement in order to contradict the self-justificatory rhetoric of British colonialism in West Africa.

THE WORLD, THE SETTLER, AND THE BODY

A reading of West African and Paris-based texts from the interwar Black Atlantic shows how thinking on the scale of the world also involved thinking on the scale of the body. The world did not negate the body: it helped to locate and explain corporeal experiences, understood in terms of space and crowding, loneliness and insecurity, life and death. Moving down to the scale of the body also involved moving up to the scale of the world. In the process, other scales—the local, national, regional, and imperial—might be reimagined and reconfigured. As Ménil's reference to "the loneliness of the black man all over the world" suggests, thinking about race and colonialism with the body as a referent could generate images that were at once individual and planetary in scale. These images constitute an important archive of thinking about the racialized body in the space of the world.

Cultural and political writing across the interwar Black Atlantic was differentially embodied, as an emerging field of research shows.[87] Scholars have brought to light a number of case studies: the idea of the "race man"; the ways in which celebrations of Black folk culture built on gendered understandings of authenticity; the valorized aesthetics of the Black male body; how Caribbean male intellectuals thought about militarism, power, and sovereignty; the forms of gender hierarchy replicated among Black anticolonial activists in London; and the "near obsession" over female sexuality in West African fiction written by men.[88] We might add to this list the vision of the Black male worker as the primary subject of colonial exploitation.

One way to read these texts connecting the racialized body and the world is to place them within a tradition of patriarchal anticolonialism. If the history of the liberal sovereign individual is also the history of the embodiment of that individual, the search for the anticolonial subject encountered the same paradox between abstract liberation and corporeal confinement.[89] Anticolonial revolution did not automatically produce sexual revolution. Historians of masculinity have described the "privileged freedom to pass at will between the public and the private" as part of the assertion of male power against an expanding domain of women's agency.[90] A similar weaponization of the public and the private can be seen in patriarchal forms of anticolonialism. As Partha Chatterjee has recounted, the world in this type of anticolonial organizing is framed as a strictly male domain—"a treacherous terrain of the pursuit of material interests"—and contrasted with the home, a cultural space protected from the dangers of the material world.[91] The historian Prasenjit Duara reminds us that the idealization of women as emblems of anticolonial national authenticity depends precisely on the denial of agency to women in the public realm. In the process, they become venerated but impassive figures—like the rustic, the child, the Aboriginal, or the royal family.[92]

Making this point should not, however, lead us into a narrow conception of the space of the world and its possibilities for anticolonialism. Those subject to hierarchies of both race and gender were not just victims of patriarchal anticolonialism. They also articulated their own political visions, including those that were global in scope. In recent years, scholars have sought to recover the archival records left by women across the interwar Black Atlantic (while recognizing that absence may be as telling as presence.)[93] Their research has shown that Black women expressed desires for global transformation or upheaval: to "turn the whole world over," and even—as UNIA member Josephine Moody proclaimed—"to set the world on fire."[94] A reexamination of the archives reveals how Black women accessed the space of the world in their own right. They did so as those who were "confronted by both a woman question and a race problem," as Anna Julia Cooper described the situation of Black American women in 1892.[95]

This scholarship vividly illuminates the variegated texture of anticolonial projects. Binaries between home and the world did not encompass the entirety of anticolonialism; neither did they exhaust the possibilities of global thinking. As Cheryl Higashida has shown, the complexity of Black women's engagements with international politics requires a nuanced understanding of gender and politics that goes beyond the rudimentary binary between nationalism and internationalism.[96] If the world could be the basis for patriarchal anticolonialism, it could also help to locate fissures and openings within that patriarchal project. To grasp this idea and its consequences more fully requires a recognition of how race, gender, and sexuality are essentially co-implicated, which means that none of these categories can be articulated without the others. By considering the imprint of the planet on the racialized body, Black anticolonial writers produced an archive that speaks to corporeal implication in matrices of power that span far beyond the individual. The way in which the body-world scale is jumped through the articulation of race also implicates other experiences of embodiment.

Queer, gender, and feminist theorists, including Black and Third World feminists; theorists of disability; theorists concerned with aging, health, and illness—all have thought about the human body as mediated and constructed by social forces, thus seeing "the matter of bodies as the effect of a dynamic of power."[97] Taken as a whole, this theoretical work might be read as a series of reflections of the interrelation of scales. Seeking to develop an understanding of the body in relation to scales beyond the body, such theory at its greatest extent relates the planet to the subject. As well as reflecting on how the matter of the body is constituted by power beyond it, these theorists have also considered how a liberatory praxis might build on a recognition of the impossibility of retrieving a "pure" self absent of the effect of social relations acting upon it—a "sex" absent of "gender," for example. We might think of this as the politics of implication, which acts in contrast to forms of politics premised on rootedness and purity. Donna Haraway, in this vein, suggests that a recognition of the self *as fully implicated in the world* frees us of the need to root politics in identification, vanguard parties, purity, and mothering."[98] Haraway's phrasing gestures towards (though it also modifies) a tradition of social reproduction Marxist-feminism, which has conceived of patriarchy with reference to accumulation on a world scale.[99] We are also reminded here of the ways in which planetary processes have shaped and defined gender itself, such that, as Hortense Spillers has influentially argued, the "theft of the body" in the context of the spatialization of the African diaspora constructs a social subject who is defined in particular ways by "the *loss* of gender."[100]

In his book *Sex, France and Arab Men*, Todd Shepard excavates a connection between decolonization, sexual Orientalism, and movements for sexual liberation in the French metropole during the 1960s and 1970s. Arab men loomed large in the consciousness of those on both sides of the battle over sex in France—whether as hyper-virile threats to France's moral order, as harbingers of a new dawn of sexual liberation, or as exemplars of a lately successful political struggle. Questions of race and empire have received scarce treatment in studies of French sexual politics and homosexuality, writes Shepard; but the prominence of the "Arab man" in the French sexual imagination points to "the central role of anticolonial movements and colonized peoples of color in making the sexual revolution."[101] By drawing a line between anticolonialism and sexual revolution, Shepard's book suggestively points to unexplored connections between political projects that have come to be seen as divergent and even irrevocably opposed.

This writing pushes us to think about the anticolonial archive within what Judith Butler calls a "gendered matrix of relations."[102] With Black interwar writing in France and West Africa as a case study, that archive might be understood as constituting a set of interventions in the politics of implication—recognizing the person as rooted in the world (understood here in its plenitude: the *whole* world). This writing about the racialized body as tied to a world-spanning colonial order constitutes a significant theoretical moment in thinking about the more general question of the body's implication in the world. By conceptualizing the effect of colonialism on the Black body and by examining processes of settlement in spatiotemporal and comparative terms, Black Atlantic anticolonial texts undermined narratives of colonial stability (in the present) and development (in the future). Their techniques of citation and interpretation enabled radical acts of comparison that functioned outside the framework of the dominant imperial discourse. Fundamentally, such acts of comparison suggested that colonial subjection carried an implicit but ineradicable threat of extirpation. In seeing colonialism as a project that bifurcated the world into two groups—the living and the always potentially dead—this analysis brought together those who had been subjected to European imperialism. All were subjected to bodily peripheralization under a planetary order. The colonized in both settler and nonsettler territories experienced a shared subjection to the fixities of racialization, and therefore a common position in a planetary system. Both groups, yoked together under the imperial order, experienced an uncertain and fractured relationship with space and time—between enforced rootedness and sudden evisceration.

5

THE TIME OF THE WORLD

And time and the world are ever in flight
W. B. YEATS

||||||||||||||||||||||||||||||||||||||||||||||||||||||||||||||||||||||||||||||||||||||||||||||||||||||||||||||||||||||||||||||||||||||||||||||||||||||||||

IN AN EDITORIAL TITLED "What is civilization?" published in
late 1927, *La Race Nègre,* the newspaper of the Paris-based
Ligue de Défense de la Race Nègre, grappled with the history, present, and future of African-descended peoples:

> We black people must convince ourselves of the historicity of
> our future role. Today, all that is expected of us is to be serv-
> ants [*on ne veut de nous qu'à titre de valets*]. But if we work consci-
> entiously to safeguard the dignity and prestige that have, for so
> long, been trampled underfoot; and if we work towards the
> affirmation of our personality and civilization—which will
> grow as a result of many external acquisitions, as long as they
> are safeguarded against certain putrid ferments—tomorrow,
> our young race will be reckoned with. We must understand
> our position as pariahs. European civilization in Africa, instead
> of making us happy and prosperous, will always invoke, as it
> were, the bloody nuptials of the [daughters of] Danaus and
> [sons of] Aegyptus.[1]

Theorists of nationalism have conjectured a particular relationship between nationalism and time. Nationalist time is empty and homogenous; it is secular, but its horizon is filled with redemptive promise. Reinhart Koselleck calls this "an unconscious secularization of eschatological expectation."[2] By constructing the "false unity of a self-same, national subject evolving through time," nationalists project their nation backwards, into the mists of time, and forwards, into an eternal future.[3] On an initial reading, La Race Nègre conforms to this model. It constructs an imagined Black national community (albeit one scattered across many territories). Through a newspaper, the archetypal product of print-capitalism, it unifies that community in both past and future. Its nationalism is also emphatically oriented to the present: it seeks to break colonized peoples out of the "imaginary waiting room of history" by insisting "on a 'now' as the temporal horizon of action."[4]

Yet written across this editorial in La Race Nègre are also contradictions and uncertainties in its treatment of time. Why does the newspaper not simply reassure its readers of the future, but asks them instead to "convince" themselves of the "historicity" of their "future role"? Why does it use the distinctly spatial term "pariah" to capture the global Black condition? Why, if its argument draws on the teleologies of Romanticism, is the relationship between Europe and Africa compared to a tragic legend from Greek mythology, in which forty-nine of the fifty daughters of Danaus killed their husbands on their shared wedding night and were condemned to the eternal filling of jugs of water?

In this chapter, I suggest that we consider more carefully the ambivalences we find in anticolonial writing on time. Drawing on the work of critics who have sought to rectify the undertheorization of time in our understanding of race and colonialism, I contend that Black anticolonial texts of the period were deliberately and radically unstable in their temporal claims.[5] Operating on the scale of the world, and with particular reference to sites of Black sovereignty that were fragile during the 1920s, 1930s, and 1940s, anticolonial writing across the Black

Atlantic pursued a temporal politics that was *conjugated*—seized, adapted, transformed—from imperial narratives. For Black anticolonialists, time and the world were inseparable. Time buttressed the disequilibrium of the colonial order; it held together the skewed order of the world. The political fact of imperialism could not therefore be undone without targeting the deep and protean temporal structures that contained and ordered the experiences of colonized subjects. If racial-colonial time was not singular but multiple, so too did anticolonial time have to be held—tensely—in a zone of temporal ambivalence. It was engaged in direct or implicit rejoinder to the inconsistent timescales of imperial rule.

Analyses of anticolonial writing have often missed this strategic self-positioning. Anticolonialists have often been depicted as either tragically replicating forms of national time or as valiantly contesting national time (with, for example, transnational, international, or diasporic time.)[6] But both of these depictions insufficiently recognize the relationship between time and the world. They rely on a spatially circumspect view that fails to see the globe as a distinct site of temporal struggle. In the process, they too easily dismiss anticolonial nationalism as falling into a temporal trap—haplessly reproducing dominant orientations toward past, present, and future. I suggest instead that we appreciate the ways in which Black anticolonial writing was often deliberately indeterminate in its approach to time. Time was, for Black anticolonialists, a battleground, not a zone of abstract speculation.[7]

Maurice Olender has perceptively written that to be racialized means to be "marked by a stagnation in time," to be "deprived of all historical mobility" and to be seen in terms of "the impossibility of change."[8] During the interwar period, Black populations were regularly written about as unassimilable and outside modernity—what Johannes Fabian has called a "denial of coevalness." This corresponds to Olender's identification of a race in terms of its lack of historical mobility.[9] But, as I explain in this chapter, stasis and stagnation were never the only temporal modalities through which race and colonialism operated. Black and African populations could also be promised convergence under colonial developmentalism. In this framing, *deferral* took the place of eternal separation for people who were not unassimilable, but whose assimilation lay in a distant horizon. Black populations could also be subject to a self-fulfilling lament for their inevitable demise under the machinery of progress: a temporal mode based on the eliminationist and future-oriented drive of settler colonialism.[10] And, finally, they could be seen as coeval—in the same timeframe as the West—but fundamentally deficient. This was a fundamentally *parodic* view, in which racialized persons and societies were mocked for being unable to measure up to the exigencies and demands of contemporaneity. Time straightjacketed colonized peoples, but the ways in which it did so were neither straightforward nor consistent.

ON VALENTINE'S DAY IN 1931, E. N. Jones explained to the readers of the *Sierra Leone Weekly News* that

> Abyssinia [Ethiopia] and Liberia are the only independent States of Africa. The white man, hawk-like watches over them and is ready to pounce upon them if needs be. The Negro, wherever he may be, is interested in them; for their rise or fall is a test of his capacity for self-government.[11]

His words echoed those of *Le Courrier des Noirs,* a Paris-based journal, about Haiti: that it was "among the most urgent causes that we have to defend," because "this small black state" had long "symbolized independence for the black peoples of the Antilles."[12]

These three precarious sites of Black sovereignty, which were the only states in the League of Nations governed by people of African descent, were closely monitored across the Black Atlantic during the

1920s and 1930s.[13] In his autobiography *My Odyssey*, Nnamdi Azikiwe described the start of his fascination with Liberia:

> It was during my stay in Hope Waddell that I first heard of a country whose executive and administrative officials were black men. It was unbelievable. A fellow student, who was a Kru, was fond of telling us that in his country the President and the governors of the countries were black men; so were all the judges, the law officers and the heads of department in the civil service. . . . His country had the opportunity to give the black race leadership; but instead of doing so, they gave impression to the outside world that they were like swine who had pearls and either did not know their value or could not make use of them.
>
> This revelation drew us closer, and I became very much interested in the Republic of Liberia.

Marcus Garvey was similarly attracted to the anomalous sovereignty of Liberia. He sent an emissary, Elie Garcia, to the country in 1920, hoping to move the headquarters of the UNIA there.[14] Ethiopia, which could claim to be the only African state unconquered by a European power after having successfully defended itself against an Italian invasion in 1896, drew keen attention and admiration across the Black Atlantic. Yet paradoxically, all of these states—admired for their recalcitrant independence—faced incursions during the interwar years that effectively vitiated their sovereignty. Haiti was occupied by the United States from 1915 to 1934. Ethiopia was occupied by Italy from 1936 to 1941. Liberia was placed under financial receivership, formally investigated by the League, and threatened with occupation between 1929 and 1936.

The rest of this chapter focuses on the racial-temporal matrix that sapped the sovereignties of Haiti, Liberia, and Ethiopia, the interwar period's only officially recognized "Black states." Any project for the liberation of Africa and its peoples had to grapple with these sites of Black sovereignty. From Accra to Port-au-Prince, anticolonialists could not avoid the subjugation of these states to different—yet always unfavorable—discourses of racialized temporality. Contemplating the global order that made Black sovereignty impossible, they returned insistently to the question of time. Yet in response to the shifting ways in which Haiti, Liberia, and Ethiopia were undermined by the White world, they did not converge on a single theory of liberation. While some championed the state as the vessel of pan-African liberation, others reflected on the tragedy inherent to the pursuit of Black sovereignty. Both sets of responses reveal a prefigurative engagement with the postcolonial state and its entrapment in enduringly colonial frameworks of domination, organized on a world scale. Haiti, Liberia, and Ethiopia foreshadowed the postcolonial condition in an era of mass decolonization. In so doing, they raised lasting questions about the prospects and limits of sovereignty within a global racial order.

"FREEDOM FOR OUR BROTHERS IN HAITI"

By 1914, Haiti had long been what J. Michael Dash named as an "inexhaustible symbol" of desire, fear, and otherness in North American writing.[15] Haiti's location in the Caribbean, its juridical sovereignty, and its Blackness all combined to give it a specially liminal temporal status in North American writing. It was at once modern and impossibly backward—"the halfway point between what we call the jungle and what we call civilization," as William Faulkner's *Absalom! Absalom!* (1938) put it.[16] Such delegitimation had a long lineage in European writing too, ever since Edmund Burke had called Haiti a "cannibal republic."[17]

Undermining Haiti's sovereignty by claiming it was "unmodern" was complicated by two inconvenient facts. First was the indisputable modernity of Saint-Domingue, given that it had been the world's most lucrative colony during the late eighteenth century. Second was the fact that Haiti had been recognized as independent by the European-dominated international order since 1804—before any other state in the Americas except the United States. As a result, Haiti's sovereignty was undercut through the specifically temporal idea of racial atavism. Haiti was not, according to this idea, simply primitive; it was *in regression*. In 1896, the British historian James Anthony Froude wrote an influential work arguing that "the Negro never rose of himself out of barbarism . . . when left free, as in Liberia and Hayti, he reverts to his original barbarism."[18] Madison Grant, the influential American eugenicist, also invoked Haiti as a country in which the collapse of European rule had seen the population "revert almost to barbarism."[19]

The image of Haiti sliding backwards in time—and threatening to drag neighboring countries with it—was the basis for an occupation that framed itself as a civilizing and modernizing mission, seeking to rationalize Haiti, and, through paternalistic guidance, bring it (back) into the modern world. Financial receivership, a mechanism through which an external power could take over the generation of customs revenues of a debtor state, was a key technique of control that was used by the United States in both Haiti and Liberia. As Emily Rosenberg points out, receivership was legitimized "in terms of rationality and benevolence"; it claimed to be "the antithesis of imperialism, arising from markets and morality rather than from an imperial state's designs for territorial aggrandizement."[20] Framing intervention in scientific and financial terms in order to dissociate it from the rapacity of colonialism, those justifying the occupation of Haiti drew plentifully on a discourse connecting race and time.

Lothrop Stoddard's *The French Revolution in San Domingo* (1914), published a year before the occupation began, drew on the example of Haiti to warn about threats to White supremacy and promote the idea that Haiti's racial conflict represented a struggle over world-historical time, between world progress or civilizational regression.[21] In *The Rising Tide of Color* (1920), published five years into the occupation, Stoddard argued that Haiti represented the "first real shock between the ideals of white supremacy and race-equality; a prologue to the mighty drama of our own day."[22] If Stoddard's writing was new in the sense that it concerned a country over which the United States now had military control, it also derivatively recapitulated what had come before— particularly the idea of racial atavism. Haiti and Liberia were examples, Stoddard wrote, of how the "black race has never shown real constructive power" and "when left to himself, as in Haiti and Liberia, rapidly reverts to his ancestral ways."[23] This idea was common among Americans involved in the occupation of Haiti. Robert Lansing, US Secretary of State from 1915 to 1920 and a chief architect of American policy in Haiti, argued in typical fashion that

> the experience[s] of Liberia and Haiti show that the African race are devoid of any capacity for political organization and lack genius for government. Unquestionably there is in them an inherent tendency to revert to savagery and to cast aside the shackles of civilization which are irksome to their physical nature.[24]

Wilson's invasion of Haiti on July 28, 1915, inaugurated a nineteen-year occupation of the republic that endured until 1934, running through five successive US presidential administrations.[25] North Americans had been writing anxiously about Haiti for over a century; but never before had they had such direct and unmediated access to it. The occupation was, as Brenda Gayle Plummer writes, "unprecedented in terms of its duration, racism . . . [and] brutality."[26] Legally entrenched by means of a treaty whose stipulations included the financial oversight of Haiti by US officials and a punitive schedule of debt repayments, the occupation defeated a peasant insurgency by late 1915 and disbanded the Haitian legislature for twelve years. A new constitution was written. For the first time, foreigners were permitted to own land in Haiti.[27]

The assault on Haiti was racializing in a temporally specific way. It made use of narratives of regression, atavism, and strange temporal liminality. Responding to this assault therefore involved at least two distinct strategies for Black writers. The first was an emphasis on Haiti's venerability. Combatting the idea of regression meant recognizing the Haitian Revolution as what C. L. R. James called "one of the great epics of revolutionary struggle and achievement."[28] James's study of the Haitian Revolution, *The Black Jacobins* (1938), is the most famous example of this interwar reappraisal of Haitian history; James himself was explicit that the book was partly a response to Lothrop Stoddard's "lies" about the Haitian Revolution.[29] Eric Williams's *Capitalism and Slavery* (1944) similarly recognized the Haitian Revolution as "a landmark in the history of slavery in the New World."[30] Aimé Césaire's key texts on Haiti were published later—prominent among which were the historical study *Toussaint Louverture: La révolution française et le problème colonial* (1960) and the play *La Tragédie du roi Christophe* (1963)—but it was his stay in Haiti in 1944 that was formative for his long-standing fascination with the history of the republic.[31]

A second, more prominent, set of Black responses to the charge of Haiti's atavism was an insistence not on Haiti's history, but on its contemporaneity. These interventions stressed Haiti's sovereign coevalness with other states. Contending with the risible but widely propagated idea of Haiti's racial atavism, they developed strategies for drawing attention to Haiti's present-day suffering under the US occupation. This strategy is visible in African American newspapers. When the occupation first began, Black newspapers in the United States generally expressed support for the modernizing mission of the Marines. This position had been influenced by wartime censorship, whose repressive apparatus targeted Black Americans in particular, but also by the apparently unimpeachable consensus that Haiti was backward and needed modernizing. This support soon withered, however, as reports from Haiti under occupation emerged.[32] In 1920, Hubert Harrison published in the *Negro World* a scathing indictment of what he called the bloody rape of the republics of Hayti and Santo Domingo . . . being perpetrated by the bayonets of American sailors and marines, with the silent and shameful acquiescence of 12,000,000 American Negroes too cowardly to lift a voice in effective protest or too ignorant of political affairs to know what is taking place.

Writing under the headline "The Cracker in the Caribbean," Harrison asked how can "we Africans of the dispersion can let the land of L'Ouverture lie like a fallen flower beneath the feet of swine?" His discursive strategy simultaneously underlined the historicity of Haiti and emphasized its subjection in the present day.[33]

A year later, the *Chicago Defender*, which had previously supported the occupation, published an article sympathetic to the Haitian delegates in Chicago who had come "with a report of the atrocities and outrages committed by the American forces."[34] A statement by M. Pierre Hudicourt, Haiti's delegate to the Second Hague Conference, was released by the NAACP and published in the Black newspaper the *New Journal and Guide* in 1922. "I consider as odious hypocrisy the pretexts of humanity and interest in the Haitian people invoked by the United States government in perpetrating upon Haiti a reign of terror and extortion, continued since 1915," read the statement. "If an individual had done to another's hurt what the United States government has done to the Haitian people, the only punishment adequate would be life imprisonment or the scaffold."[35] By May 1930, the Baltimore *Afro-American* was attributing the occupation straightforwardly to "the ancient U.S. theory that a Negro has no rights which a white man is bound to respect."[36] The transformed understanding of what was happening in Haiti in these newspapers—from modernization under American largesse to pillage under American empire—reflects a shift in the underlying temporal basis for conceptualizing Haiti: from backwards, even atavistic, to unquestionably contemporary.

African American writers drew connections between the occupation of the republic and the struggles of Black people in the United

States, emphasizing the simultaneity of Haitian and African American suffering. They pointed out that "white southerners" constituted the Marine force that was "occupying Haiti."[37] In March 1921, the official magazine of the NAACP, *Crisis*, published an open letter to President Warren G. Harding, in which three domestic demands—the right to vote, the right to "travel without insult," and an end to lynching—were allied with "freedom for our brothers in Haiti."[38] By building connections with Black nationalists outside the country, Haitian Garveyites like Eliézer Cadet and Elie Garcia made the occupation into an urgent matter for pan-African thinking and organizing. Like other Haitians living abroad, they challenged the idea that Haitian history offered a tale of regression and collapse.[39] Joseph Mirault, a Haitian newspaper correspondent in New York, reminded readers of the *Negro World* that "as you know, and as everybody knows, the American Occupation to justify its presence in Haiti has to carry out that kind of propaganda to make the world believe that we are still in a state of savagery."[40]

Drawing attention to Haiti's presentness could also take other routes. Haitian women like Theresa Hudicourt and Eugénie Sylvain, collaborating with the International Commission of Women of the Darker Races, worked to put the occupation of Haiti onto the agenda of international women's organizations.[41] Connecting struggles for gender equality with anticolonialism, they asserted that Haiti's independence was, just like the rights of women, an urgent international question.[42] Novels about the occupation written by Haitians sought to immerse the reader in the day-to-day realities of life under North American rule. They did so with a particular interest in gender, centering the power-, class-, and race-freighted relationships between, especially, American men and Haitian women.[43] *La Race Nègre* suggested that Haiti could rightfully intervene in contemporary politics on the African continent, emphasizing its modernity and formal equality with other states. Its writers suggested that Haiti come to the assistance of Ethiopia when it was invaded by Italy, as well as administer a League of Nations mandate over Cameroon.[44]

By valorizing Haiti's history and underlining Haiti's present-day subjugation, Black writers launched a dual-pronged assault on the slander of Haitian atavism. At times, they made use of the citational practices that were so prominent in West Africa to incisively capture the ways in which Haiti was seen as a global threat to White supremacy. When, for example, an American senator complained at the League of Nations that "colored countries" would soon outnumber "white" ones, mocked Liberia as a "joke nation," and derided Haiti as a country of "baby killers and creatures of the forest," the *Afro-American* simply reported the tirade without additional comment.[45] For Black anticolonialists, Haitian sovereignty was defended by insisting on both the dignity of Haiti's history *and* its intractable modernity. Any regression in Haiti in political or economic terms was, these writers argued, a direct result of imperialist aggression. The idea of racial atavism sought merely to disguise contemporary despoilation through historical fantasy.

"HANDS OFF ABYSSINIA"

No single event was more significant for the interwar Black Atlantic than Italy's invasion of Ethiopia on October 3, 1935.[46] The invasion was met with unparalleled mobilization. In Paris, Black, anticolonial, and left-wing organizations set aside their differences and created a popular front in defense of Ethiopia. In London, the George Padmore and C.L.R. James–led International African Friends of Abyssinia was formed, the League of Coloured Peoples entered a newly radical phase, and Sylvia Pankhurst's influential *New Times and Ethiopian News* was established.[47] Across West Africa, Hands Off Abyssinia committees were set up, relief funds were collected, and mass demonstrations held. In Cape Town and Durban, Black dockworkers refused to handle Italian goods.[48] In the Caribbean, there were mass petitions, vocal public meetings and riots, alongside the birth of the Rastafari movement in the United States, the Pan-African Reconstruction Association began trying to raise volunteers for Ethiopia, while African American groups in Harlem organized the Provisional Committee for the Defense of Ethiopia, drawing thousands to their rallies.[49] "Almost overnight," wrote one prominent African American historian, "even the most provincial among the American Negroes became international-minded."[50] For Kwame Nkrumah, recalling the moment he heard of the invasion as a young student in London: "At that moment it was almost as if the whole of London had suddenly declared war on me personally."[51] For W. E. B. Du Bois, writing at the time: "Black men and brown men have indeed been aroused as seldom before."[52]

It is easy to forget, in light of the strength of feeling generated by these oppositional defenses of Ethiopia, that Italy's invasion was marked not just by silent complicity but by active and powerful support. Anticolonial engagements with Ethiopia—whose occupation began soon after Haiti's ended—were forced to contend with the claims of those sympathetic to the occupation. When border skirmishes, provoked by Italy, erupted at Wal Wal in December 1934, Ethiopia had appealed to the League of Nations for assistance. But Britain and France, then concerned with the threat of German rearmament, showed little interest. A secret British report in June 1935, which found scant reason to defend Ethiopian sovereignty, was conveniently leaked to the Italian government.[53] And the agreements signed between Mussolini and the French foreign minister, Pierre Laval, in January 1935, included a surreptitious recognition of Italian primacy in Ethiopia.[54] The long-planned Italian invasion came on October 3, 1935, without a declaration of war. Ethiopia was incorporated into the short-lived Africa Orientale Italiana from 1936 to 1941.

If Haiti was imagined in atavistic terms as having regressed after the end of French rule, then Ethiopia during the Italian invasion was the subject of a temporal discourse that represented the country in settler-colonial terms: an ancient but dying civilization that was being dragged into the modern world through an act of violent colonial replenishment. This language was distinctly fascist in its focus on modernization, speed, power, and will. But it also drew extensively upon the "extinction discourse" that had long accompanied settler-colonial projects.[55] A deep sympathy for the future that Italy wished to build in Ethiopia was expressed in books and articles, including those written by non-Italians.[56] This writing reveals and exemplifies a temporal discourse that was, in important ways, different from that which was mobilized against Haiti.

Consider the work of William Watts Chaplin. An American war correspondent who arrived in Ethiopia on a ship carrying blackshirts and the Italian general Pietro Badoglio, Chaplin began his reporting with a paean to Italian modernization in Eritrea, where "the roads grow visibly" in a spectacular feat of engineering.[57] Chaplin fêted "the civilizing influence of Mussolini's men."[58] "Determined whites," he explained, were "spreading the gospel of cleanliness and health and justice by peaceful argument where possible, by force of arms where that is considered necessary." Ethiopians were "savage blacks and "wild creatures, while Italian colonizers "remind one of America's early settlers who went about their daily tasks with a rifle ever at hand lest the redskins suddenly descend on them."[59] Ethiopian music, meanwhile, was reminiscent of "the swan song of savagery, the death rattle of barbarism" in the face of "the white man's civilization."[60]

Chaplin was scarcely alone in imagining that Italy's invasion, genocidal ambitions, and attempted settlement of Ethiopia (and Libya) heralded a bright future of renewed settlement, in which lesser races would, once again, be swept aside by more powerful ones. Italian colonization in Africa became an explicit model for the future-oriented policy of the Third Reich in Eastern Europe, with high-ranking Nazi officials closely studying Italian interwar colonialism in Africa, an expansionist policy which they saw as "the quintessence of fascist modernity."[61] Neither was Chaplin alone in seeing similarities between

Italy's occupation of Ethiopia and the history of the United States. The New York correspondent of *Il Corriere della Sera* argued that the United States was likely to support Italy, given the North American power's extensive experience with "the primitive psychology of the colored race." He compared Ethiopia's admission to the League of Nations with the emancipation of enslaved African Americans, which, he wrote, had not been enough in seventy years to change the "semi-barbarism" and "incurable immaturity" of that community. Segregation in the United States showed that "America knows the Negro well and understands how to treat him. . . . Now," he added, "many Americans are curious to know if, as would be logical, one could institute a Jim Crow diplomatic car on the international train which leads to Geneva."[62]

For Black writers in diverse Atlantic locations, this discursive assault on Ethiopia's sovereignty, which accompanied the Italian occupation, elicited an array of responses. One set of engagements directly confronted the discourse of Fascist modernism. It sought to undermine the linearity of that discourse using a language saturated with religious symbolism, circularity, and historicity. This is especially evident in much of the poetry about the war written by African American poets, including Langston Hughes, Owen Dodson, Marcus B. Christian, and J. Harvey L. Baxter. The literary scholar Jon Woodson has pointed to ways in which the Ethiopia conflict was presented in this poetry "as a war between two competing modes of time."[63]

But not all writing by Black authors on Ethiopia evoked circular and transcendent temporalities. Another set of interventions focused on Ethiopia's *simultaneity*, insisting on its contemporaneous relevance to the anticolonial struggle. This latter type of writing was especially evident across West Africa, where, as S. K. B. Asante's study *Pan-African Protest* has shown, the invasion was "among the main influences in the awakening of racial and political consciousness," a turning point at which "unequivocal demands for self-determination began to be made and signs of militancy began to appear."[64] Criticisms of the colonial

regime became markedly more hostile. The West African press "under-
went a great transformation, becoming less parochial and more pan-
African in content," with a decisive impact on the direction of West
African politics after the Second World War.[65] These pan-West African
and pan-African affinities fueled by the invasion often carried with them
expressions of global anticolonial simultaneity: a necessary response to a
discursive assault on Ethiopia that was both future- and past-oriented.

   In this set of interventions, Black writers depicted Italy's invasion as
collapsing the façade of interwar international society, revealing a world
still ordered by violence and race. The League of Nations, in this critical
reading, was a dissembling device. It was what the Indian social scien-
tist Benoy Kumar Sarkar called a new version of "the reactionary regime
of the Congress of Vienna, the Holy Alliance, and the dictatorship of
Metternich," or what The Sierra Leone Weekly News derided as "The
League of European Brotherhood."[66] This view fueled a widespread and
deep cynicism about the prospects of solidarity between Europe and
Africa. It also contributed to a reconceptualization of the political affinities of Africans and African-descended peoples—in West Africa, the
Caribbean, Britain, France, and the United States—as standing alongside the other subjects of a European-dominated racial order by virtue
of their shared experience of such domination, thereby facilitating pan-
Africanism, nationalism, and a strong proto-Third Worldism.[67]

   A striking illustration can be found in an address to the League of
Nations by a Haitian general, Alfred Auguste Nemours, which was published in the Paris-based journal Africa. Insisting that that "the era of
colonial wars is over, in Africa just as in America, just as the period of
the exploitation of one race by another is also over," Nemours lambasted
the widespread acquiescence to Italy's invasion as evidence of systemic—
but nevertheless fundamentally anachronistic—racism.[68] In place of a
Fascist future, he invoked an alternative history and teleology oriented
around the Haitian and French Revolutions. His speech, published
in Black newspapers, conveyed a powerful sense of the anticolonial

simultaneity that was enabled by communicative technologies. "Speaking in the name of the Blacks of Haiti," he said, "I know that all the millions of Blacks and men of color, scattered throughout the world, are observing a minute's silence to listen to me attentively."[69]

Many other writers insisted on the *nowness* of Ethiopia, a position that was embedded in readings of global history and utopian projections for a "colored" future.[70] In an essay on the crisis, W. E. B. Du Bois argued that "the black world" knew that the invasion was "the last great effort of white Europe to secure the subjection of black men." But Italy's victory, he warned, would be "costly" because "the whole colored world"— "all that vast mass of men who have felt the oppression and insults, the slavery and exploitation of white folk, will say: 'I told you so!'"[71] Joel Augustus Rogers, the prominent Jamaican historian, expressed a related view in his influential pamphlet *The Real Facts about Ethiopia* (1936). In words very similar to those of Stoddard, whom he cited as a "far-seeing thinker," Rogers framed the Ethiopian crisis as the latest instance in a long saga of European domination over the rest of the world.[72]

"For the past four centuries," wrote Rogers, "the European, or white race, has been colonizing in all the lands of the darker races" and had "wounded their pride, aroused their deepest hate, and created in the hearts of darker people, totally unknown to one another a common hostility to white peoples."[73] Challenging the view that Ethiopia was not really "black," and thus of no concern to African-descended peoples in the Americas, Rogers insisted that there were "only two varieties of mankind, the black and the white", a resolutely global reading of race that—as we have seen across the interwar Black Atlantic, particularly in Garvey's arguments—grouped together all colonized peoples (including, Rogers specified, the "dark-skinned people of India").[74] "The avalanche is on its way," he concluded, "and it will not stop until the last vestiges of the brutal and debasing color-line imposed on the world by the white race shall have been shattered into irretrievable fragments."[75]

By emphasizing the presentness of Ethiopia, Black anticolonialists worked to wrest its future away from a settler and fascist vision. In so doing, they often reworked their understandings of their own futures under colonial regimes. Across the Black Atlantic, and especially in Britain's West African and Caribbean colonies, activism over the Ethiopia crisis weakened political positions that had imagined a future for Black subjects in imperial structures. Concomitantly, pan-African, African nationalist, Black nationalist, pan-"colored," and proto-Third Worldist affinities were strengthened and reinforced. When the British governor of St. Vincent expressed frustration that people on the Caribbean island were ignoring "geography and ethnology" in their determination to support the Ethiopians as a nationalist cause, he obliquely pointed to the expansion of an imaginative geography that, in reaching out to Ethiopia, detached itself from Britain.[76] As Sir William Arthur Lewis, the St Lucian economist, wrote, "West Indians felt that in that issue the British Government had betrayed a nation because it was black, and this has tended to destroy their faith in white government, and to make them more willing to take their fate in their own hands."[77] For H. O. Davies, the Secretary of the Nigerian Youth Movement: "we became convinced, after the Italian annexation of Ethiopia, that our liberty lies in 'self-determination.'"[78]

LIBERIA: "NATIONHOOD BEFORE RACEHOOD"

Unlike Haiti or Ethiopia, Liberia did not experience direct occupation during the interwar period. But its sovereignty came under severe strain in other ways. Its governing class, which was mostly descended from African American settlers, had for many decades engaged in hostilities with the Indigenous groups of the "interior," who formed a large majority of the country's overall population. Liberia endured constant financial pressure starting with its independence in 1847, and its rulers eventually turned to the export of Indigenous labor, agreeing to supply contract workers to the Spanish cacao plantations on the island of Fernando Po. The poor treatment of these laborers made this agreement increasingly unpopular with Liberians during the 1920s and it was terminated in 1927 (though workers continued to be supplied privately to the island).

That year, accusations by Liberian politician Thomas Faulkner that these laborers had been enslaved for the financial benefit of a network of government officials received international attention. A committee of the League of Nations was convened to investigate the allegations. Its report found that slavery as classically understood did not exist in Liberia, but that the shipment of workers to Fernando Po, as well as to Gabon, was carried out "under conditions of criminal compulsion scarcely distinguishable from slave-raiding and slave-trading." Liberia was already subject to an American financial receivership. The League investigation involved serious consideration of turning the country into a territory administered under the League of Nations mandate system. It was only in 1935, when President Barclay signed a new agreement with American financial interests, that the crisis was finally averted.[79]

Liberia faced a chronopolitical assault similar in some ways to that which was levelled at Haiti. The idea that race had propelled these states atavistically backwards in time to a pre-sovereign condition was used in both cases to justify intervention. But Liberia's peculiar situation gave rise to discourse that was delegitimizing in a specific way. The West African republic was depicted as *parodying* a form of sovereignty that existed properly elsewhere: acting it out without achieving it, in particular by failing to achieve "civilization," and therefore making a mockery of the institution itself. The resulting language was framed, unusually, in terms of comparative simultaneity. For Henry Fenwick Reeve, who published *The Black Republic* in 1923, Liberia's rulers had failed "to keep in line with the great civilizing efforts of other Governments on the west coast of Africa" "the spirit of pomposity runs through the entire warp and woof of their civic life"; and they were simply "incapable of civilized government."[80] "The Great Powers," he warned, "have no use for a second 'Haiti,' or San Domingo on the Continent of Africa, however pure its aspirations may be in theory."[81] Liberia's supporters in Africa recognized the power of this discourse. The country's "detractors" believed that as a "Negro Republic," it "could be nothing but a caricature of self-government," complained the *Sierra Leone Weekly News* in 1928.[82] Even the pan-African pioneer Martin Delaney had once described the country as a "parody" and "a poor miserable mockery—a burlesque on a government."[83]

While the pan-African view on Liberia became more supportive, with limited exceptions the European and American commentators on interwar Liberia continued to employ this language of parody and ersatz.[84] Sidney de la Rue, an American financial administrator who was posted to Liberia, wrote that while there existed "a semblance of the form of government brought from America, . . . it is probable that there never was a plan of government less suited to the psychology of the tribesmen than the one under which Liberia has labored."[85] The examples of Liberia and Haiti were cited by British colonial administrators, both during the interwar period and after the Second World War, to warn against the consequences of decolonization in West Africa.[86] And in the House of Lords in 1934, Liberia was described in the following words: "Almost from the very start there has been trouble and no real progress in civilisation has been made. There is a pretentious imitation of American political institutions, but beyond that it hardly goes, and . . . the position of the country to-day is wholly deplorable."[87]

This was a decidedly *synchronous* conception of Liberia's place in global time. It compared Liberia to other—"real"—states in order to demonstrate Liberia's deficiencies. A linear and evolutionary vision of state-building and historical progress was invoked precisely in order to point to Liberia's failure to really achieve statehood. Far from being denied, coevalness was weaponized. In a vision of frantic and competitive state-building, sovereignty was sapped from those who failed to keep up. This was a colonial-racial temporality that did not assign Liberia an allochronic "stagnation in time" but a stagnation in the *present*.[88] Explicitly or implicitly, Liberia's supposedly parodic existence was placed at the door of its inescapable racial limitations.

How did Black writers respond? Countering the idea that Liberia was parodying sovereignty—a kind of delegitimizing contemporaneity—many of them insisted on the possibility and the necessity of Liberia "succeeding" as a sovereign African state. This view, which pitched Liberia forwards into the future, led to rhetorical support for violent state-building processes within the country: from Henry Sylvester Williams, the pioneering pan-Africanist; to W. E. B. Du Bois, who referred to "war-like Liberia tribes"; and to Nnamdi Azikiwe, who argued in his 1934 book about Liberia that "the pacification of the bellicose tribes is an achievement that cannot be minimized."[89]

Prefiguring a form of "subaltern realism," these defenses of Liberia's political class could lead commentators to minimize and even legitimize its brutal exercise of power.[90] Though at times privately critical of Liberia's government, these figures insisted that the racially motivated origins and implications of the attacks on the country necessitated a strategic public defense of its sovereignty. George Padmore, who was famously at loggerheads with his superiors at the Comintern over Liberia, wrote privately in 1934 that "Liberia has her faults, but since white politicians are no better than black ones, it is our duty to save the 'black baby from the white wolves.'"[91] Du Bois had similarly argued the previous year that while "Liberia is not faultless" its "chief crime is to be black and poor in a rich, white world; and in precisely that portion of the world where color is ruthlessly exploited as a foundation for American and European wealth."[92] Analyses in West African newspapers similarly pointed to the race-based hypocrisy in singling out Liberia for criticism at the League of Nations. Liberia's travails reflected "a general agreement among the white races to keep the black races down," wrote a regular columnist in the *Sierra Leone Weekly* News. "The same spirit which, in the Mediaeval times, unified the nations of Europe into one vast brotherhood of Christendom against non-Christian nations . . . still exists in these modern days in the new guise of a confederacy of the white races of the world—Whitedom against Blackdom." Liberia had been victim to a "great delusion": that of putting "nationhood before racehood. So long as she was humoured and tolerated as a 'Sovereign State' by the Great Powers, she felt highly flattered and cared not a rush what befell the rest of the Race."[93] But the country had now realized the impossibility of nationhood in a world that continued to be ordered by race.

This adoption of a tragic mode in relation to Liberia points to another angle on its interwar difficulties. Rather than seeking to justify the domination of Indigenous peoples in pursuit of state-building, this approach reflected on the impossibility of Liberian success in a global system that was premised upon the denial of Black sovereignty. A strongly structuralist tone emerged in this writing. In temporal terms, it embraced—but subverted—the synchronicity through which Liberia was condemned. Revealing the web of global relationality that kept Liberia weak and impoverished, it gave way to an informed pessimism about the prospects for an African republic in a world cleaved by racial and colonial stratification.

Why had a League of Nations mandate had not been raised for other "murderous and persecuting nations"? the *Sierra Leone Weekly News* asked in 1931.[94] Could the reason be linked to how "the assertion" of Liberia's rights "as an independent Sovereign State" and "the maintenance of the final control in the exercise by all within her territories of their rights and liberties must necessarily prove disturbing, if not irritating, to those who claim superiority by virtue of their race and colour"?[95]

Who can think of what has transpired and is still transpiring in South and East Africa, who can think of the attitude of the white settlers in those African territories, and is not forced to stare in bewildering and "astounding" amazement at the faces of these White Prosecutors of Black Liberia?

And if, not dumb-founded and stupefied at such amazing inconsistency be moved to ask "What does it all mean? Why all these angry demonstrations in the name of Righteousness and Justice, against a weak poverty-stricken Black Republic?"[96]

Looked at in relation to the "white civilised nations of the world," Liberia showed "the tragedy of the situation," explained the *Sierra Leone Weekly News*. The West African republic had become a part of "the grand chain of what is known as the Comity of Nations"; but its poverty had placed it at a structurally weak part of that chain. It had simply become a vessel for global capital—"a link in the chain of international force of world-wide development."[97]

The most sustained and complex writing on Liberia from this perspective came from George W. Brown, an African American scholar. In his book *The Economic History of Liberia* (1941), based on his London School of Economics doctoral thesis, Brown produced an economic history that was at once a rigorous account of Liberia's economy in historical perspective—it remains a landmark in the field—and a contemplation of the tragic nature of Liberia's relationship with a Western-dominated and racialized global order.[98] *The Economic History of Liberia* traced the historical trajectory of Liberia's political economy: from independence in 1848 to the use of coffee cultivation as a means of generating revenue, the turn to loans from European capitals on exceedingly poor terms, the revolts of Liberia's Indigenous peoples, and the brutal practices used by European countries to conscript Liberian workers.[99]

Well before the current "labor crisis," Brown pointed out, France had recruited Liberian laborers to work on the Panama Canal and serve in the French Colonial Army, and high-ranking French officials had encouraged unfree labor practices. Workers had been flogged, beaten, tied up, and kept in compounds before being shipped abroad. Threats of collective punishment, including the burning of entire villages, had been used to ensure compliance. Repeated encroachments on Liberia's territory—at one point, France annexed almost the entirety of its coastline—characterized the latter two decades of the nineteenth century. Even the United States' declaration of "special interest" in Liberia in 1897 did not end the constant "threats of annihilation to Liberia's sovereignty."[100] At the turn of the century, Liberia was left with little option but to grant concessionary rights to foreign companies, beginning with the Union Mining Company in 1902–4. Threatened with bankruptcy in 1911, it had agreed to a major international loan, with its revenues then being subject to international supervision. Brown placed Liberia's interwar predicament within this essential context: its impossible existence as a colonial state without the attendant metropolitan resources, a situation which had pushed Liberia's elite to exploit its Indigenous population as a reservoir of labor and tax revenue.

For Brown, Liberia's problems had to be placed within the historical context of its essentially tragic political economy, which had made of its rulers a comprador elite. "Puppets or pawns in the big game of international finance, they serve as little more than clerks or tellers who pass on to the foreign brokers the contributions from the mass of virile Africans, retaining for themselves little more than is adequate and necessary for sustenance."[101] Now that Ethiopia was under occupation, Liberia was now the "last of the Black Governments in the Black Country."[102] And yet, surrounded as it was by hostile "white powers," it "could not stand for an hour against the embittered might of the mechanized war machines of any world power."[103] Liberian sovereignty was totally subject to a "triumvirate of power": the superintendent of the Firestone Plantations, the manager of the Bank of Monrovia, and the financial adviser appointed by the US government. The economy had become dominated by foreign capital, while an inadequate education system depended heavily on White philanthropists.

One had to accept, wrote Brown, that "in the strict letters of political science, Liberian sovereignty is not intact, and to that degree her independence is not absolute."[104] Yet his characterization of the country was not entirely pessimistic. He saw a future for it in the Indigenous Liberian peasants who he thought represented another form of economy and mode of existence. "As long as he lives under his communal economy; as long as he resists all efforts to uproot him and develop him into a wage earner," wrote Brown, "the Western onslaught is powerless to penetrate his culture or to beat down and destroy his economy."[105]

BLACK SOVEREIGNTY IN A WHITE WORLD

Though at significant cost, Haiti, Liberia, and Ethiopia all emerged from the Second World War with their sovereignties intact or regained. Within two decades, they had ceased to be unique representatives of Black sovereignty. In 1957, Ghana became the first in a cascade of new African seats to arrive at the United Nations. The anticolonial drive to understand, defend, and emblematize Haiti, Liberia, and Ethiopia—ubiquitous during the interwar years—diminished. In one sense, however, the expansion of the state across Africa, Asia, and the Caribbean should have rendered the struggles of these three states *more*, not less, significant. The concerted attacks on the three sites of Black sovereignty in the interwar order foreshadowed the ways in which formal decolonization could exist alongside global stratification. This contradicted the idea that decolonization constituted a true normative revolution in world politics.[106]

Unavoidably modern states between 1914 and 1945, Haiti, Liberia, and Ethiopia saw their juridical sovereignties rebuffed with powerful temporal discourses—regression, parody, stasis, vanishing, extinction, failure. The radical indeterminacy of these discourses reflected a duplicitous and shifting colonial order. Though the world technically evened out its temporalities in exiting from colonialism, creating a global synchrony of undifferentiated political forms, the international order that emerged after the Second World War in fact drew profoundly on the stratifications of political time that had emerged during the colonial period.

When postcolonial states emerged onto the world stage after World War Two, the language of temporal failure that had been pioneered in relation to Haiti, Liberia, and Ethiopia could be generalized, allowing for the maintenance of hierarchy within juridical equality.[107] For many Black writers, the fragile situation of these states illuminated what Karen Salt calls "the circumscribed contours of black sovereignty."[108] Haiti, Liberia, and Ethiopia's inability to survive the period intact called into question the promises of fairness and progression offered by the League of Nations.[109] By contending with the delicate presence of Black states in this interwar order, Black anticolonialists sought to understand how independence could be sapped through the mobilization of time. Beyond a formally colonial order, uneven temporalities have continued to permit global juridical equality to exist alongside deep fractures and vertiginous stratifications.

HOW SHOULD WE RESPOND to the unevenness of time on the scale of the world? How is race to be resisted when it is subsumed within dissembling discourses of history, scientific progress, governance, and modernity? One contemporary response to these questions has been to attack at their source the very notions of progress and history that are seen to underwrite this differentiating discourse—a critique which often finds itself reassessing Hegel.[110] Yet the anticolonial defenses of Haiti, Liberia, and Ethiopia, attuned to the divergent and contradictory nature of attacks on these states, typically sought not consistency but strategic viability in terms of their representations of time. Undoing the knots that tied each of these states to some version of racial time meant paying careful attention to dominant discourses and undercutting them on their own terms. If anticolonial writing is emplotted, as David Scott has influentially argued using the work of Hayden White, those plots could be layered, various, and contradictory—perhaps more like musical forms with polyrhythmic structures than novels or epic poems.[111] Dominant forms of time structured the lives of colonized peoples in ways that could be contested and resisted, but not ignored or bypassed.[112] Any case for "unlearning" history must therefore remain attentive to the ways in which historicism or the idea of development do not constitute the whole range of ways of representing time for the purposes of imperial domination.[113]

A defense of Haiti, Liberia, or Ethiopia did not necessarily imply a hopeful outlook on the institution of sovereignty or the postcolonial state. Certainly for those, like Nnamdi Azikiwe, who themselves became heads of state, the existence of Black states in a hostile world was encouraging. But other reflections on the invisible chains that weighed down these states and their divided populations came much closer to the tragic structuralism of dependency.[114] When the Ghanaian anticolonialist Kobina Sekyi attacked the "artificiality" of African states that were not based on traditionally African forms of political organization, he evinced a kind of cultural romanticism combined with a tragic lament of the unstoppable expansion of the Western state and its dominating subjectivities.[115] And while the muscular and virile language used in defense of these states is representative of the ways in which anticolonialism could take on patriarchal forms, this mode of response was always threatened by the activity of those whose defenses of Black sovereignty also sought to undermine gendered power.

Black Atlantic anticolonialists devoted significant attention during the 1920s, 1930s, and 1940s to combatting the representations—governed by what Edward Said identified in *Orientalism* as "a battery of desires, repressions, investments, and projections"—of sites of Black sovereignty.[116] If theories of race were global but "everywhere worked out in the language of the nation-state," as the historian Christopher

Bayly observed, the precise inverse was also true.[117] Theories of the state were everywhere worked out in the global language of race. Nowhere was this clearer than in the conceptualization of sites of Black and African sovereignty. All were bound in world-spanning temporal chains. Imaginative and political writing about Haiti, Liberia, and Ethiopia during the interwar period insistently connected the specificity of each state to the impersonality of the whole world and its organizing structures. Haiti, Liberia, and Ethiopia proleptically showed that statehood represents no easy escape from the hierarchizing temporal power of race.[118]

EPILOGUE

EPILOGUE

A CENTURY AFTER THE Paris Peace Conference, the globalist optimism that characterized the end of the First World War is no longer widespread. Dipesh Chakrabarty has recently suggested that we now live in a planetary age rather than a global one. The globe is "a humanocentric construction"; the planet is a concept that "decenters the human." Unlike the globe, the planet existed before humans and will continue to exist after they are gone. "To encounter the planet in thought is to encounter something that is the condition of human existence and yet remains profoundly indifferent to that existence."[1] This sense of dislocation is related to a mood that Emily Apter calls "planetary dysphoria"—a depressive and melancholic state of extreme nonoptimism about the future of the world, at least when it comes to our place within it.[2] The world has become, one philosopher writes, "increasingly unthinkable."[3] Others contend that a "universe-laden language" deriving from "the astronaut's view of humanity" is incapable of responding to the present moment.[4] From a different vantage point but with a curiously similar outcome, globalism has come under attack from a recrudescent conservatism.[5]

Like planetary dysphoria, postcolonial dysphoria inhabits a previous moment of optimism and finds in it a new despondency. In *Foreign Office* (2015), the artist Bouchra Khalili revisits the period from 1962 to 1972, when Algiers was a center of world revolution. A series of photographs depict in states of emptiness and decay the buildings and offices in the city that once hosted liberation movements: a conference room in Hotel El-Safir, the residence of a Black Panther Party delegation in 1969; the stairwell of a building, labeled as the headquarters of the delegation from the People's Movement for the Liberation of Angola; a corridor where the Democratic Front for the Liberation of Palestine was based.[6] Khalili's elegiac vision is mirrored in the work of other contemporary artists whose images, films, and installations point to a generalized collapse of hope.[7] As Angela Davis put it recently, Third Worldism has "been virtually eliminated" as a force in international politics.[8] Postcolonial dysphoria discovers the impossibility of former hope just when it has become most urgent.

YET OUR NEW PLANETARY AGE does not supersede the global age that came before it. It requires us instead to sift through the globalisms that we have inherited and locate those that can form the basis of world-encompassing collective action.[9] Black Atlantic writers during the 1920s and 1930s emphasized the world's wholeness at the same time as they underlined its divisions.[10] Frequently drawing attention to the oneness of the world and the shrinking, through modernity, of its once ungraspable size, Black anticolonialists also insisted that the planet was violently divided by race. Theirs was a form of surreptitious, ambivalent globality. It embraced the scale of the world but was skeptical of the unified human agent that had been imbued by dominant globalities with the possession of the earth.

Bracketed by Ghana's independence in March 1957 and the formation of the Organisation of African Unity in May 1963, the pan-African project for a united polity on the continent represents the clearest attempt at maneuvering Black Atlantic critique into international politics.[11] But the consequences of interwar Black anticolonial thought were not limited to institutions. Traces of what Cedric Robinson described as "an accretion" of "collective intelligence gathered from struggle" can be found across the supervening decades.[12] Fanon's work, which called for "a restructuring of the world," is only one instance of a tradition that continued not to flee the global but to seize, remake, and adapt its encompassing scale.[13] Any attempt to relegate the study of the global—"how the world hangs together"—to futility must grapple with the enduring oppositional power of these underground globalities.[14] They are expressed across what Jesse McCarthy calls a "dense transatlantic feedback loop" that animates the cultural circuits of the Black Atlantic, and, through them, the world beyond.[15]

THE PROVINCIALIZING IMPULSE OF LOCALISM remains a powerful and seductive political discourse.[16] By contrast, the archives of interwar Black Atlantic writing contain many odes to cross-border traversal. If the European states involved in the colonization of Africa "tacitly and by implication took it that Africa would always be willing to be bled for the benefit of Europe," wrote an editorialist for the *Gold Coast Leader* in July 1920, "it never occurred to the schemers that the African might some day cry halt." They were wrong. "Never before were the signs of the times clearer than the present as to the coming together of Africans throughout the world. Instinctively it is being felt that in race solidarity is the coming strength of a people who have once again in the cycle of the ages to contribute substantially to the new civilisation that is about dawning."[17]

This "coming together of Africans throughout the world" is precisely what alarmed the colonial authorities. When, some years later, a copy of the Paris-based *Le Cri des Nègres* was discovered under a bench of a fourth-class train carriage traveling from Dakar to Kaolack, a letter was quickly sent to a number of high-level administrators of French West Africa. "It should be noted," remarked the letter, "that this constitutes the first example of a dissemination which, if continued, would be susceptible to unfortunate consequences."[18] "One can even wonder," went another missive from French colonial intelligence, "if the Powers which have a Black population within their home territories or colonies should not come together to exchange information."[19] Such glimpses into imperial surveillance point to the ways in which imperial powers often seek to block subaltern traversal across different sites of their authority. They remind us that a counterpolitics of scale is forged not in an abstract setting but precisely in the face of the provincializing strategies adopted by the rulers of the world.

Notes

INTRODUCTION

1. Marilla (or Marillia) Van, listed as the author of this article and others in the *News*, was probably a pseudonym for a Sierra Leonean political figure. I am grateful to David Harris and Rob Hammond for their assistance in trying to locate the person behind the pseudonym. For a discussion of anonymity and pen-names in colonial West Africa, see Newell, *The Power to Name*.

2. Marilla Van, "Random Jottings: The Pan-African Congress," *Sierra Leone Weekly News* [henceforth *SLWN*], June 21, 1919.

3. "The Year 1918," *SLWN*, January 11, 1919. "Negro Claims: The Future of the Black Races," *SLWN*, January 25, 1919.

4. "Editorial," *SLWN*, March 8, 1919.

5. Kelley, "But a Local Phase of a World Problem," 1077.

6. "Editorial Notes," *Gold Coast Leader* [henceforth *GCL*], February 5, 1919.

7. Hubert Harrison, "Our Larger Duty," *New Negro* 3, August 3, 1919, in Perry, *A Hubert Harrison Reader*, 100–1.

8. "A New Venture in London for the Welfare of Africa," *SLWN*, April 5, 1919. These interwar observations recall the "shrinking" of the world "from a previously awesome scale to a manageable space" that took place during the late nineteenth century. Bell, *Idea of Greater Britain*, 29.

9. Quotations from "Ring Out the Old: Ring in the New," *SLWN*, January 4, 1919; "Racial Unity," *GCL*, July 24–31, 1920; and "A Suicidal Policy," *SLWN*, August 25, 1928. The second of these articles depicted African unity in world-historical terms: "Never before were the signs of the times clearer than the present as to the coming together of Africans throughout the world . . . . We desire now to found for ourselves a place in the history of mankind more abiding than any that has gone before. And it is also easy to see that by promoting the unity of the Ethiopian race we shall be indirectly promoting the unity of the entire human race." For similar celebrations of pan-African unity in the West African press of this period, see also "Men and Matters," *Comet*, November 13, 1936; "An Epoch," *GCL*, January 31, 1920; and "Scrutineer," *GCL*, July 24–31, 1920.

10. "International Relations," *GCL*, April 2, 1927.

11. For the near universality of depictions of the world in human cultures, see Aslanian et al., "AHR Conversation," 1448.

12. Marx, *Capital*, vol. 1, 231.

13. Cosgrove, *Apollo's Eye*, 16–18.

14. Said, *Culture and Imperialism*, 283.

15. Viswanathan, *Power, Politics, and Culture*, 270.

16. Butler, *The Psychic Life of Power*, 104. Others have emphasized the importance of contingency and ambivalence for identities formed under unequal power. See, paradigmatically, Bhabha, "Of Mimicry and Man"; and with a more normative orientation, Brown, "Wounded Attachments"; and Rao, *Third World Protest*. Brent Hayes Edwards has helpfully suggested seeing articulations of politics and political affinity in Black internationalist cultures as "prosthetic" interventions, rather than "definitive" statements of rigid and unchanging ideas. Edwards, *The Practice of Diaspora*, 14.

17. Fanon, *Black Skin, White Masks*, 4. Penny Von Eschen, in *Race against Empire*, documents the role of governmental authorities in the United States in fragmenting the global ambitions of African American political organizing during the 1940s and 1950s.

18. Lefebvre, *La production de l'espace*, 31.Though the concept of "worldmaking" has recently been used by scholars referring to the international system, that term was not originally intended to carry any connotations of the international or global. Duncan Bell rightly points out that seeing "global intellectual history as a species of world making does not assume or prescribe any particular spatial scale"; Bell, "Making and Taking Worlds," 257. Gayatri Spivak discusses "the 'worlding' of what is now called 'the Third World'" using what she calls a "vulgarization" of Heidegger; Spivak, "Three Women's Texts and a Critique of Imperialism," 243, 260n1. Here there is a deliberate and suggestive slippage between the two senses of the "world"—which is, however, untheorized. In Getachew's recent *Worldmaking after Empire: The Rise and Fall of Self-Determination*, the relationship between the not necessarily global concept of worldmaking and the specifically global project of anticolonialism is also implied but not explicitly discussed.

19. Arboleda, *Planetary Mine*, 15.

20. Chakrabarty, *Climate of History in a Planetary Age*, 85.

21. "That black lives are necessarily geographic, but also struggle with discourses that erase and despatialize their sense of place, is where I begin to conceptualize geography," writes McKittrick in *Demonic Grounds*, 4. "Often, but not always, the only recognized geographic relevancy permitted to black subjects in the diaspora is that of dispossession and social segregation." See also the edited volume by McKittrick and Woods, *Black Geographies and the Politics of Place*.

22. McKittrick, *Demonic Grounds*, 20.

23. Bose and Manjapra, *Cosmopolitan Thought Zones*. We can see Black global thought as a critical Southern response to the powerful representational practices of the North (see Doty, *Imperial Encounters*), reminding us, as Edward Said emphasized in *Culture and Imperialism*, that the colonized world was never simply a receptor of representations. My identification of this body of thought contrasts with the tendency of studies on Black Atlantic political and economic thought to focus on academic work produced during the postindependence years. See Girvan, "Caribbean Dependency Thought Revisited"; Bernal, Figueroa, and Witter, "Caribbean Economic Thought"; Vitalis, *White World Order, Black Power Politics*. Works like Martin's *African Political Thought* similarly explore African anticolonial thought largely at the level of state leaders.

Of the Black Atlantic thinkers active during the 1920s and 1930s, the work of W. E. B. Du Bois has been exceptional in receiving serious—though still rare—attention within the field of international political thought. See Getachew and Pitts, "Introduction."

24. The historian Manu Goswami points out that a "scalar reorientation from the self to the world" was also central premise of a body of anticolonial thought in India. Goswami, "Imaginary Futures and Colonial Internationalisms," 1468.

25. See chapter 2 for a discussion of structuralist thought in interwar West Africa.

26. Taylor, "A Materialist Framework for Political Geography." For precursors, see Lefebvre, *La production de l'espace;* Amin, *Accumulation on a World Scale;* and Wallerstein, *Modern World-System.*

27. Howitt, "Scale," 138. See especially Massey's influential 1984 study, *Spatial Divisions of Labor,* and Neil Smith's article "Geography, Difference and the Politics of Scale." Other key contributions include Angelo and Goh, "Out in Space"; Brenner, "The Limits to Scale?"; Brenner, "The Urban Question"; Marston, "The Social Construction of Scale"; Marston, Jones, and Woodward, "Human Geography without Scale"; Swyngedouw, "Globalisation or 'Glocalisation'?"; Kurtz, "Scale Frames and Counter-Scale Frames"; Howitt, "Scale and the Other."

28. Marston, Jones, and Woodward, "Human Geography without Scale," 422.

29. Derickson, "Masters of the Universe," 557.

30. He continues: "There is no global view! And if there is no global view, you are always inside. The Globe is a sort of a remnant of a political theology." Latour, cited in Kurki, *International Relations in a Relational Universe,* 166.

31. Swyngedouw, "Globalisation or 'Glocalisation'?," 33.

32. Anderson, *Zone of Engagement,* 205. Emphasis in original.

33. I have written about the simultaneous proliferation of national and pannational ideas during the Belle Epoque in Younis, "'United by Blood.'"

34. Getachew, *Worldmaking after Empire,* chap. 1.

35. See, for example, Breuilly, *Nationalism and the State,* 282–87.

36. Ambivalent Black Atlantic nationalists argued, for example, that "whether race or nation Negroes are defenceless everywhere" ("Whither Is the Youth

League Bound?" *SLWN*, August 6, 1938); and that "Europe really knows no such thing as Nationality; she knows only Empire" (Kobina Sekyi, cited in Langley, *Ideologies of Liberation in Black Africa*, 244.)

37. For an overview of the field, see Olaniyan and Sweet, "Introduction"; on diaspora-in-the-making, see Patterson and Kelley, "Unfinished Migrations," 26. Amid a rich literature on the conceptualization of the African diaspora, see especially Lemelle and Kelley, *Imagining Home*; Edwards, *The Practice of Diaspora*; Hall, Stuart, "Cultural Identity and Diaspora."

38. Cosgrove, *Apollo's Eye*, 18.

39. Headley, "The Sixteenth-Century Venetian Celebration of the Earth's Total Habitability," 24. See also Bartelson, *Visions of World Community*, 67.

40. Walter, *Colonial Violence*, 235.

41. "Whereas other societies, domestic and international, had conceived that they bounded heaven and earth, or that they stretched from sea to sea, the nineteenth-century society of 'civilized' states possessed the capacity to do so in practice for the first time." Gong, *Standard of "Civilization" in International Society*, 5.

42. Shaw's *Theory of the Global State*, 19, explores the emergence of a "common consciousness of human society on a world scale," whose foundations are located in the sweeping destruction of World War II. For precursors, including Ibn Khaldun and Herodotus, see Conrad, *What Is Global History?*

43. Headley, "The Sixteenth-Century Venetian Celebration of the Earth's Total Habitability," 25.

44. Wynter, "Unsettling the Coloniality of Being/Power/Truth/Freedom," 259.

45. Foucault, *Ethics*, 316.

46. Ferreira da Silva, "Globality," 33.

47. Coronil, "Towards a Critique of Globalcentrism." Isaac A. Kamola has recently posited an intriguing relationship between the commodification of higher education and the academic reimagining of the world as a single market during the 1990s. Kamola, *Making the World Global*.

48. Arturo Escobar defines imperial globality as "an oppressive globality in which manifold forms of violence increasingly take on the function of regulation of peoples and economies." Escobar, "Beyond the Third World," 209. On the forms of oppression and hierarchy connected to global coloniality, see

Mignolo, *Darker Side of Western Modernity*, 18–19. On the connection between globality and racialized conceptions of development, see Ferreira da Silva, "Globality," 36.

49. Lefebvre, "Reflections on the Politics of Space," 31.

50. Palumbo-Liu, Robbins, and Tanoukhi, *Immanuel Wallerstein and the Problem of the World*, 9.

51. Césaire, *Discourse on Colonialism*, 27.

52. My line of reasoning here differs from recent arguments seeking to show that traditions internal to Europe offer critical ammunition for an anticolonial politics. Vico, Herder, Hegel, Heidegger, and debates in German idealism in general, have variously been offered up as examples of anticolonial options within the Western philosophical tradition. See Noyes, *Herder;* Brennan, *Borrowed Light;* Muthu, *Enlightenment against Empire.* By contrast, my argument, though it is interested in historical political writing, focuses not so much on *traditions* of thought as on the *methods* for procuring critical insight. In other words, I am focused on strategy rather than lineage.

53. Robbins, "Single? Great? Collective?," 797.

54. Van Munster and Sylvest, *The Politics of Globality since 1945*, 3.

55. Said, *Culture and Imperialism*, 283. On separate lineages, see Mignolo, *The Darker Side of Western Modernity*, xvi. For this reason, in his study of globality Denis Cosgrove calls the colonial encounter "at once tragically destructive and mutually transformative." Cosgrove, *Apollo's Eye*, 24.

56. Mbembe, "The Society of Enmity," 34.

57. "Man is world-forming," as Heidegger puts it. The concepts of *Weltanschauung* (worldview), *Lebenswelt* (lifeworld) and *Weltbild* (world-picture)—associated respectively with Wilhelm Dilthey, Edmund Husserl, and Martin Heidegger—invoke "worlds" in this sense, as does Nelson Goodman's influential idea of world-making and Heidegger's notion of worlding. Heidegger, *Fundamental Concepts of Metaphysics*, 185; Goodman, *Ways of Worldmaking.*

58. Stuart Hall's paradigmatic article, "Race, Articulation, and Societies Structured in Dominance," drawing on Althusser, adopts this way of thinking about articulation. He also usefully expands on his use of the term in an interview with Grossberg, "On Postmodernism and Articulation." In addition to Hall's work, I have found exceptionally helpful the discussion of articulation

given by Brent Hayes Edwards in *The Practice of Diaspora*, 11–15. Drawing on the French word *décalage*, Edwards points to the ways in which difference and unevenness can be articulated through a diasporic discourse. "Articulation is always a strange and ambivalent gesture," he writes, using as a metaphor the joints of the body, "because finally, in the body it is only difference—the separation between bones or members—that allows movement." (15)

59. I capitalize White not to confer the identity legitimacy but precisely to denaturalize it as an adjective applied to people. Recognizing White as a proper noun—the keystone around which spans the chromatic order of race—means rejecting the idea that "white" is a mere descriptor of skin color. This point is made in more detail by, among others, Kwame Anthony Appiah, in his article "The Case for Capitalizing the B in Black," *The Atlantic*, June 18, 2020. There is an absence of scholarly literature on the White Atlantic, but there are tantalizing references to it in Mills, "Unwriting and Unwhitening the World," 210; Stam and Shohat, *Race in Translation*, xv. I do not mean to suggest here that the White Atlantic was monolithic, simply that it was an identifiably coherent discourse that bore a relationship to imperial power.

60. Perry, *A Hubert Harrison Reader*, 101. Such comments recall what Duncan Bell has written about the importance of technological change not only in helping to meet political goals, but also in shaping the goals themselves. Bell, *Idea of Greater Britain*, 65.

61. Perry, *A Hubert Harrison Reader*, 122, 126.

62. Perry, *A Hubert Harrison Reader*, 101.

63. I develop these points more fully in chapter 5.

64. In the mid-1850s, for example, Martin Delany wrote that the oppression of distinct "classes of people" took place in "every quarter of the habitable globe," pointed out that "the white races are but one-third of the population of the globe," and told fellow Africans in the diaspora that "all the world now gazes at us." Levine, *Martin R. Delany*, 189, 210, 252.

65. Rosenboim, *The Emergence of Globalism*, 1–2.

66. Gómez, *The Tropics of Empire*, 44.

67. Pitts, *Boundaries of the International*. See also Chimni, "Third World Approaches to International Law"; Anghie, *Imperialism, Sovereignty and the Making of International Law*.

68. This division of the League of Nations into three key areas is taken from William Rappard's 1925 account of its operation in *International Relations as Viewed from Geneva*, as cited and discussed in Pedersen, *The Guardians*, 8–10. A standard criticism came from the *Sierra Leone Weekly News* in the wake of the League's failure to prevent Italy's invasion of Ethiopia: the organization, remarked the newspaper, was nothing but "an instrument to perpetuate white supremacy." Thomas Dosumu-Johnson, "The Negro Race: Its Place in Civilization," *SLWN*, March 3, 1934.

69. Vitalis, *White World Order, Black Power Politics*.

70. See Edwards, "Review."

71. See Kelley, "Introduction."

72. On technology and the imperial imagination, see especially Bell, *Idea of Greater Britain*. Belich, *Replenishing the Earth*, and Cronon, *Nature's Metropolis* provide insights into the power of booster literatures. It was Cecil Rhodes who dreamed of interstellar colonialism. See Rhodes, *Last Will and Testament of Cecil John Rhodes*, 190.

73. Azikiwe, *My Odyssey*, 34; Nkrumah, *Autobiography of Kwame Nkrumah*, 18, 37. Jomo Kenyatta did not write an autobiography but, according to C. L. R. James, he recounted how: "Kenya nationalists, unable to read, would gather round a reader of Garvey's newspaper, *The Negro World*, and listen to an article two or three times. Then they would run various ways through the forest, carefully to repeat the whole, which they had memorised, to Africans hungry for some doctrine which lifted them from the servile consciousness in which Africans lived." Grimshaw, *C. L. R. James Reader*, 300.

74. "Editorial Notes," *GCL*, August 21, 1929,

75. Digby-Junger, "The *Guardian, Crisis, Messenger*, and *Negro World*," 263–64.

76. Carr and Hart, *The Global 1920s*, 39. As Carr and Hart point out, thousands of veterans of the US Civil War were also still alive in 1919.

77. On the forcible recruitment of *tirailleurs sénégalais*, see Lunn's oral history, *Memoirs of the Maelstrom*.

78. The elder May's Methodist training involved eighteen months' study in London at a training college of the British and Foreign Mission School Society. Spitzer, *Lives in Between*, 50–52; Lynch, "Edward W. Blyden," 384. On May *pater*'s death, see *African Law Reports*, 56; Marke, *Origin of Wesleyan Methodism in*

Sierra Leone. On the *Sierra Leone Weekly News,* see Wyse, *H. C. Bankole-Bright and Politics in Colonial Sierra Leone,* 24.

79. Spitzer, *Lives in Between,* 159–60. Spitzer mentions that the colonial authorities used May's conviction to abolish the African-governed Freetown City Council in 1927 and replace it with a European-dominated body. Cornelius May had himself studied in England for seven years.

80. "1937: A Retrospect," *SLWN,* January 1, 1938.

81. Azikiwe, *My Odyssey,* 177.

82. The interwar period, which I focus on in this study (I include the years during the two World Wars), is widely recognized as a golden age for Black Atlantic newspapers. Penny Von Eschen, in *Race against Empire,* 8, writes that World War II and its immediate aftermath represent a "golden age in black American journalism." Rosalynde Ainslie, in *Press in Africa,* 32, 73, calls the 1930s "an exceptionally fertile period" for the press in Nigeria and Ghana, noting that the independence period paradoxically "diminished the number of African-controlled newspapers." See also Omu, *Press and Politics in Nigeria.*

83. "Men and Matters. Two Sick Men of Africa, and After?," *Comet,* March 2, 1935.

84. For an analysis of international relations literature in terms of this division between "narrow" and "deep" perspectives on hierarchy, see Zarakol, *Hierarchies in World Politics,* 4–7. A range of accounts—especially those drawing on postcolonial and Marxist traditions—have stressed hierarchy's deep and constitutive nature (see e.g., Grovogui, *Beyond Eurocentrism and Anarchy.*) Other works identify such hierarchies in the history of international law. See Anghie, *Imperialism, Sovereignty and the Making of International Law;* Koskenniemi, *The Gentle Civilizer of Nations.*

85. As Alexandra Reza writes, "decolonisation is treated as history, not theory"; Reza, "African Anticolonialism as Cosmonationalism," 10. The reference here is specifically to scholars of decolonization in international relations: Georg Deutsch, Neta Crawford, and Henri Grimal. A disciplinary divide between theory (as a product of the contemporary academy) and history (as a source of empirical data for theory) is also evident in the nevertheless valuable and enriching account of hierarchy in the field of international relations edited by Zarakol, *Hierarchies in World Politics.*

86. If existing approaches to international hierarchy often focus on the powerful at the expense of the subordinated, one of the results of this

imbalance has been a failure to comprehend the textured and experiential aspects of such stratification and the different ways in which it was comprehended by populations living under colonial rule. This did not always transform into systematized political doctrines or state-led political projects and it took place across an intellectual space that traversed any single empire or language. Drawing on Raymond Williams, we might call this a structure of anticolonial feeling—the solution from which movements against imperialism were precipitated. See Williams and Orrom, *Preface to Film*, 21. For an examination of the phrase across Williams's writing, see Matthews, "Change and Theory in Raymond Williams's Structure of Feeling." Brent Hayes Edwards points out the similarities with Ralph Ellison's description of Black culture as "a concord of sensibilities." Rowell, "An Interview with Brent Hayes Edwards," 796.

87. Magee, *Empire and Globalisation* (on "cultural economies"); Belich, *Replenishing the Earth* (on "replenishing"); Lake and Reynolds, *Drawing the Global Colour Line* (on settlement); Bell, *Idea of Greater Britain* (on "greater England"); Rosenberg, *World Connecting* (on imperial coalitions).

88. Wright, "Foreword," 12. Nico Slate's *Colored Cosmopolitanism*, 3, explores "global solidarities of color," but, as with other works on anticolonial internationalism, his focus is on antihierarchic activity rather than hierarchic theory.

89. See, respectively, the succession of literary periodicals founded by young Haitians in response to the US occupation of Haiti (discussed in chapter 5); the introduction to René Maran's novel *Batouala* (discussed in chapter 4); African American poetry in response to the Italian invasion of Ethiopia (discussed in chapter 5); and Samuel Johnson's *History of the Yorubas* (discussed in chapter 2).

90. At the same time, formal distinctions matter: they reflect important decisions about what Jacques Rancière calls the different "ways of doing things with words"; Rancière, "The Politics of Literature," 13. Writing about Negritude, Carrie Noland reminds us that "poetry circulates in a realm distinct from that of a newspaper or official party organ"; Noland, *Voices of Negritude in Modernist Print*, 236.

91. I draw here on Quentin Skinner's criticism of the "reification of doctrines," Pierre Bourdieu's critique of scholastic reason, and the work of literary scholars using field theory. See Skinner, "Meaning and Understanding in the

History of Ideas," 11; Bourdieu, *Pascalian Meditations;* Ahearne and Speller, "Pierre Bourdieu and the Literary Field."

92. For nationalism as a theory of political legitimacy, see Gellner, *Nations and Nationalism,* 1. For nationhood as the goal of nationalism, see Smith, *Nationalism,* 21. For taxonomies of nationalism, see Breuilly, *Nationalism and the State,* 62. These scholars recognize, of course, that nationalism is a product of certain features of modernity: capitalism, communications technologies, industrial societies, changing conceptions of time and space. Much of the work of nationalism studies has been to examine these quintessentially modern phenomena. The ideology of nationalism is also widely recognized as weakly theorized and self-contradictory. Nevertheless, nationalism is given a form of coherence by representing it as an ideology that can be defined according to a series of principles—implicitly contrasting it with forms of *inter-* or *pan-*nationalism, despite its historical association with both.

93. Melville, *Redburn,* 214. Tellingly, this world-containing American blood was contrasted by Melville—in an anti-Semitic aside—to insular, hermetic, "Hebrew" blood. For an outstanding study of Whiteness as a project at once national and global, see Lake and Reynolds, *Drawing the Global Colour Line.* Whiteness in the context of the United States has been studied extensively: see the works by Roediger, *The Wages of Whiteness;* Jacobson, *Whiteness of a Different Color.* For a provocative examination of settler nationalisms in the "Angloworld," see Belich, *Replenishing the Earth.* On the notion of Greater Britain, which hoped to revitalize Britain's links with its settler colonies and territories, see Bell, *Idea of Greater Britain.* On pan-Latinism, see Giladi, "The Elaboration of Pan-Latinism in French Intellectual Circles."

94. The spatial imaginaries of anticolonial imaginaries have received less attention than their dominant counterparts. For a recent and convincing critique of the differential treatment meted out by scholars to African nationalisms as compared to their European counterparts, see Larmer and Lecocq, "Historicising Nationalism in Africa."

95. Fanon, *The Wretched of the Earth,* 2.

96. A vibrant tradition of anticolonial anarchism attests to a rich body of antistatist thought that emerged alongside the critique of empire. See, for example, Anderson, *Under Three Flags;* Harper, *Underground Asia.* But anticolonialists also often searched for new forms of nationalism, while critiques of the

postcolonial state were themselves—as Neil Lazarus has written—often "undertaken precisely in the name of alternative nationalisms, of different national imaginings." Lazarus, *Postcolonial Unconscious*, 70.

97. Though there is a richly detailed literature on pan-Africanism, theoretical hostility has dominated general discussions of pan-nationalism. The only major comparative monograph on pan-nationalisms, Snyder's *Macro-Nationalisms*, suggests that "in most cases . . . they reveal an aggressive impulse seeking to extend control over contiguous or non-contiguous territory in the name of territorial imperative" and "almost always there is an element of domination— the mother nationalism demands control of her children everywhere"; they are, then, "an outcome of aggressive nationalism"; Snyder, *Macro-Nationalisms*, 4. Tom Nairn dismisses pan-Arabism, pan-Hellenism, and pan-Slavism as "conservative ideological trances employing a rhetoric of racial solidarity to stifle popular and national trouble-makers"; Nairn, *Faces of Nationalism*, 170. John Breuilly's less hostile analysis nevertheless sees pan-Arabism and pan-Africanism as examples of "unification nationalisms" that were ultimately unsuccessful, though they "played an important role as intellectual forerunners of territorial nationalism"; Breuilly, *Nationalism and the State*, 287. (For a rare comparative discussion of pan-movements that is not imbued with negativity and a sense of failure, see Goebel, *Anti-Imperial Metropolis*, 265–66. I am grateful to Brent Hayes Edwards for alerting me to this point.)

98. Kelley, *Race Rebels*, 124. Edwards also points out that "discourses about black *national* autonomy . . . played a formative role in the formulation of black *internationalist* initiatives"; Edwards, *Practice of Diaspora*, 10. See also Minkah Makalani's analysis of Cyril Briggs: "an intellectual who pursued a political vision that drew on both socialism and black nationalism but who refused to be restricted by them"; Makalani, *In the Cause of Freedom*, 47.

99. Abrahams, *The Coyaba Chronicles*, 45.

100. This point has often been made in the scholarship on Black Atlantic interwar print cultures. See Peterson and Hunter, "Print Culture in Colonial Africa," 5–8; James, "Transatlantic Passages," 50; Putnam, "Circum-Atlantic Print Circuits and Internationalism from the Peripheries in the Interwar Era"; Newell, *Power to Name*, 48.

101. On the sharply differentiated nature of Black citizenship in the United States, see Saidiya Hartman's concept of the "burdened individuality" experi-

enced by African Americans after emancipation. Hartman, *Scenes of Subjection*, chap. 4.

CHAPTER 1: THE NATION AND THE WORLD

1. Garvey was a Jamaican newspaper editor and political activist who founded an organization—the United Negro Improvement Association (UNIA)—and an associated newspaper, the *Negro World*. The UNIA looked to unite all those of African descent for the purpose of collective uplift. Perhaps the largest mass movement of African-descended peoples in modern history, while its official history was short—it quickly declined after its peak in the early-to-mid-1920s, and especially after Garvey was deported from the United States to Jamaica in 1927—its traces remained visible many decades later in the language and iconography of African nationalisms, the Rastafari movement, the Nation of Islam, forms of Black music including hip hop and jazz, among many other manifestations. *The Marcus Garvey and Universal Negro Improvement Association Papers*, edited by Robert A. Hill and currently running to thirteen volumes, offer a finely detailed and comprehensive scholarly resource on Garvey and Garveyism. See also the recent edited volume, Stephens and Ewing, *Global Garveyism*, for a helpful introduction and survey.

2. See Wigger's recent study on this panic, *The "Black Horror on the Rhine."*

3. "Are Moroccans and Algerians Negroes?" *Negro World*, January 20, 1923.

4. "Are Moroccans and Algerians Negroes?" *Negro World*, January 20, 1923.

5. Moses, *Creative Conflict in African American Thought*, 291.

6. Slate, *Colored Cosmopolitanism*.

7. Robert A. Hill has explained that starting in July 1921, Garvey undertook a "retreat from radicalism" as he tried to placate the US government, which threatened his immigration status. His ideas about national loyalty moved from a radical skepticism about Black belonging in the West to reiterative insistence on the "loyalty" of UNIA members to their respective states. Articulations of anticolonial solidarity and pan-Africanism did not disappear (as this chapter will show), but they did suffer from the distinct forms of repression faced by Garvey and the UNIA. Hill, *Marcus Garvey and Universal Negro Improvement Association Papers*, 1:lxxxiv.

8. Harold, *Rise and Fall of the Garvey Movement in the Urban South;* Rolinson, *Grassroots Garveyism;* Vinson, "'Sea Kaffirs'"; Vinson, *The Americans Are Coming!;* Ewing, *Age of Garvey;* Ewing, "Caribbean Labour Politics in the Age of Garvey, 1918–1938"; Taylor, "'Negro Women Are Great Thinkers as Well as Doers'"; Roll, "Garveyism and the Eschatology of African Redemption in the Rural South."

9. Ewing, *Age of Garvey,* 6–7, 132.

10. Blain, *Set the World on Fire,* 2–3.

11. Two recent and salutary exceptions, which examine the spatial politics of Garveyism and the UNIA, are Jagmohan, "Between Race and Nation"; Bledsoe and Wright, "Pluralities of Black Geographies." My approach differs from both in that I focus on archival close reading of the texts of Garveyism, especially the *Negro World.* In that sense, I want to try and bridge the methodological gap between historians, on the one side, and social scientists and geographers, on the other, and to suggest that a *political* reading of Garveyism might nevertheless benefit from the archival techniques of historians.

12. The term "racial chauvinism" was used by the Comintern during its Third Period (1928–33). See Lemelle and Kelley, *Imagining Home,* 36. For Garveyism's "Eurocentric undercurrents," see Watson, "Raciology, Garveyism and the Limits of Black Nationalism in the Caribbean Diaspora," 88.

13. "Miscegenation will lead to the moral destruction of both races," he declared in 1925; Hill, *Marcus Garvey and Universal Negro Improvement Association Papers,* 6:216. On his antisemitism, see Hill and Bair, *Marcus Garvey: Life and Lessons,* lvii; on his meeting with the Ku Klux Klan, see Ewing, *Age of Garvey,* 118.

14. "Far from revolutionary, these appeals are, in fact, eminently conservative. Conservatism is a politics of cultural conservation; conservatives live in a world of racial, national, and ethnic distinctions." Gilroy, "Black Fascism," 82.

15. Edwards, *The Practice of Diaspora,* 118.

16. Gilroy, *Against Race,* 72.

17. This broader definition is now often associated with post-1960s developments in antiracist organizing, such as the Black Consciousness movement in South Africa and the antiracist movement in Britain. See Mgbako, "'My Blackness Is the Beauty of This Land'"; Narayan, "British Black Power." But a study of the *Negro World* (and indeed the history of Haiti) shows that its roots lie much earlier.

18. Gilroy, "Black Fascism," 91.

19. Lewis, *Marcus Garvey*; Watson, "Raciology, Garveyism and the Limits of Black Nationalism in the Caribbean Diaspora," 89.

20. Moses, *Golden Age of Black Nationalism*, 267.

21. Hill and Bair, *Marcus Garvey*, xxiv–xxxx.

22. Harold, *The Rise and Fall of the Garvey Movement in the Urban South*, 41; Rolinson, *Grassroots Garveyism*, 73; Ewing, *Age of Garvey*, 112. An earlier study gives a peak circulation figure of fifty thousand; Moses, *Creative Conflict in African American Thought*, 252.

23. The obituary of a man from Louisiana, who died aged 116 and who had been formerly enslaved, "explained his love of hearing the Garvey speeches read from the front page, as he had never learned to read." Rolinson, *Grassroots Garveyism*, 117.

24. Marable, *Malcolm X*, 52.

25. Rolinson, *Grassroots Garveyism*, 76; Cronon, *Black Moses*, 45.

26. Ewing, *Age of Garvey*, 91.

27. TNA CO 23/285/1. These issues date from October 11 and 25, 1919; another issue in the same folder dates from November 1, 1919.

28. "A Lesson from India and China," *Negro World*, November 1, 1919.

29. Vincent, *Black Power and the Garvey Movement*, x.

30. "Colored Peoples Everywhere Asserting Their Rights to Self-Determination," *Negro World*, December 1, 1923. Another article in 1919 suggested that "Negroes must now combine with China, India, Egypt, Ireland and Russia to free themselves in the future." Hill, *Marcus Garvey and Universal Negro Improvement Association Papers*, 2:495.

31. See *Negro World* issues of May 16, 1925; June 20, 1925; July 4, 1925; November 14, 1925.

32. For other publications influenced by *The African Times and Orient Review* *(ATOR)*, see Winkiel, *Modernism, Race and Manifestos*, 162 (though Winkiel mistakenly refers to ATOR as *"The Ethiopian Times and Orient Review"*); see also Geiss, *Pan-African Movement*, 224. Hill, *Marcus Garvey and Universal Negro Improvement Association Papers*, 1:314. Ali would later go on to found *The Comet*, based in Lagos (see chapter 2).

33. Ali would later work for Garvey—he became a regular contributor to the *Negro World*, heading its Africa section. The relationship ended bitterly. Later, Ali "was still telling anyone in London who would listen that because of

Garvey's 'laziness and general worthless character' he had been discharged from his messenger job in 1913." Cronon, *Black Moses*, 43. Ali also wrote a satiri-cal, fictionalized portrait of Garvey in "Ere Roosevelt Came." Hill, *Marcus Garvey and Universal Negro Improvement Association Papers*, 2:liv; Hill, *Marcus Garvey and Universal Negro Improvement Association Papers*, 6:55.

34. "Editorial," *ATOR*, July 1, 1912, iii.

35. "Editorial," *ATOR*, July 1, 1912, iii.

36. Short biographical features encouraged pride in figures of African descent (a Sierra Leonean author, a Guyanese inventor); a Persian writer denounced European imperialism in his country; a Japanese historian cri-tiqued the "increasing dependence of Asia upon Europe"; Booker T. Washing-ton wrote a long profile of the Tuskegee Institute; Pan-Islamism was explained and defended on "political" grounds. Another regular feature was a press round-up, titled "Darker Races in the Press of the World." See *ATOR* issues of July 1912, August 1912, and October 1912; see also Esedebe, *Pan-Africanism*, 67–70.

37. "The Need for Inter-Racial Unity," *ATOR*, November 1912.

38. Esedebe, *Pan-Africanism*, 69.

39. Perry, *A Hubert Harrison Reader*, 92.

40. Perry, *Hubert Harrison*, 7, 295; Hill and Bair, *Marcus Garvey*, xix. Hill and Blair mention that A. Philip Randolph, Chandler Owen, and W. A. Domingo were other "stepladder orators" who "began speaking along Lenox Avenue" in 1916 and who, "along with Garvey, converted the black community of Harlem into a parliament of the people during the years of the Great War and after" (xix).

41. Perry, *A Hubert Harrison Reader*, 227–28.

42. "Why I Am a Garveyite," *Negro World*, January 8, 1927.

43. Hill, *Marcus Garvey and Universal Negro Improvement Association Papers*, 2:91.

44. "Hon. Marcus Garvey, Foremost Orator of the Race, Delivers Brilliant Speech in Philadelphia," *Negro World*, November 1, 1919.

45. Perry, *A Hubert Harrison Reader*, 92.

46. Perry, *A Hubert Harrison Reader*, 90. In 1912, *ATOR* reported that an Afri-can American flag had been designed by Bishop J. Lennox of the Zion African Episcopal Church after he had been shocked by hearing an abusive song that

mocked the absence of a Black flag. His flag supposedly depicted eleven stars (representing the holy disciples, except Judas) in a field of purple and surrounded by twelve bars of red, white, and blue. "New Flag for Afro-Americans," *ATOR*, October 1912. But the vexillologist Stephen A. Knowlton has shown this to be an incorrect report, based probably on a fraudulent press release and perhaps intended to mock Black "pretensions" to statehood. Knowlton, "'Show Me the Race or the Nation without a Flag, and I Will Show You a Race of People without Any Pride,'" 33. Nevertheless, Garvey would later refer to the same abusive song when explaining the origin of his own flag. Garvey, *More Philosophy and Opinions of Marcus Garvey*, 56.

47. Cited in Knowlton, "'Show Me the Race or the Nation without a Flag, and I Will Show You a Race of People without Any Pride,'" 39. The interview took place on August 8, 1920. There is a continuity with later iterations of Black nationalism. As Knowlton suggests with reference to the work of T. N. Phu, the visual iconography of the Black Panther Party, which included flags, gestured to contemporaneous anti-imperial struggles in Asia and Africa (51).

48. Hahn, *Political Worlds of Slavery and Freedom*, 133. Its officials acted, in the words of Manning Marable, as "a nobility in exile." Marable, *Malcolm X*, 19.

49. Hill, *Marcus Garvey and Universal Negro Improvement Association Papers*, 2:499.

50. Hill, *Marcus Garvey and Universal Negro Improvement Association Papers*, 2:495.

51. Letter from Captain John B. Trevor to Brigadier General Malborough Churchill, April 5, 1919. Hill, *Marcus Garvey and Universal Negro Improvement Association Papers*, 1:401–2.

52. Hill, *Marcus Garvey and Universal Negro Improvement Association Papers*, 1:493.

53. Hill, *Marcus Garvey and Universal Negro Improvement Association Papers*, 2:333.

54. Hill, *Marcus Garvey and Universal Negro Improvement Association Papers*, 1:304. See Gallicchio, *African American Encounter with Japan and China*, for an outstanding study of African American interest in Japan—and, later, China—as potential leaders of a pan-"coloured" global revolt.

55. Quinn-Judge, *Ho Chi Minh*, 21.

56. "Editorial," *Negro World*, February 24, 1923.

57. In Wright's novel, a Black man, furious at prejudicial treatment, is thrown into a UNIA-influenced reverie. He "saw millions of black soldiers marching in black armies; he saw a black battleship flying a black flag; he himself was standing on the deck of that black battleship surrounded by black generals." Wright, *Lawd Today!*, 143–44. For a discussion of this passage, see Dawahare, *Nationalism, Marxism, and African American Literature between the Wars*, 126.

58. "Hon. Marcus Garvey in First Public Appearance Stirred Large Crowds at Philadelphia Meeting." *Negro World*, October 11, 1919.

59. And—in the same article—"the sword will decide to whom belongs the right." "Hon. Marcus Garvey, Foremost Orator of the Race, Delivers Brilliant Speech in Philadelphia," *Negro World*, November 1, 1919. "The war has taught us that education in these days must necessarily be extended farther than the use of the pen," ran a letter published in the same year, "it must also embody the use of the sword and the rifle." "J. A. Martineau Sees Danger in the Annexation of the West Indies to the U.S.A." *Negro World*, October 25, 1919.

60. "Hon. Marcus Garvey, Foremost Orator of the Race, Delivers Brilliant Speech in Philadelphia," *Negro World*, November 1, 1919.

61. Nationalism was, Garvey contended, "the symbol of race equality, race achievement and race supremacy." Only a "race with its own government and its own country is assured recognition and respect . . . . We cannot go very far without a country." "Nationalism is the Symbol of Race Equality," *Negro World*, September 1, 1923.

62. "Editorial," *Negro World*, April 21, 1928.

63. Satter, "Marcus Garvey, Father Divine and the Gender Politics of Race Difference and Race Neutrality," 45.

64. "Europeanness" is "a defining logic of race . . . materially, discursively and extra-corporeally." Hesse, "Racialized Modernity," 646.

65. On "the impossibility of black sovereignty," see Salt, *The Unfinished Revolution*, 94; Getachew, *Worldmaking after Empire*, 52; Younis, "Grand Machinery of the World," 279; Glover, "'Flesh Like One's Own,'" 237. Nisancioglu's "Racial Sovereignty" gives a detailed theoretical account of the relationship between race and sovereignty.

66. Shilliam, "What about Marcus Garvey?"

67. "Greatest Meeting in History of Universal Negro Improvement Ass'n Held in Liberty Hall," *Negro World*, October 25, 1919.

68. "Hon. Marcus Garvey in First Public Appearance Stirred Large Crowds at Philadelphia Meeting," *Negro World*, October 11, 1919.

69. Watson, "Raciology, Garveyism and the Limits of Black Nationalism in the Caribbean Diaspora," 87.

70. In an article for the *New York Call* in 1911, Harrison enjoined his readers to "confess the naked truth that there is nothing innate in race prejudice. But it is diligently fostered by those who have something to gain from it." Perry, *A Hubert Harrison Reader*, 56. Harrison had prominently broken with the Socialist Party of the USA on this point. Perry, *Hubert Harrison*, 7.

71. Satter, "Marcus Garvey, Father Divine and the Gender Politics of Race Difference and Race Neutrality," 47.

72. Wintz, *African American Political Thought*, 127.

73. Dorman, "Skin Bleach and Civilization," 62–65.

74. Mbembe, *Critique of Black Reason*, 156.

75. See Slate, *Colored Cosmopolitanism*, chap. 2.

76. Garvey, *Tragedy of White Injustice*.

77. Ellis, *Race, War, and Surveillance*, 44.

78. "The World in Unrest," *Negro World*, November 1, 1919.

79. "Hon. Marcus Garvey in First Public Appearance Stirred Large Crowds at Philadelphia Meeting," *Negro World*, October 11, 1919.

80. "Negro Race Going Forward to the Point of Destiny," *Negro World*, March 24, 1923. Threats about the extirpatory power of White supremacy were common in the newspaper. See, for example, "Hon. Marcus Garvey, Foremost Orator of the Race, Delivers Brilliant Speech in Philadelphia," *Negro World*, November 1, 1919, for a sustained argument about why "to the white man blood is thicker than water," and why the prospect of lasting domination underneath White supremacy was a fate worse than death. See also Hill, *Marcus Garvey and Universal Negro Improvement Association Papers*, 2:466. See also "Editorial," *Negro World*, October 11, 1919, for a warning about the power of White "mobs." Elsewhere, UNIA members were warned about the threat of the reimposition of slavery. "Mrs. Capers, Black Cross Nurse, Thrills Charleston Audiences," *Negro World*, March 17, 1923.

81. Untitled article, *Negro World*, March 28, 1925.

82. The "white man," Garvey wrote elsewhere, was "thinking all the time, never resting, never sleeping." Garvey, *More Philosophy and Opinions of Marcus Garvey*, 25.

83. Brantlinger, *Dark Vanishings*, 2.

84. See Hill and Bair, *Marcus Garvey*, xxiii.

85. "Hon. Marcus Garvey, Foremost Orator of the Race, Delivers Brilliant Speech in Philadelphia," *Negro World*, November 1, 1919. "The Views of the U.N.I.A. on the Race Problem Are Upheld," *Negro World*, March 24, 1923.

86. A letter to the newspaper described this oppression in the context of the history of Africans in the Caribbean: "The Anglo-Saxon race of those islands, although in the minority, took the reins in one hand and the whip in the other. Our burden was heavy and our journey was long, and we groaned under the pressure of our oppressors without any relief." "West Indians—What of the Future," *Negro World*, October 11, 1919.

87. "If White People Accepted the View of the Absolute Need for Subserviency of the Black Race for the White, What Justification Can There Be for the Use of Black Troops by One White Nation against Another White Nation?" ran one headline in the *Negro World* on October 11, 1919.

88. Digby-Junger, *"The Guardian, Crisis, Messenger, and Negro World,"* 280.

89. As Garvey himself suggested: "the voice of conscience" was "playing on that pale face all the time"; "having stolen everything he has from one dark race or another, he only lives in dread of the day when the dark races will come together as one man and demand it back from him." "Hon. Marcus Garvey, Foremost Orator of the Race, Delivers Brilliant Speech in Philadelphia," *Negro World*, November 1, 1919. See also "Socialism and the Negro," *Negro World*, October 11, 1919; "The Riots Once More," *Negro World*, October 11, 1919. Meanwhile, for the moral claim pertaining to "colored" peoples, see for example "Thousands of Loyal Members Fill Liberty Hall," *Negro World*, May 5, 1923. This article argued that "this white man's civilization" had "succeeded in destroying itself" and that "out of the debris and the ashes of that civilization will arise a newer and better civilization" which the "colored races are peculiarly suited to establish, especially those who have not been contaminated with the vices of white civilization."

90. It is true that Garvey hoped the UNIA would establish a territorial base in Liberia: he sent a delegation to President C. D. B. King in 1920, proposing a far-reaching partnership between the African republic and his organization. But the failure of this proposal meant that actually existing Garveyism was *in effect* deterritorial: it did not have to deal with the contradictions that would

have ensued between its transnational ambit and a national base in West Africa. See M'bayo, "W. E.[ths}B. Du Bois, Marcus Garvey, and Pan-Africanism in Liberia," 39–41; for an examination of the deterritorial sovereignty of the UNIA, see Shilliam, "What about Marcus Garvey?" Adom Getachew also describes Garvey's nationalism as "deterritorial." Getachew, *Worldmaking after Empire*, 25.

91. M'bayo, "W. E. B. Du Bois, Marcus Garvey, and Pan-Africanism in Liberia," 24; Watson, "Raciology, Garveyism and the Limits of Black Nationalism in the Caribbean Diaspora," 87. This view of Garveyism's scope does not require us to contradict Graves's view that Garvey was unoriginal as a political thinker. Graves, "Social Ideas of Marcus Garvey," 67.

92. Carnegie, "Garvey and the Black Transnation," 51.

93. On Black women's literary responses to that movement, see Dubey's careful study *Black Women Novelists and the Nationalist Aesthetic*.

94. See Narayan, "Huey P. Newton's Intercommunalism."

CHAPTER 2: THE STRUCTURE OF THE WORLD

1. "The Back of the White Man's Mind," GCL, March 19, 1921.

2. Expressions of anti-African racism in the British press were commonly cited in newspapers along the West African coast as evidence of imperial disdain. These citations often traveled from one West African newspaper to another. In June 1919, for example, a British *Sunday Chronicle* article argued that White women had to be protected from the supposedly uncontainable urges of Black men. The article was cited in the *Gold Coast Leader* and, from there, in the *Sierra Leone Weekly News*, each time attracting a novel critique. For the original article, see: A. E. G., "The Black Menace: Why the Colour Line Must be Clearly Drawn," *Sunday Chronicle*, June 15, 1919. The *Gold Coast Leader* commented on the article on August 16; from there, it was mentioned in the *Sierra Leone Weekly News*. "Can England with Her Present Policy in Ruling the Nations Be Destined to Be the Last of the Ruling Nations?" SLWN, October 11, 1919. I. T. A. Wallace-Johnson's famous article, "Has the African a God?," which attracted sedition proceedings, was also premised on the citation of European racist discourse—though here it was ventriloquized rather than directly quoted. "To the European," Wallace-Johnson had written, "he (the African) is

classified as a monkey." See "Has the African a God?" *African Morning Post*, May 15, 1936.

3. Newell, *The Power to Name*, 55.

4. Jenkins, "Gold Coast Historians and Their Pursuit of the Gold Coast Pasts," 35.

5. "The Back of the White Man's Mind," *GCL*, March 19, 1921.

6. See, *inter alia*, Fauvelle, *Golden Rhinoceros*.

7. Peterson and Hunter, "Print Culture in Colonial Africa," 3. See also Hofmeyr and Peterson, "Politics of the Page."

8. Writing about the period 1776–1860 in the British Caribbean, for example, Christopher Taylor makes the point that "the lack of a West Indian political economy is the product less of ignorance, creole indolence, or the contingencies of history than it is itself an argument" that "quietly articulates a fierce polemic." Taylor, *Empire of Neglect*, 9. And Manu Goswami explains that "nationalists in colonial India attempted to find a space between what they indicted as the excessive abstraction of classical political economy and the 'self-serving materialism' of colonial economic policies." Goswami, *Producing India*, 221.

9. On the "planetary system," see Moretti, "Conjectures on World Literature," 54. The literary critic Emmanuel Obiechina points out that West African novels "appeared after the novels on Africa written by non-Africans," and were therefore always in some sense a reaction to this earlier literature *about* Africa from the outside. Obiechina, *Culture, Tradition and Society in the West African Novel*, 261. In West Africa, as elsewhere, the interwar period saw many ventures into new forms of vernacular writing: D. O. Fagunwa pioneered the Yoruba-language novel with *Ògbójú Ọdẹ nínú Igbó Irúnmọlẹ̀* (1938); Pita Nwana wrote *Omenuko*, the first novel in Igbo (1933); Kobina Sekyi wrote a play, *The Blinkards* (1915), in English and Fante; and Ferdinand Kwasi Fiawoo wrote a play in Ewe, *Toko Atolia* (1942). Along with others, like the musicologist J. H. Kwabena Nketia, these figures have since been canonized as the founders of vernacular West African traditions that flourished in the postindependence period, as seen, for example, in the influence of Fagunwa on figures like Wole Soyinka and Amos Tutuola. See Izevbaye, "West African Literature in English," 478; Emenyònu, *The Rise of the Igbo Novel*. Interwar innovations in West African forms took place alongside the deepening of a West African tradition of writing in English. Two of the best-known instances are Sekyi's novella *The*

Anglo-Fanti, serialized in 1918, and the novels and pamphlets which came to be known as Onitsha market literature, the publication of which began soon after the Second World War in eastern Nigeria. West African newspapers had also published folktales in English since the 1880s and 1890s. Newell, *The Power to Name*, 115; Obiechina, *An African Popular Literature*.

10. Recognizing this interrelation should not mean underplaying the importance of intra-African conversations taking place within African writing, as Evan M. Mwangi has reminded us; Mwangi, *Africa Writes back to Self*. At the same time, though, even such apparently constant notions as tradition and authenticity were themselves implicated the global encounter between African and European forms. Ato Quayson thus helpfully suggests that, rather than assuming an organic relationship between tradition and African literature, we should instead think in terms of mediation and "interdiscursivity"— evaluating "the strategic location of each of the writers in relation to indigenous resources as well as to larger historical realities." For example, rather than seeing Yoruba traditions like the three-tiered Yoruba universe—*Orun* (Sky), *Ilé* (Earth), *Aiyé* (World)—as self-contained, we should consider how they interacted with Western visions of the world. Quayson, *Strategic Transformations in Nigerian Writing*, 10–11.

11. Not all newspaper writing was overtly political. West African newspapers included "nonpolitical" columns, often written by and aimed at women, covering "women's issues." As Stephanie Newell has pointed out, with the exception of writing by Gladys May Casely Hayford—J. E. Casely Hayford's daughter, who contributed to the *Gold Coast Leader*—those who wrote under female names almost exclusively wrote on such topics. Newell, *The Power to Name*, 160. West African writing of this period was overwhelmingly produced by men, though sometimes under female pseudonyms. Newell points to the prominence of the theme of marriage across colonial West African fiction, which was "underwritten by the topic of female sexuality to the point of near obsession" (128). In chapter 4, I examine the relationship between the gendered body and the world in interwar Black Atlantic writing.

12. The Gold Coast historians Carl Christian Reindorf, John Mensah Sarbah, and J. B. Anaman all produced books on the colony's history before the First World War, and historical accounts had also been published in English-language newspapers by—among others—J. H. Brew, T. Laing, S. R. B. Attoh Ahuma, and

others. In Nigeria, Samuel Johnson completed *The History of the Yorubas* in 1897, although it was not published until 1921. The itinerant pan-African intellectual E. W. Blyden wrote extensively about West African history after moving to Liberia from the Caribbean in 1850. See Jenkins, "Gold Coast Historians and Their Pursuit of the Gold Coast Pasts." On the emergence of Nigerian nationalist historiography, see Zachernuk, "Of Origins and Colonial Order."

13. A good example of these "apolitical" histories is J. B. Danquah's *Gold Coast: Akan Laws and Customs and the Akim Abuakwa Constitution*, published in 1928.

14. These books are described by one historian as West Africa's "first major literary works of a nationalist character to appear since Blyden's writing in the late nineteenth century." Coleman, *Nigeria*, 250.

15. See Simms, "Western Christianity."

16. De Graft-Johnson, *Towards Nationhood in West Africa*, 45. Reviewers of the book expressed predictable disdain for de Graft-Johnson's own "educated" status. The German Africanist Diedrich H. Westermann complained that de Graft-Johnson's "outlook is European throughout" and his book "overburdened with quotations from Thucydides, Tolstoi, Virgil, Plutarch, Tacitus, Sophocles, and many others." Westermann, "Review: Towards Nationhood in West Africa by I. W. de Graft Johnson."

17. De Graft-Johnson, *Towards Nationhood in West Africa*, 73.

18. De Graft-Johnson, *Towards Nationhood in West Africa*, 49. Von Puttkamer is quoted as "General von Putt Kamer."

19. V. Y. Mudimbe has argued that, despite the importance of *Towards Nationhood in West Africa* as a nationalist text, de Graft-Johnson "still envisaged the future of West Africa in terms of the British Empire"; Mudimbe, "African Gnosis Philosophy and the Order of Knowledge," 172. Mudimbe's view is accurate with respect to the book's officially attested imperial loyalties. But it does not account for moments, like the von Puttkamer citation, in which European imperialism in Africa is represented as a project of rapacious exploitation.

20. De Graft-Johnson, *Towards Nationhood in West Africa*, 48.

21. De Graft-Johnson, *Towards Nationhood in West Africa*, 48.

22. On scale jumping, see Smith, "Contours of a Spatialized Politics."

23. See Adi, "Bandele Omoniyi." Adi points out that Omoniyi is one of the century's earliest examples of a "politically active West African student" (581). I

am grateful to Hakim Adi for discussing Omoniyi's book with me via email in June 2020, when archives were closed due to the Covid-19 pandemic.

24. The journal *Wasu* developed the idea of a "West African nationality" by drawing on West African (especially Yoruba) history, culture, folklore, and language. Adi, *West Africans in Britain*, 36.

25. Adi, *West Africans in Britain*, 27–30. Solanke's press analysis earned him the appreciation and support of Amy Ashwood Garvey.

26. Ladipo Solanke, "Open Letter to the Negroes of the World," *GCL*, August 8, 1925.

27. Solanke, *United West Africa, or Africa at the Bar of the Family of Nations*, 66.

28. Comparison with Japan was not new to West African writing. The historian John Mensah Sarbah had compared "Fanti patriots" to the Japanese during the Meiji Restoration. Sarbah's claim was then quoted with approval by De Graft-Johnson in *Towards Nationhood in West Africa*, 25.

29. Solanke, *United West Africa, or Africa at the Bar of the Family of Nations*, 62.

30. Adi, *West Africans in Britain*, 34–39.

31. Wilson, *Origins of West African Nationalism*, 274, 314.

32. Noyes, *Herder*, 9.

33. For example, Cooper's influential survey of economic thought about Africa and the world, "Africa and the World Economy" (1981), presented these ideas as arriving in the African context from the late 1960s through the work André Gunder Frank, Samir Amin, Walter Rodney, and Immanuel Wallerstein. There was no acknowledgement in his essay that structuralist thinking about African economics had already existed on the continent before the 1960s. Similarly, Crawford Young wrote in another survey of the "migration of dependency theory from Latin America" to Africa during the 1960s and 1970s. Young did acknowledge the "rich history" of pan-African political thought on the subject of African liberation. But he scanted the economic dimensions of such thought, thus reinforcing the idea that specifically economic thought arrived in Africa in the 1960s. Young, "Nationalism, Ethnicity, and Class in Africa," 425, 461. Meanwhile, scholars writing about the economic history of Africa have typically seen colonial-era African writing as—at best—a source of data rather than a source of theory. See, for example, Austin, "Reciprocal Comparison and African History."

34. See, *inter alia*, Samuels, Biddle, and Davis, *A Companion to the History of Economic Thought*, which evades Africa, the Caribbean, and the African

diaspora. The work of A. G. Hopkins is exceptional for considering West African political figures of the interwar period as both economic agents and as progenitors of economic thinking and policy. See his illuminating 1966 article "Economic Aspects of Political Movements in Nigeria and in the Gold Coast 1918–1939."

35. See Mukonoweshuro's study *J. E. Casely Hayford*, which places Casely Hayford within a class that was "a mediating link between the colonial economy, dominated by the merchant bourgeoisie, and the pre-capitalist hinterland" (5). Because of this class position, Mukonoweshuro argues, the interwar nationalist movements in the region did not seek a radical transformation of the colonial order (95).

36. For an overview, see Kay, *Latin American Theories of Development and Underdevelopment*.

37. Born to a privileged Cape Coast family in 1866, Casely Hayford had become interested in pan-Africanist ideas in his youth while at Fourah Bay College in Sierra Leone. He studied law in Britain between 1893 and 1896, returning to the colony as a barrister and political commentator who quickly became involved in West African oppositional politics. His books included an experimental hybrid work, *Ethiopia Unbound: Studies in Race Emancipation* (1911)—dedicated to "The Sons of Ethiopia, The World Wide Over"—and a defense of Indigenous African land tenure, *The Truth about the West African Land Question* (1913).

38. Irele and Jeyifo, *Oxford Encyclopedia of African Thought*, 1:214. DiGiacomo, "Assertion of Coevalness," has recently argued for seeing *Ethiopia Unbound* in the context of global modernism.

39. Mukonoweshuro, *J. E. Casely Hayford*, 5.

40. For insightful surveys of this Belle Époque economic dislocation, see Bickford-Smith, "Betrayal of Creole Elites"; Spitzer, *Creoles of Sierra Leone*, 69–84.

41. Wilson, *Origins of West African Nationalism*, 320.

42. Wilson, *Origins of West African Nationalism*, 258.

43. Using methods of compulsion, such as quota systems, export-oriented farming created periodic shortages of food crops for local consumption. Mamdani, *Citizen and Subject*, 162; Ajayi and Crowder, *History of West Africa*, 2:522; Holmes, "Economic and Political Organizations in the Gold Coast 1920–1945." For a discussion of the effects of this shift on women in colonial Ghana, see

Grier, "Pawns, Porters, and Petty Traders." On cocoa in western Nigeria, see Berry, "Supply Response Reconsidered." Mining peaked later: in Sierra Leone, for example, iron and diamond mining began in the 1930s. See Greenhalgh, *West African Diamonds*.

44. Quoted in Kimble, *A Political History of Ghana*, 364. The bill was the latest in a series dating back to 1894 which attempted to assign the management of uncultivated land to the British government. See Berry, "Hegemony on a Shoestring," 341–43; Kimble, *Political History of Ghana*, chap. 9; Agbosu, "The Origins of Forest Law and Policy in Ghana during the Colonial Period."

45. "The Negro's Place in the Sun: By H. B. Philpott, in Reynold's Newspaper," *GCL*, July 27, 1918.

46. Africanus, "Sir Frederick Lugard," *GCL*, February 5, 1919.

47. "The Future of Togoland," *GCL*, December 6–13, 1919.

48. See, for example, "The Economic Slavery of the African," *GCL*, December 5, 1925.

49. I have written about this explosion in racial thought elsewhere: Younis, "'United by Blood.'" Other newspapers referred to an "Octopus system which with tentacles round our vitals is sucking our very life blood out of us"; "1921," *SLWN*, Jan 7, 1922. These words paralleled de Graft-Johnson's characterization of the Gold Coast Sedition Bill (1934) as "an octopus whose tentacles will sap the vitality of African intelligence and, unless opposed, and strenuously opposed, will affect posterity till the end of time"; Shaloff, "Press Controls and Sedition Proceedings," 245–46.

50. Ahinnana, "Our Youth," *GCL*, October 27, 1923. See also "The Firestone Lease," *GCL*, November 14, 1925.

51. While "nonnatives" enjoyed the benefits of British common law, "natives" were, by definition, subject to customary law. As a legal category, British citizenship was only established with the British Nationality Act of 1948. But the earlier colonial division nevertheless represents a kind of racialized citizenship policy: "a colonial form of jus sanguinis through racial descent," as Christopher Lee has argued. For "it is clear that the doctrine of jus sanguinis held a particular grip on access to certain benefits available to those with 'non-native' status, advantages that were racially determined and ultimately constituted a more exclusive form of citizenship." Lee, "Jus Soli and Jus Sanguinis in the Colonies," 520–22.

52. Untitled article, *GCL*, July 26, 1919.

53. "A Coloured Empire," *GCL*, August 2–9, 1919.

54. "Scrutineer," *GCL*, July 26, 1919.

55. "The Land Question," *GCL*, August 8, 1925.

56. The *Sierra Leone Weekly News* dated the "pagan and unrighteous idea that Africans exist for the purpose of wealth production . . . for the white man" to around 1900 and connected the idea to the theories of European race thinkers like Haeckel and Treitschke. "The African and the League Mandate," *SLWN*, October 18, 1919.

57. Mamdani, *Citizen and Subject*, 37.

58. On the strict limitation of African participation in government, consider Nigeria: just four Africans were elected as members of the Legislative Council in almost the entire interwar period (1923–46); policy influence at the level of the central executive was not open to Africans before 1943; and Africans were almost totally excluded from the councils and boards advising the colonial government on specific problems. Such near-exclusion "was an explicit policy of the British administration"; Coleman, *Nigeria*, 153–56. In the realm of customary rule, however, many traditional leaders came to enjoy more authority than they had held in the precolonial period. Far from resolving the land question, indirect rule in West Africa opened the door to a wide range of novel disputes on jurisdictional grounds. Controversies included how to define "strangers," who were liable to pay tribute, and whether the rent from cash crops like cocoa was the personal income of a "chief" or public revenue. Berry, "Hegemony on a Shoestring," 343. See also Crowder, *Colonial West Africa*, 199; Harris, *Sierra Leone*, 22. For a comparison of French and British systems of indirect rule, see Crowder, "Indirect Rule."

59. "Editorial Notes," *GCL*, August 21, 1926. Fanon, *Wretched of the Earth*, 51.

60. There were "signs all over the globe, that the coloured races are asking themselves why a small fraction of the Earth's population should be allowed to lord it over them," observed the *Sierra Leone Weekly News*. "Great Negro Offshoot from the European War," *SLWN*, March 18, 1922.

61. Smith, "Contours of a Spatialized Politics," 66.

62. Belich, *Replenishing the Earth*, 115.

63. Weiss, *Framing a Radical African Atlantic*, 93.

64. Gocking, "J. E. Casely Hayford," 385.

65. Cole, *Ghana's Concert Party Theatre*, 72; Shaloff, "Press Controls and Sedition Proceedings," 242.

66. Gump, "Grumbler's Row: What is Civilization?" *African Morning Post* [henceforth *AMP*], June 4, 1935.

67. Dusé Mohamed Ali, "That Question of Colonies," *Comet*, November 2, 1935.

68. See Derrick, *Africa's Agitators*, 307–15.

69. Wuta-Ofei wrote to Padmore on December 29, 1931 asking for help obtaining a printing press, "which will (a) get the masses together + (b) make their voices heard by the world." He mentioned that he had already approached Marcus Garvey for help with the same task. Weiss, *Framing a Radical African Atlantic*, 519–23.

70. A helpful and comprehensive list of these articles is provided in Leslie James, "What We Put in Black and White," 266–313.

71. See Spitzer and Denzer, "I. T. A. Wallace-Johnson and the West African Youth League." I. T. A. Wallace-Johnson wrote for *Negro Worker* from its inception and in 1933 became a member of its editorial board. Spitzer and Denzer credit him with bringing Marxist concepts to West African political thought (435). On Bankole, see Hanretta, "'Kaffir' Renner's Conversion"; Weiss, "Making of an African Bolshevik."

72. As a result of this contact, they were placed under secret surveillance by the colonial authorities. Newell, *The Power to Name*, 75; Weiss, *Framing a Radical African Atlantic*, 522–23.

73. Kobina Sekyi, "Our White Friends," *GCL*, June 3, 1922. On cultural economy, see Magee, *Empire and Globalisation*, 16.

74. "Commercial Morality," *West African Pilot* [henceforth *WAP*], December 17, 1938.

75. Kofi Pekiyi, "Africans Utilise Cocoa Beans," *AMP*, March 18, 1938.

76. High-profile industrial accidents exposed the violence of West Africa's mining economy. Forty-one miners died in one accident at a Gold Coast mine in Prestea in 1934. Derrick, *Africa's Agitators*, 309; Bush, *Imperialism, Race and Resistance*, 105, 112.

77. The 1937–38 crisis—the more successful of the two—ultimately affected 94 percent of cocoa purchases in the Gold Coast. Rohdie, "The Gold Coast Aborigines Abroad," 390; Frankel, *Cocoa in Ghana;* Howard, "Differential Class

Participation in an African Protest Movement"; Meredith, "The Colonial Office, British Business Interests and the Reform of Cocoa Marketing in West Africa," 287–300; Alence, "The 1937–1938 Gold Coast Cocoa Crisis."

78. "Exploitation Exposed," *AMP*, October 29, 1937; A. Abraham, "An Attempt to Enslave," *AMP*, February 5, 1938. For other critical articles on the cocoa pool, see "The Pool and the Lobster," *AMP*, February 5, 1938; O.A. Alakija, "As I See It: Economic Armageddon," *WAP*, January 5, 1939.

79. Kofi Pekiyi, lamenting what he saw as the insufficiency of the Gold Coast response to the crisis, which had involved burning cocoa beans rather than selling them at the fixed price, imagined that "most of the whites" would say at "their lunch and dinner tables": "Yes, what can the niggers who are solely contingent, weak minded of invention and manufacturing do? Though they are determined they will after all yield to us." Kofi Pekiyi, "Africans Utilise Cocoa Beans," *AMP*, March 18, 1938.

Histories of West Africa have sometimes tried to downplay this language. A good example is the classic study by David Kimble, *A Political History of Ghana.* After arguing that "the history of the Gold Coast can only be fully interpreted in the light of the rise of nationalism" (xv), Kimble admits that "the basic difference of colour," though "not initially regarded as of fundamental importance," did come to play a major role. But he puts this down to a misunderstanding ("false notions of superiority and inferiority—on both sides") and then adds it immediately to the tally of "national feeling" (506). Later, he observes that "Gold Coast politicians were seeing themselves in some kind of global perspective" for the first time, pointing in particular to the spread of the *Negro World* across the Atlantic (544). Yet the significance of this development is quickly waved away with the assertion that there was a "relative lack of racial bitterness in the Gold Coast," perhaps because "nationalist aspirations were so consistently expressed in the form of constitutional demands" (550).

80. Du Bois, *The World and Africa and Color and Democracy,* 156–58. Du Bois's writing, particularly his essay "The African Roots of War" of 1915, is rightly seen as providing a richly textured, contemporaneous alternative to the Leninist theory on imperialism. See, for example, Marable, *W. E. B. Du Bois.* Du Bois's achievements are indisputable, but the view of imperialism as racially exploitative cannot be attributed to him alone.

81. Nat, "Black and White in West Africa," *SLWN*, April 27, 1934.

82. J. A. Wachuku, "Universal Disarmament," *WAP*, October 14, 1938.

83. Adi, *West Africans in Britain*, 45.

84. Adi, *West Africans in Britain*, 45.

85. "Gold Coast and Jamaica," *AMP*, June 20, 1938.

86. "The Dependent African," *AMP*, November 8, 1937.

87. Kwesi Toi, "Eight Years Ago," *AMP*, December 29, 1937.

88. Moses Armah, "Our Quiet Half Hour," *AMP*, May 7, 1938.

89. Marx, *Capital*, 1:875.

90. "Rambling Talks," *SLWN*, July 2, 1938. For a discussion of this article, see Spitzer, *Creoles of Sierra Leone*, 191–93.

91. "General Black Restiveness," *WAP*, March 15, 1938.

92. Everett F. S. Davies, "The Emotion Called Fear," *WAP*, July 18, 1938.

93. "Are We Civilized?" *WAP*, September 18, 1938.

94. In 1943, for example, J. B. Danquah, the prominent Ghanaian politician and cofounder of the UGCC, clarified: "When I say 'we' I mean the Gold Coast. I do not mean black men. I do not mean Negroes. This is not a question of race at all." Iliffe, *Africans*, 259.

95. As one historian writes in a discussion of Nigerian expatriates during this period, pan-African ideas and ambitions "no longer framed the vision of Nigerians abroad as they once had. Instead, segments grouped by various criteria—as insiders, ethnic minorities, or radicals—now vied for a place on the national stage." Zachernuk, *Colonial Subjects*, 145.

96. Nkrumah's youthful reading of Garvey and his close later relationship with Padmore were formative. See Basil Davidson's biography of Nkrumah, *Black Star*.

CHAPTER 3: THE WHITENESS OF THE WORLD

1. Schneider, *Quality and Quantity*, 236; Georges Dequidt and Georges Forestier, "Les aspects sanitaires du probleme de l'immigration en France." Lothrop Stoddard's *The Rising Tide of Colour*, originally published in 1920, debuted in France in 1925. Vacher de Lapouge was, along with Gobineau, an important French influence on Nazi eugenics. Among his ideas was a revolution in sex in which selectionist breeding would, like military service, be performed by men in patriotic service to the nation. See Mottier, "Eugenics and the State," 220.

2. Camiscioli, *Reproducing the French Race*, 1; Lewis, *Boundaries of the Republic*, 1; Thomas, *French Empire between the Wars*, 1–30; Ezra, *Colonial Unconscious*. For key works on immigration in interwar France, see Rosenberg, *Policing Paris;* Noiriel and Tilly, *French Melting Pot*.

3. Conklin, *Mission to Civilize*, 130.

4. Rosenberg, *Policing Paris*, ix.

5. Rosenberg, *Policing Paris*, ix; Stovall, "The Color Line behind the Lines," 739–40.

6. Ezra, *Colonial Unconscious*.

7. Schneider, *Quality and Quantity*, 1–5.

8. See Watson, "Birth Control and Abortion in France since 1939."

9. "A Coloured Army," *Gold Coast Nation*, October 19, 1916. "Editorial Notes," *GCL*, November 18, 1922.

10. Du Bois, *W. E. B. Du Bois on Asia*, 33.

11. Schwarz, *White Man's World;* Lake and Reynolds, *Drawing the Global Colour Line;* Roediger, *The Wages of Whiteness;* Jacobson, *Whiteness of a Different Color*. Many works in this field do acknowledge the formative role of Black approaches to Whiteness in their own critical approaches, but nevertheless usually center Whiteness as understood by its proponents rather than detractors. By contrast, this chapter operates in the tradition of Roediger's edited collection *Black on White*, which presents Black writing on Whiteness.

12. Roediger, *Class, Race and Marxism*, chap. 2; see also Roediger, *Black on White*. For an overview of Whiteness studies during the 1990s, see Kolchin, "Whiteness Studies."

13. Wynter, "Sambos and Minstrels," 150. Emphasis added.

14. *La Race Nègre* was the newspaper of the political group Ligue de défense de la race Nègre (LDRN), which was formed by Lamine Senghor and Tiemoko Garan Kouyaté out of a split from the Communist-supported group Comité de défense de la race Nègre (CDRN). The CDRN had published its own newspaper, *La Voix des Nègres*. For an illuminating discussion on the word *"Nègre"* and its translation into English, see Edwards, *Practice of Diaspora*, 25–38.

15. N.P.J., "La représentation parlementaire coloniale ou la panacée chimérique?" *La Race Nègre* [henceforth *LRN*], April 1929. Interwar colonial politics has often been divided into assimilationist versus anti-assimilationist (or nationalist) camps, with reference to the respective hopes of various groups

and figures for expanding political rights within the French imperial structure. Like many others, I do not think these labels are adequate. What is called "assimilationist" often refers to projects with strong elements of cultural nationalism; "nationalists," meanwhile, might simultaneously make demands for political rights within the French system. As a shorthand to refer to these positions, I use "assimilationist" and "anti-assimilationist," in quotation marks.

16. In June 1921, the PCF created the Comité d'études coloniales as a forum for theoretical discussions on colonialism. The Comité d'études coloniales was accompanied by a mass-based organization, the Union Intercoloniale, which also published the anticolonial journal Le Paria between 1922 and 1926. On the Comintern and Black movements in France, see Dewitte, Mouvements Nègres, especially chap. 3; Murphy, "Defending the 'Negro Race.'"

17. On the breakup of the Union Intercoloniale, see Goebel, Anti-Imperial Metropolis, 188–214; Liauzu, Aux origines des tiers-mondismes, 99–136; Sagna, "Des pionniers méconnus de l'indépendance," 277–93. On Lamine Senghor, see Murphy, "Tirailleur, facteur, anticolonialiste"; Murphy, "Defending the 'Negro Race'"; Dewitte, Mouvements Nègres, chap. 4.

18. "Condamnation des Nord-Africains," LRN, Nov–Dec 1934.

19. Ludovic-Morin Lacombe, "Haïti: Communisme et Nationalisme," LRN, Nov–Dec 1934. This article, which dismissed the "white parvenu" as a "porter" with airs and graces, was not the only instance of a vein of classism in La Race Nègre.

20. "Notre ligne politique," LRN, Nov–Dec 1934.

21. After 1931, Tiemoko Garan Kouyaté left La Race Nègre in an acrimonious split; its editor became Emile Faure. Faure was born in Saint-Louis, Senegal. He became a leading Black activist in France and evinced a strong emphasis on cultural and racial nationalism. In 1938, he undertook a rapprochement with the Left and worked with Daniel Guérin to try and build a common plan of action with Kenyatta and Padmore in London. After the war, he was deported to the Ivory Coast. See Gérard, European-Language Writing in Sub-Saharan Africa, 363n64. These statements in La Race Nègre might be read as prefiguring some of Césaire's more radical statements in Discourse on Colonialism, 36, about the irredeemability of the "European bourgeois"; but Césaire did not apply such statements to European workers.

22. Krausz, Reconstructing Lenin, 169. Emphasis in original.

23. Ali Baba, "L'Impérialisme et la politique coloniale," *Le Paria*, December 1923.

24. Fanon, *Toward the African Revolution*, 82.

25. Pascal Dumont, "Solidarité," *A.O.F.*, June 26, 1919.

26. Goebel, *Anti-Imperial Metropolis*, 226.

27. Marcus Garvey had, on his expulsion from the United States, set up an office in the same building as *La Dépêche Africaine*, in Paris' seventh arrondissement; Sharpley-Whiting, *Negritude Women*, 36. Edwards, *The Practice of Diaspora*, 149.

28. Paul Morand, "L'Aristocratie Blanche Contres les Peuples de Couleur," *La Dépêche Africaine* [henceforth *LDA*], July 1928. In 1929, these extracts would be published in a new book by Morand, titled *Hiver caraïbe*. Like Gobineau, Morand was a racist who was nevertheless genuinely popular among some Black intellectuals for his willingness to valorize—however patronizingly—Black cultures.

29. Sweeney, *From Fetish to Subject*, 119–24.

30. The newspaper nevertheless maintained that the "colonial empire of France is indivisible and unalienable." Pierre Taittinger, "Pour la plus grande France," *LDA*, July 1928. Morand's vision reflected that of Stoddard, who had warned of the "tremendous and steadily augmenting outward thrust of surplus colored men from overcrowded colored homelands" which were "already populated up to the available limits of subsistence." Stoddard, *The Rising Tide of Color against White World-Supremacy*, 231.

31. "Au pays du lynch," *Le Cri des Nègres* [henceforth *CDN*], January 1934.

32. "Un appel de journalistes Haïtiens: Aidez-nous dans notre lutte contre la dictature de Président Sténio Vincent!" *CDN*, June 1934.

33. Dewitte, *Mouvements Nègres*, 369. "Appel," *Le Colonisé*, November 15, 1936.

34. "Aprés [sic] 35 ans de luttes contre l'oppression coloniale," *Africa*, December 1, 1935.

35. Sharpley-Whiting, *Negritude Women*, 58.

36. Paulette Nardal, "L'Eveil de la conscience de race," *La Revue du Monde Noir*, April 6, 1932. For a discussion of this article, see Gérard, *European-Language Writing in Sub-Saharan Africa*, 366–67.

37. Aimé Césaire, "Nègreries," *L'Étudiant Noir*, March 1935.

38. "Madagascar," *LRN*, Feb–March 1930.

39. See Stovall, *White Freedom*.

40. Camiscioli, *Reproducing the French Race*, 14.

41. Gary Wilder, for example, suggests that being able to "refigure the nation-state as imperial" is a challenge to "methodological nationalism" because "treating empire as an irreducible unit of analysis and refiguring France as an imperial nation-state" is a methodology that "confounds conventional distinctions among national, transnational, and international phenomena"; Wilder, *French Imperial Nation-State*, 5–6. Yet though he explicitly cites Wallerstein, the "world-system" is profoundly absent from Wilder's work, which traverses the boundaries of France only insofar as it incorporates French colonies and overseas territories. A similar issue arises in Michael Goebel's study of anti-imperialism in interwar Paris. Goebel downplays the importance of race for colonial subjects in interwar France by arguing that race was enmeshed with other discriminatory practices; he proposes instead the concept of "everyday ethnicity." As Wallerstein explained, dichotomizing race and ethnicity neglects the global scale that produces both of these closely intertwined categories. Goebel, *Anti-Imperial Metropolis*, 58–62; Balibar and Wallerstein, *Race, Nation, Class*, chap. 4.

42. In particular, see Childers, *Seeking Imperialism's Embrace*; Wilder, *Freedom Time*; Cooper, *Citizenship between Empire and Nation*; Shepard, *The Invention of Decolonization*.

43. Drayton, "Federal Utopias and the Realities of Imperial Power," 402.

44. Camiscioli, *Reproducing the French Race*, 2–6, 15.

45. Camiscioli, 9.

46. Saada, *Empire's Children*, chap. 7.

47. Two studies written during the 1920s—Roberts, *The History of French Colonial Policy, 1870–1925*; Buell, *The Native Problem in Africa*—give a contemporaneous perspective on French colonial policy and its driving imperatives. Later studies assessing assimilation and its alternatives in French imperialism include Thompson, *French West Africa*; Betts, *Assimilation and Association in French Colonial Theory*; Johnson, *Emergence of Black Politics in Senegal*; Crowder, *Senegal*; Wilder, *French Imperial Nation-State*.

48. Betts, *Assimilation and Association in French Colonial Theory*, 122.

49. Conklin, *Mission to Civilize*, 211.

50. Lake and Reynolds, *Drawing the Global Colour Line*, 4.

51. Such consequences ranged from a hardening color bar to the spread of indirect rule. They meant the difference between an Africa "improving" under imperial tutelage—as was claimed by proponents of colonial rule—and an Africa that was being degraded and weakened by imperial rule—as anticolonialists claimed. In the Lagos-based *Comet*, for example, White prestige was said to have emerged with the end of Queen Victoria's reign, the appointment of Joseph Chamberlain as Secretary of State for Colonies, and Britain's rapprochement with the Boers after the Anglo-Boer War. "That Eternal Colour Question," *The Comet*, September 28, 1935.

52. Gilpin, *War and Change in World Politics*, 31.

53. Matera, Bastian, and Kent, *The Women's War of 1929*, 60.

54. "Great Negro Offshoot from the European War," *SLWN*, March 18, 1922. On the maintenance of British supremacy in West Africa through the idea of racial difference and hierarchy, see Zachernuk, *Colonial Subjects*, 104.

55. "The African and the League Mandate," *SLWN*, Oct 18, 1919.

56. "A Suicidal Policy," *SLWN*, August 25, 1928. "Keeping the Black Man Down," *SLWN*, January 17, 1931.

57. "The Racial Question in Africa," *SLWN*, July 20, 1929.

58. "The Civic Equality of Africans," *SLWN*, April 4, 1931.

59. "The William Wilberforce Centenary," *SLWN*, September 16, 1933.

60. "Rambling Talks," *SLWN*, September 30, 1933.

61. The language in which such diminishment was characterized—the ebbing of loyalty to the "lords of the lower world"—drew upon the phraseology of the New Testament to connote the demystification of White superiority as a quasi-religious experience. The phrase evokes a gloss to Colossians 2:3 in a New Testament translation of 1812, which refers to "the worship paid by the ancient heretics, disciplines of Simon and Menander, to the angels: whom they believed to be the makers and lords of the lower world." (Geddes and Robertson, *New Testament*, 310.)

62. Sekyi wrote extensively about his views on colonialism, society and forms of political organization, from a broadly conservative and organicist viewpoint. See Irele and Biodun, *Oxford Encyclopedia of African Thought*, 1:323; Baku, "An Intellectual in Nationalist Politics"; Derrick, *Africa's Agitators*, 275; Langley, *Ideologies of Liberation in Black Africa*, 240–54. For Sekyi's pan-African contacts, see Asante, "The Neglected Aspects of the Activities of the Gold Coast Aborigines Rights Protection Society," 36–37.

63. J. Withers-Gill, "Editorial Comments, Aspirations, and Potentialities: A Bath of the Obvious," *African World*, June 25, 1921.

64. Kobina Sekyi, "Our White Friends," *GCL*, October 8, 1921. For the full series "Our White Friends," see the *Gold Coast Leader* from October 8, 1921 until the end of 1921, and thereafter in the following 1922 issues: February 4–11, 1922, March 4, June 3, June 17–20, August 1, October 28, November 18, and December 12.

65. Kobina Sekyi, "Our White Friends," *GCL*, October 15, 1921.

66. Kobina Sekyi, "Our White Friends," *GCL*, October 15, 1921 and October 22, 1921. The article series includes a lengthy digression into climactic influences on White and Black social institutions, personalities, worldviews, and cultures, part of which drew on Sekyi's experiences of studying in London, and which defended participative West African cultural practices against the atomized and privatized culture that Sekyi saw in England. The installment from November 26, which describes Sekyi's view of England, drawn from his personal experience as a student at University College, London, describes, for example, how "to a more communistic person, the white Britisher . . . seems both amusing and pitiable." Kobina Sekyi, "Our White Friends," *GCL*, November 26, 1921.

67. Kobina Sekyi, "Our White Friends," *GCL*, October 15, 1921.

68. Kobina Sekyi, "Our White Friends," *GCL*, December 12, 1922.

69. "Our white friends are very adroit in evading issues," remarked the *African Morning Post* in a discussion of the cocoa pool. The ridicule of educated Africans had "been followed up as a policy by our White friends on every conceivable opportunity," lamented J. W. de Graft Johnson, for which the "only possible aim could be to discredit the educated African in the eyes of the world." De Graft-Johnson, *Towards Nationhood in West Africa*, 45.

70. "That Aryan Bogey," *The Comet*, August 11, 1934. Elsewhere, Ali dismissed "the senseless vapourings of anthropologists"; Dusé Mohamed Ali, "About It and About—That Eternal Colour Question," *The Comet*, September 28, 1935. Dusé Mohamed Ali, "About it and About—That Eternal Race Puzzle," *The Comet*, October 31, 1936.

71. "The Pan-African Congress in Paris," *SLWN*, June 14, 1919.

72. Césaire, *Collected Poetry*, 69. Translation modified. Césaire began writing the poem in late 1935; it was first published by the journal *Volontés* in August 1939. I have benefited from translations by N. Gregson Davis and John Berger. I

examine only this first edition of the *Cahier*, but the poem was palimpsestically reworked over the following decades. For a comprehensive account of this process of accretion, see Arnold, "Beyond Postcolonial Césaire."

73. Macharia, *Frottage*, 38.

74. Smith, "The Negro Writer," 297.

75. Searching for "white world" in a major online corpus of American English yields a maximum of ten references a year before 1850. Between 1880 and 1900, there are over one hundred references a year. See Mark Davies, *The Corpus of Contemporary American English: 600 Million Words, 1990-present*, https://www.english-corpora.org/coca/. For a typical reference just before Douglass to the "white world," which confined the term to its pastoral connotations, see J. A. Symonds's influential essay on Switzerland, "Davos in Winter," *Fortnightly Review* 30 (1878): 74–87.

76. Douglass, "The Color Line," 575.

77. Drumont, *La Fin d'un Monde*, iv.

78. Stoddard, *The Rising Tide of Color against White World-Supremacy*, vi.

79. Spengler, *The Hour of Decision*, 218.

80. "Whoever will take the time to read and ponder Mr. Lothrop Stoddard's book on 'The Rising Tide of Color,'" said President Warren G. Harding during a speech in Birmingham, in 1921, "must realize that our race problem here in the United States is only a phase of a race issue that the whole world confronts." Three years later, the Johnson-Reed Immigration Act imposed strict racial restrictions on immigration to the United States. Spiro, *Defending the Master Race*, 178; Okrent, *The Guarded Gate*.

81. In 1926, Madison Grant's *The Passing of the Great Race* was published in French. Stoddard's *The Rising Tide of Color* was issued in French in July 1925, translated by the obscure poet Abel Doysié, who had also translated Stoddard's *The New World of Islam* (1921). It also appeared the same year in German. In 1934, Spengler's *The Hour of Decision* appeared in French as *Années décisives*. A notable example of the interwar declinist writing in French is *Le crépuscule des nations blanches* (Twilight of the white races), published by the Swiss writer Maurice Muret in 1920.

82. In January 1935, in the French left-wing literary magazine *Europe*, the critic and novelist Jean-Richard Bloch suggested that the United States and the Soviet Union represented opposing strategies of destroying the "infection" of

untrammeled liberal capitalism that threatened "to kill the white world"; Jean-Richard Bloch, "Vers la fin d'un monde," *Europe*, January 15, 1936. For André Duboscq, a prominent journalist and sinologist of the period, the "white world" was a useful concept in works like *Le Pacifique et la rencontre des races* (The Pacific and the meeting of races, 1929). See also Henri Daniel-Rops, *Le monde sans âme*, 1932, who writes of *"une ruée barbare qui vaincrait le monde blanc"* (23).

83. Du Bois, *Writings*, 549–803. Du Bois won a highly publicized public debate with Stoddard in Chicago in 1929.

84. "The black world gets only the pittance that the white world throws it disdainfully," he wrote in 1920. Du Bois, *Darkwater*, 45.

85. The White world was also specifically invoked in texts written by black women. Terrell, *A Colored Woman in a White World*.

86. Du Bois, *Darkwater*, 45.

87. Césaire, *Cahier d'un retour au pays natal*, xlvii; Césaire, *Journal of a Homecoming*, 44. The *Cahier*'s white world has usually been understood in terms of the poem's internal patterning and symbolic system. In this view, the blueness, harshness, and grandiosity of the "white world" locate it as Negritude's dominant but ultimately pitiable opposite. Khalfa, "Aimé Césaire, *Cahier d'un retour au pays natal*," 128. It has also been common to cite this stanza without elaborating on its imagery. In his famous essay on Negritude, for example, Sartre specifically reproduces this stanza without commenting on its image of the white world. Sartre, *Black Orpheus*, 15. Abiola Irele is right to emphasize that the *Cahier* "is an eminently contestatory poem," one that is "not merely an inscription of the world" but that also seeks to transform the world it describes. Abiola Irele, "Introduction" in *Journal of a Homecoming / Cahier d'un retour au pays natal* by Aimé Césaire, xlvii.

88. See Du Bois's description of the "religion of whiteness" as delusional and self-betraying; the sardonic treatment of White supremacist discourse in Marcus Garvey's *Negro World;* Hubert Harrison's advice in 1920 that Lothrop Stoddard's book should be "widely read by intelligent men of color from Tokio to Tallahasse"; and the *Gold Coast Leader*'s recommendation in 1921 that its readers should discover "what is at the back of the white man's mind." Du Bois, *Darkwater*, 31; "White Supremacy Whistling to Keep Its Courage Up," *Negro World*, December 1, 1923; Perry, *A Hubert Harrison Reader*, 306–9; "The Back of the White Man's Mind," *GCL*, March 19, 1921.

89. We can read the rebarbativeness of this stanza in terms of Césaire's broader opposition to what Carrie Noland has called the idea of "language as transparent vehicle"; Noland, *Voices of Negritude in Modernist Print*, 18. Césaire's "mystic flesh," for example—not easy to visualize—could be a reference to the French decadent novelist Marcel Batilliat, who wrote a novel called *Chair mystique* in 1897.

90. Harrison argued that the anti-Black violence following the First World War showed "that while white people spoke of patriotism, religion, democracy and other sounding themes, they remained loyal to one concept above all others, and that was the concept of race." Perry, *A Hubert Harrison Reader*, 83. "Until the white men of this country can put patriotism ahead of race," he wrote in his diary, "I shall not." Perry, *A Hubert Harrison Reader*, 370.

91. McKay, *A Long Way from Home*, 233.

92. Gates and Jarrett, *New Negro*, 149–54. Schuyler moved sharply to the Right during the McCarthy period.

93. Crowder, *Colonial West Africa*, 16.

94. Fanon, "Antillais et Africains," 261.

95. Fanon, *Black Skin, White Masks*, 179.

96. Baldwin, "Princes and Powers." Elsewhere, he wrote: "The power of the white world is threatened whenever a black man refuses to accept the white world's definitions." James Baldwin, "Power beyond Words," *Negro Digest*, December 1963. And: "This world is white no longer, and it will never be white again." Baldwin, *Collected Essays*, 129.

97. These are the concluding words to Raoul Peck's (2017) film about James Baldwin, *I Am Not Your Negro*. See also the accompanying book, which reproduces the text; Baldwin and Peck, *I Am Not Your Negro*, 132.

98. A recent example: "It is our relation to the white world that is the problem." Hartman, *Wayward Lives, Beautiful Experiments*, 44.

99. Rose, "'Fear of a Black Planet.'"

CHAPTER 4: THE BODY AND THE WORLD

1. Bwin Hwe Kan, "Think and Look Ahead, by a Negro," *GCL*, January 17–24, 1920.

2. Kan, "Think and Look Ahead, by a Negro."

3. "What of the Future?" *GCL*, May 27, 1922.

4. "Editorial Notes," *GCL*, June 2, 1923. Compare with Hitler's proclamation, two decades later, that "the Volga must be our Mississippi." See Bernhard, "Hitler's Africa in the East," 3; Etkind, *Internal Colonization*, 133.

5. "The Regeneration of Africa, by Alfred Wiggleworth," *SLWN*, October 6, 1923.

6. "The South African Situation," *GCL*, September 1, 1923.

7. Hurtado, Cronon, and Lamar, *Intimate Frontiers*; Stoler, "Tense and Tender Ties," 832. A powerful argument for studying colonialism in a way that sees gender and race as inseparable is given by Anne McClintock in *Imperial Leather*. See also, nonexhaustively, Whitlock, *The Intimate Empire*; Ambaras, *Japan's Imperial Underworlds*; Kwon, *Intimate Empire*.

8. McClintock, *Imperial Leather*, 3.

9. Though our subjects differ, I am inspired by Keguro Macharia's reconsideration of categories of kinship and sexuality with reference to interwar African and Afro-diasporic texts in *Frottage*.

10. Fanon, *Black Skin, White Masks*, 4. Weheliye, *Habeas Viscus*, 2.

11. Lloyd, "The Indigent Sublime," 163; Fanon, *Black Skin, White Masks*, 116, translation amended. We are reminded here of what Foucault called "that old sovereign right to kill." Cited in Mbembe, *Necropolitics*, 71.

12. It would thus also be to replicate "a world that has dehumanized and erased the possibility of black interior lives," as McKittrick puts it. McKittrick, *Demonic Grounds*, 32.

13. Miller, *Nationalists and Nomads*, 10.

14. Sharpley-Whiting, in *Negritude Women*, challenges the "masculine genealogy" of Negritude; as part of that project, in Nardal, *Beyond Negritude*, she also translates Paulette Nardal's essays. For further reflections on this alternative genealogy, see Edwards, *Practice of Diaspora*, 122.

15. "To be or not to be," *LRN*, February 1932; emphasis in original. Among the means being used to destroy Africans, *La Race Nègre* pointed to forced labor and famine, and even suggested that the European health service in Africa was responsible for plague. *"But the principal factor behind the extinction of our race,"* explained the newspaper, *"is the systematic destruction of all forms of Black organisation.* The action of conquering Europeans resembles the effect of dynamite or six Lebel bullets to the head. Its objective is always to destroy local

organisation and to disperse the community, by aiming for the head." Emphasis in original.

16. In other articles, *La Race Nègre* returned to the theme of colonial extermination. It explained how French colonialism in Equatorial Africa had brought about "the devastation of entire regions" and "a methodical decimation of the inhabitants." The newspaper noted in particular the devastating drop in the Congo's population under Belgian rule, which they estimated at ten to twenty million dead: "the death of a race." S.B. "Cinquante ans de colonisation en A.E.F.: Les misères et les souffrances de tout un peuple nègre," *LRN*, September 1930. And it observed with alarm the scale of land theft by the "colonizing State" in different areas of Africa, snatching land from African peasants—"thousands of hectares of concessions are distributed, violently, to white strangers, right under their very noses, a process against which they have no right of appeal." "Le sort des nègres à travers le monde," *LRN*, November–December 1930.

17. Elkins and Pedersen, "Introduction," 1.

18. Betts, *Assimilation and Association in French Colonial Theory, 1890–1914*, 112.

19. Thomas, *The French Empire between the Wars*, 4–11, 35.

20. Wolfe, *Traces of History*, 28.

21. See especially Merchant, *The Death of Nature*. Anne McClintock, in *Imperial Leather*, 24, reminds us that "the imperial conquest of the globe found both its shaping figure and its political sanction in the prior subordination of women as a category of nature."

22. I have discussed the career of Lamine Senghor in the previous chapter. *La violation d'un pays* was prefaced by Paul Vaillant-Couturier, a PCF militant, who argued that the story was representative of the history of colonialism. Senghor's pamphlet has been studied in terms of its political vision and allegorical style, but his references to the prospect of colonial genocide have largely passed unnoticed. Edwards, *Practice of Diaspora*, 229–34; Guernsey, "Lamine Senghor's *La violation d'un pays* as a Precursor to Cultural Nationalism."

23. Senghor, *La violation d'un pays*, 23. We do not know the reach of *La violation d'un pays*, but a scholar has located at least one incident recorded in the French colonial archives of its illicit transmission in West Africa. Spiegler, "Aspects of Nationalist Thought among French-Speaking West Africans," 126. See also Edwards, *Practice of Diaspora*, 231.

24. "Le Congrès de Bruxelles," *Le Courrier des Noirs*, November 1927. Emphasis added.

25. Tiemoko G. Kouyaté, "Politique Africaine," *Africa*, December 1, 1935.

26. Edwards, *Practice of Diaspora*, 279.

27. See Jennings, "Writing Madagascar Back into the Madagascar Plan."

28. I. Béton, "Les revendications coloniales d'Allemagne," *Le Colonisé*, December 20, 1936.

29. Mbembe, *Necropolitics*, 26, 38, 66, 74, 96.

30. On settler sovereignty, see Veracini, *Settler Colonialism*, 54; Ford, *Settler Sovereignty*.

31. René Ménil, "Généralités sur l'écrivain de couleur antillais," *Légitime Défense*, June 1, 1932, 8. Ménil argued that French colonial conquest in the Caribbean had made ample use of ideology—especially Christianity—as a tool of asserting control, ensuring that Antilleans absorbed French culture and rejected "the particular genius of Antilleans of color." Progressively, the Antillean of color "disowns his race, his body, his fundamental and particular passions"; he becomes, then, a tragic figure, neither truly himself nor truly accepted by the French. As a poet who is alienated from his own forms of cultural expression, he paints landscapes that can only invoke ennui. For an early and influential scholarly discussion of this text, see Kesteloot, *Black Writers in French*, 20. When *Légitime Défense* was reissued in 1978, Ménil later criticized it for its excessive naïveté; as Edwards suggests, Ménil's own reassessment may be the "most lucid and unsparing critique of *Légitime Défense*." Edwards, *Practice of Diaspora*, 193–94.

32. Wright, *Lawd Today!*, 143–44. Emphasis in original. The character, Jake, goes on to imagine a "black battleship surrounded by black generals." I have discussed this scene in chapter 1. For a broader examination of this passage, see Dawahare, *Nationalism, Marxism, and African American Literature between the Wars*, 126; on the novel more broadly, see Costello, "Richard Wright's *Lawd Today!* and the Political Uses of Modernism." Though *Lawd Today!* was written in 1935, it was not published until 1963.

33. The *Cahier* was revised multiple times, most prominently in 1956, but these lines are part of the original 1939 text, which was published in the Paris-based Surrealist journal *Volontés*. Césaire, *Collected Poetry*; translation amended. See also Césaire, *Original 1939 Notebook of a* Return to the Native Land, in which Eshleman and Smith translate "*un homme seul*" as "a lone man."

34. The poem was published in Senghor's collection *Chants d'ombre*. It reflects upon the end of war in Europe as the "snow of peace" descends, and is framed as a prayer for godly forgiveness of France, exploring the narrator's feelings towards those he wants to forgive even though "they will barter black flesh" [*troqueront la chair noire*]. Senghor had enlisted in the French army in 1939 and was made a prisoner of war in 1940; he spent two years in prison camps before being released on medical grounds. See Constant and Mabana, *Negritude*; Senghor, *Selected Poems of Léopold Sédar Senghor*, 45. I have also benefitted from the translation by Ellen Conroy Kennedy in Kesteloot, *Black Writers in French*, 110.

35. Sekyi-Otu, *Fanon's Dialectic of Experience*, 82. Cited in McKittrick, *Demonic Grounds*, 26.

36. "Some of Our Problems," *SLWN*, April 27, 1929.

37. Furthermore, this was a trans-Atlantic image: Wright did not move to Paris until 1946.

38. Mbembe, *Necropolitics*, 10. Elsewhere, Mbembe writes of a process by which "people of African origin" are transformed "into living *ore* from which metal is extracted." Mbembe, *Critique of Black Reason*, 40.

39. Wolfe, *Traces of History*, 29.

40. McKittrick, *Demonic Grounds*, 45.

41. "To think about distant places, to colonize them, to populate or depopulate them: all of this occurs on, about, or because of land. The actual geographical possession of land is what empire in the final analysis is all about." Said, *Orientalism*, 74.

42. For a discussion of the critical reception of *Batouala*, see Allen, *René Maran's Batouala Jazz-Text*. For my translations I have adapted the 1922 English edition, translated by Adele Szold Selzer. Maran, *Batouala*, 1922. I have also drawn upon Lilyan Kesteloot's book *Black Writers in French*, in which Ellen Conroy Kennedy translates some extracts of *Batouala*. On Maran's biography, see Dennis, "René Maran Story."

43. Maran, *Batouala*, 1921, 21.

44. Maran, *Batouala*, 1921, 77.

45. Maran, *Batouala*, 1921, 11. The historian Philippe Dewitte suggests that this preface is the first example in print of a Black Frenchman attacking the hypocrisy of official French discourse. Dewitte, *Mouvements Nègres*, 69–70.

46. Wilder, *French Imperial Nation-State*, 165. See Senghor's essay, "René Maran, precurseur de la Négritude" in Senghor, *Liberté* 1. Maran's fame spread across the Black Atlantic. Debates about *Batouala* appeared in the *Negro World* in 1922, while both Du Bois and Locke wrote about Maran in their contributions to Alain Locke's *New Negro* anthology. See Wilder, *French Imperial Nation-State*, 163–66; Malela, Buata B., *Les écrivains afro-antillais à Paris*, chap. 1.

47. Kesteloot, *Black Writers in French*, 210–11.

48. Césaire, *The Collected Poetry*, 47, 55, 59, 60.

49. Jacques Roumain, *When the Tom-Tom Beats*, 72–73. Roumain was an influential critic of the US occupation of Haiti who, in July 1927, had cofounded *La Revue Indigène* in Port-au-Prince. See Shannon, *Jean-Price Mars, the Haitian Elite and the American Occupation, 1915–35*, 66; Joseph, *Thinking in Public*.

50. McKittrick has pointed out ways in which "the production of scales beyond the body . . . occurs vis-à-vis the exploitation of black labor." McKittrick, *Demonic Grounds*, 77. Mbembe also sees enslavement as turning the Black body into "an essential cog in a planetary-scale process of accumulation." Mbembe, *Necropolitics*, 170.

51. Senghor, "Le Réveil des nègres," *Le Paria*, April 1926; "Le mot 'Nègre,'" *La Voix des Nègres*, January 1927. These articles have been widely discussed: see Murphy, "Defending the 'Negro Race'"; Dewitte, *Mouvements Nègres*, 144–45; Edwards, *Practice of Diaspora*, 33. As the historian David Murphy points out, this is "a racial identity that is based not on shared racial characteristics but . . . on a shared sense of oppression." Murphy, "Defending the 'Negro Race,'" 168.

52. "Ce qu'est notre Comité de Défense de la Race Nègre," *La Voix des Nègres*, January 1927.

53. S. B., "Cinquante ans de colonisation en A.E.F.: Les misères et les souffrances de tout un peuple nègre," *LRN*, September 1930.

54. McKittrick, *Demonic Grounds*, 93. The image of Toussaint Louverture buried, surrounded and submerged in whiteness can be read as a direct reference to Toussaint's snowy imprisonment in Fort-de-Joux at the end of his life. It can also be seen as a celebration of what Césaire described elsewhere as the Haitian general's ability to see assimilation as a "mask of subjection." Walsh, *Free and French in the Caribbean*, 117.

55. Cooper, *Voice from the South*, 112.

56. Cited in "Editorial Notes," *GCL*, July 5, 1919.

57. In a Stoddardian vein, Taylor predicted a "vast world struggle" between "white" and "coloured" races. Taylor, "Distribution of Future White Settlement," 386, 402.

58. Belich, *Replenishing the Earth;* Crosby, *Ecological Imperialism,* 300; Ferguson, *Empire,* 112.

59. Buzan and Lawson, *Global Transformation,* 52.

60. This pro-settlement thought ranges from the nineteenth-century advocates of "Greater England," like J. R. Seeley and Charles Dilke, to the later activities of internationally oriented racial segregationists like Phillip Kerr, Lionel Curtis, and Jan Smuts. Bell, *Idea of Greater Britain;* Thakur, Davis, and Vale, "Imperial Mission, 'Scientific' Method." Some have isolated these racial affinities as a causal factor in international relations that can explain, for example, the Anglo-American "great rapprochement" after the American Revolution. Vucetic, *Anglosphere.*

61. See especially Elkins and Pedersen, *Settler Colonialism in the Twentieth Century.* The historian Patrick Bernhard has argued that the Third Reich's vision of a new *Volksgemeinschaft,* fundamental to its colonization project in Eastern Europe, was modeled in important respects on Fascist Italy's expansionism in Africa. Bernhard, "Hitler's Africa in the East." Adam Tooze highlights the "striking similarity" between Italy's agrarian settlement scheme in Africa and Japan's settlement project in occupied Manchuria during the 1930s. Tooze, "Interwar Agrarian Crisis and the Second World War," 395.

62. See, *inter alia,* Elkins and Pedersen, *Settler Colonialism in the Twentieth Century.*

63. Compare with other African countries that *did* see such settlement, and therefore have received scholarly treatment: Zimbabwe and Malawi (briefly yoked together under the Federation of Rhodesia and Nyasaland), South Africa, Kenya, Algeria, Mozambique, and Angola—not to mention borderline cases such as Ethiopia under its brief Italian occupation and the secessionist Congolese province of Katanga. See especially Elkins and Pedersen, *Settler Colonialism in the Twentieth Century;* in addition see Bateman and Pilkington, *Studies in Settler Colonialism;* Wolfe, *Settler Colonialism and the Transformation of Anthropology;* Veracini, *Settler Colonialism.*

64. Lorenzo Veracini writes that "a settler sovereignty is characterised by an exclusive interpretation of a settler peoplehood, a specific understanding of

sovereign capacities and their location, and by the conviction that the settler colonial setting is charged with a special regenerative nature." Veracini, *Settler Colonialism*, 54.

65. Lord Lothian, "The Question Mark of Africa," *SLWN*, January 24, 1931.

66. See chapter 2 for a more detailed examination of these developments; they are summarized in Bickford-Smith, "Betrayal of Creole Elites."

67. "The Parting of Ways," *GCL*, July 25, 1925.

68. Odeziaku, "Needless Noise," *Comet*, July 23, 1938. The writer who used the pen-name Odeziaku was actually an English poet and novelist, John Moray Stuart-Young, who had moved to Nigeria and become a palm-oil trader with distinctly pro-African and anticolonial political sympathies. See Newell, *The Forger's Tale*. There is something self-ironizing, then, about his use of the phrase "visiting White alien."

69. "The South African Situation," *GCL*, September 1, 1923.

70. "The Racial Question in Africa," *SLWN*, August 3, 1929.

71. "The White Man's Grave or the Black Man's Resurrection or Which Other?" *SLWN*, July 12, 1930.

72. "Return of Governor Byrne," *SLWN*, September 27, 1930. George Padmore used exactly the same terminology in a book published six years later: "Why is Africa always the dumping-ground for the surplus of Europe, while at the same time Australia closes its door to coloured peoples of Asia and Africa?" Padmore, *How Britain Rules Africa*, 9.

73. "Some of Our Problems," *SLWN*, April 27, 1929.

74. Heline nevertheless repeated the imperialist claim that "no backward people can hold its territory indefinitely. Theodore Heline, "Ethiopia: A Pivotal Point in a Changing World," *The Comet*, November 7, 1936.

75. Donald Friend, "Contrast in Domination," *WAP*, April 13, 1939.

76. "Editorial Notes," *GCL*, June 27, 1925

77. In 1930, the *Sierra Leone Weekly News* reported that the prominent South African statesman General Jan Smuts had said, at a public meeting in New York, that the "Negro" was "next to the ass, the most patient of animals." He had also warned his audience "against attempts to Europeanise the Negroes of South Africa"—"a policy which Bolshevizes the Negro," he had explained, "because Africans were a 'child people.'" "Round and about Notes," *SLWN*,

February 22, 1930. In 1935, the same newspaper condemned the "process of unification and even of absorption that is going on condoned and sanctioned by the Colonial Office with respect to East and South Africa," arguing that "the aggressive nature of a dominant foreign race the more necessitates protection of native lands." "Rambling Talks," *SLWN*, February 16, 1935.

78. "Scrutineer," *GCL*, July 24–31, 1920.

79. "Black and White," *GCL*, May 30, 1925. Dusé Mohamed Ali, "About it and About . . ." *Comet*, February 22, 1936. The next month, Ali published quotations from Sir Abe Bailey, a South African mining magnate, who had argued that "White supremacy and white civilisation are doomed if they depend solely on the protection of the colour of the white man's skin." Ali commented dryly that the Boers relied not on intellect but on the "cowhide whip" and "guns."

80. "Extirpation Policy," *WAP*, September 12, 1938.

81. Zik, "Inside Stuff: Around the World," *WAP*, December 21, 1938.

82. George Padmore, "Anglo-Boer Conflict in South Africa," *AMP*, June 4, 1935.

83. Cudjoe, *Aids to African Autonomy*, 40.

84. Cudjoe, *Aids to African Autonomy*, 33.

85. Cudjoe, *Aids to African Autonomy*, 36.

86. On structures of feeling, see Williams and Orrom, *Preface to Film*, 21.

87. On Black Atlantic archives and their boundaries and limits, see Hartman, "Anarchy of Colored Girls Assembled in a Riotous Manner"; Tinsley, "Black Atlantic, Queer Atlantic."

88. Carby, *Race Men*; Smethurst, *New Red Negro*, 57; Tumblety, *Remaking the Male Body*, 36; Stephens, *Black Empire*; Matera, *Black London*, chap. 5; Newell, *Power to Name*, 128.

89. Stepan, "Race, Gender, Science and Citizenship," 64.

90. Tosh, *A Man's Place*, 2.

91. Chatterjee, *Empire and Nation*, 122. Dipesh Chakrabarty, in *Provincializing Europe*, 208, similarly writes of a "culturally conceived opposition between the world and the word, between 'worldly responsibilities'—the world of chores, dominated by needs—and the noninstrumental pleasure of company and conversation." Rao, in *Third World Protest*, explores this home-world dialectic in his search for an ethic of postcolonial solidarity.

92. Duara, "The Regime of Authenticity," 295–96.

93. A nonexhaustive list would include Blain, *Set the World on Fire;* Higash- ida, *Black Internationalist Feminism;* Joseph-Gabriel, *Reimagining Liberation;* Sharpley-Whiting, *Negritude Women;* Dove, *Selected Writings of a Pioneer West African Feminist.*

94. Historians Keisha N. Blain and Tiffany M. Gill recount a trip taken by an educator and activist, Mary McLeod Bethune, to Europe in 1927: the "first time this daughter of sharecroppers had ever left the United States." Returning from her trip, Bethune shared the news of her travels "through her extensive work with black women's organizations and clubs. She admonished her organ- izational sisters to follow in her footsteps, claiming that traveling abroad was a way for black women to expand their understanding of the world beyond the United States . . . [and reaffirming] what she told the members of the National Association of Colored Women (NACW) just one year earlier: that black women are 'not merely a national influence, but also a significant link between the peoples of color throughout the world.'" For Bethune, "if more black women embraced [this] vision, they could indeed 'turn the whole world over.'" Blain and Gill, *To Turn the Whole World Over,* 1.

95. Cooper, *Voice from the South,* 134. On the limits and openings in Cooper's worldliness, see respectively Jun, *Race for Citizenship,* chap. 2; May, "'It Is Never a Question of the Slaves.'"

96. Higashida, *Black Internationalist Feminism.*

97. Butler, *Bodies That Matter,* xii–xiii. See Lee, *Living Alterities;* Gilleard and Higgs, *Ageing, Corporeality and Embodiment;* Hall, *Feminist Disability Studies;* Alcoff, *Visible Identities;* Mohanram, *Black Body;* Conboy, Medina, and Stan- bury, *Writing on the Body.* Typically focused on the human, the implications of this thinking extend beyond any single species.

98. Haraway, *Manifestly Haraway,* 58. Emphasis added.

99. Federici, *Caliban and the Witch;* Mies, *Patriarchy and Accumulation on a World Scale.*

100. Spillers, "Mama's Baby, Papa's Maybe," 67, 77. Spillers adds that this involved "a willful and violent (and unimaginable from this distance) severing of the captive body from its motive will, its active desire."

101. Shepard, *Sex, France, and Arab Men, 1962–1979,* 69. Shepard points out that anticolonial movements and people of color were not only the subjects of

Orientalist representation: they were also *participants* in a dialogue about gender, race, sexuality, and decolonization—though not on equal terms.

102. Butler, *Bodies That Matter,* xvi.

CHAPTER 5: THE TIME OF THE WORLD

I am grateful to *Millennium: Journal of International Studies* for allowing me to reuse here some of the material and arguments I published in that journal in 2018. See Younis, "Race, the World and Time."

1. "Qu'est-ce que la civilisation?" *LRN,* November–December 1927.

2. Koselleck, *Futures Past,* 50. Benedict Anderson has influentially suggested that nationalism is based on modern conceptions of time as homogenous, secular, and empty, which are emblematized in the products of print-capitalism: the newspaper and its calendrical regularity, the novel and its plotted simultaneity. Anderson, *Imagined Communities.* The time of nationalism operates on the godless and abstracted level of what Dipesh Chakrabarty calls "History 1": "the universal and necessary history posited by the logic of capital." Chakrabarty, *Provincializing Europe,* 250.

3. Duara, "Regime of Authenticity," 289, 291.

4. Chakrabarty, *Provincializing Europe,* 8.

5. Helgesson, "Radicalizing Temporal Difference"; Lloyd, *Under Representation.* I have drawn especially on Helgesson's argument that postcolonial understandings of temporality are marked by an aporia between two different—both valid—ways of understanding time. My argument also addresses the problem that David Lloyd identifies in *Under Representation,* 70: that temporal understandings of race and racism have been neglected by scholars in favor of models "cast principally in spatial terms." Some valuable exceptions that do address imperial temporalities include Mueller, "Temporality, Sovereignty, and Imperialism"; Hutchings, *Time and World Politics;* Klinke, "Chronopolitics." Manu Goswami has written instructively about the "specific temporal politics" of anticolonialism; Goswami, "Imaginary Futures and Colonial Internationalisms," 1463. Though I focus on political writing, I have found helpful Mark Currie's study of anticipation in narrative, *About Time.*

6. Yogita Goyal offers an incisive summary of one of the key binaries that has characterized analyses of anticolonial time: "While nation time is linear

and developmental (even if interrupted by what Arjun Appadurai calls disjuncture and difference), diaspora has seemed to offer a more discontinuous and fractured sense of time. While nation time links past, present, and future in a march toward progress, diaspora time emphasizes the breaks and discontinuities in such a movement, recalling the trauma of the Middle Passage and looking forward to the Jubilee." Goyal, "Africa and the Black Atlantic," x.

7. Christopher Miller wrote about hybridity and nationalism that we cannot realistically "be either 'for' or 'against' [them] . . . in a systematic and absolute way, since both are real." Miller, *Nationalists and Nomads*, 7. My argument extends this insight to the representation and articulation of time.

8. Olender, *Race and Erudition*, xix.

9. Fabian, *Time and the Other*, 25. For a related critique of anthropological notions of time, see Greenhouse, *A Moment's Notice*, 3.

10. This idea is deftly conveyed by the term "proleptic elegy" in Brantlinger's landmark study of settler discourse, *Dark Vanishings*.

11. E. N. Jones, "Liberia," *Sierra Leone Weekly News* [*SLWN*], February 14, 1931. Jones was a Sierra Leonean politician, banker, and reverend; he also went by the name Lamina Sankoh.

12. "Haïti aux Haïtiens," *Le Courrier des Noirs*, November 1, 1927.

13. Egypt joined the League in 1937 after the signing of the Anglo-Egyptian treaty. Comparative analysis of Haiti, Liberia, and Ethiopia virtually disappeared after the Second World War. The scarce exceptions include Putnam, *The Insistent Call;* Ross, "Black Americans and Haiti, Liberia, the Virgin Islands, and Ethiopia"; Getachew, *Worldmaking after Empire*. Within postcolonial studies there have been several engagements with Haiti, such as Kaiama L. Glover's *Haiti Unbound*, but little interest in Liberia or Ethiopia.

14. Akpan, "Liberia and the Universal Negro Improvement Association"; Azikiwe, *My Odyssey*, 32.

15. Dash, *Haiti and the United States*, 1.

16. Quoted in Godden, "'Absalom, Absalom!,' Haiti and Labor History," 686. See also Balthaser, *Anti-Imperialist Modernism*, 118–46.

17. Fitzpatrick and Jones, *The Reception of Edmund Burke in Europe*, 190.

18. Quoted in Sherwood, *Origins of Pan-Africanism*, 28.

19. Spiro, *Defending the Master Race*, 242.

20. Rosenberg, "Ordering Others," 406.

21. Stoddard, *The French Revolution in San Domingo*. For a discussion, see Riley, *Performing Race and Erasure*, 109.

22. Stoddard, *Rising Tide of Color against White World-Supremacy*, 227.

23. Stoddard, *Rising Tide of Color against White World-Supremacy*, 100–1.

24. Schmidt, *United States Occupation of Haiti*, 62–63. As Schmidt shows, such language was common among US soldiers and officials involved in the occupation of Haiti.

25. On the US occupation of Haiti, see the outstanding study by Schmidt, *United States Occupation of Haiti*. Also essential are Plummer, *Haiti and the United States*; Dash, *Haiti and the United States*; Renda, *Taking Haiti*; Castor, *L'occupation américaine d'Haïti*; and the recent work by Dalleo, *American Imperialism's Undead*. Other works on the occupation examine its effects on specific elements of Haitian society: on the church, Pamphile, *La Croix et Le Glaive*; on education, Pamphile, *L'éducation en Haiti sous l'occupation américaine 1915–1934;* on peasants, Millet, *Les paysans haïtiens et l'occupation américaine d'Haïti, 1915–1930.*

26. Plummer, *Haiti and the United States*, 101.

27. Schmidt, *United States Occupation of Haiti*, 99.

28. James, *The Black Jacobins*, xi.

29. Renault, "Toward a Counter-Genealogy of Race."

30. Williams, *Capitalism and Slavery*, 202.

31. Césaire's letters from the period also indicate, however, a growing frustration with a "historical" approach to Haiti. "In particular," he wrote to André Breton on April 4, 1944, referring to a text on Haiti which he had sent Breton, "the historical dimension, or the historicity already sufficiently reduced, must be completely eliminated." Véron, "Césaire at the Crossroads in Haiti," 438.

32. For African American newspaper articles supporting the occupation in its opening stages, see "Speaking of Haiti," *The Chicago Defender*, September 4, 1915, 8; C. Brown, "Little Haiti and Her People: Conditions Are Such That the Country Could Be Made a Paradise—American Occupation Will Help," *Afro-American*, April 8, 1916, 4. While previous studies have emphasized the effect of the Cayes massacre of December 1929 in transforming African American attitudes to the occupation—see, for example, Putnam, *Insistent Call*, 59–61—I show here that reporting on Haiti began to shift much earlier, from around 1919. Reports from the occupation drew attention to the overt racism expressed

by the occupying Marines, an all-White force disproportionately drawn from the Southern United States. On US Marines in Haiti, see Renda's *Taking Haiti*, 53–62. On the repression of African Americans during World War I, see Ellis, *Race, War, and Surveillance*.

33. Perry, *A Hubert Harrison Reader*, 239.

34. "Haitians Say U.S. Made Them Suffer," *The Chicago Defender*, May 14, 1921. Haitian delegations continued to receive sympathetic coverage in the African American press: see "Haitian Denounces American Invasion," *New Journal and Guide*, February 4, 1922, 3.

35. "Haitian Denounces American Invasion," *New Journal and Guide*, February 4, 1922, 3.

36. "Get Out of Haiti," *Afro-American*, July 26, 1930, 6.

37. "30,000 Blacks Occupy Rhineland: Americans Criticise French for Sending Colored Troops into White Country; Frenchman Replies, Asks America Why Uncle Sam Sent White Troops into The Black Republic of Haiti," *Afro-American*, May 7, 1920, 1. The US Army was not desegregated until the 1940s. See Renda, *Taking Haiti*, 53–56.

38. Detweiler, *Negro Press in the United States*, 146.

39. Plummer, "Garveyism in Haiti during the US Occupation," 80. Garcia would later travel to Liberia, representing the UNIA.

40. "Voodooism in Haiti," *Negro World*, April 7, 1923.

41. McPherson, "Personal Occupations," 586.

42. Anti-occupation political activity also seems to have acted as an incubator for feminist organizing, as suggested by the flourishing of women's political organizations after the end of the US occupation. McPherson, "Personal Occupations," 584–85, 598. Theodora Holly, the daughter of a prominent African American bishop who had emigrated to Haiti in 1861, criticized the occupation in the Black newspaper *New York Age*. The women's organization L'Oeuvre des Femmes Haitiennes pour l'Organisation du Travail was established by a group of African American women. Plummer, "The Afro-American Response to the Occupation of Haiti," 138.

43. Haitian male novelists typically represented the occupation as a struggle over masculinity, symbolized by the class-freighted competition between Haitian and American men for Haitian women. But we find different explorations of the occupation's gendered implications in two novels written by

Haitian women: Virgile Valcin's *La blanche négresse* (1934), in which a French-Haitian woman married to an American is—disastrously—revealed to be of African descent; and Annie Desroy's *Le Joug* (1934), which centers on the lives of two couples (one American, one Haitian) during the occupation. Kaussen, *Migrant Revolutions*, 94n4; Chancy, *Framing Silence*, 49–50.

44. Ludovic-Morin Lacombe, "Haïti: Son devoir envers l'Ethiopie," *LRN*, Jan–Feb 1936. Spiegler, "Aspects of Nationalist Thought among French-Speaking West Africans," 237. The Haitian activist Jean Barau also wrote in *La Race Nègre* about the crisis now "paralyzing the economic life of the country." Jean Babau, "L'impérialisme yankee en action," *LRN*, February–March 1930.

45. "More Colored Nations Than White Ones," *Afro-American*, May 30, 1919, 1.

46. There is a vast literature on the Italo-Ethiopian War and its international ramifications. For an overview, see Steiner, *The Triumph of the Dark*, chap. 2; Strang, *Collision of Empires*.

47. Spiegler, "Aspects of Nationalist Thought among French-Speaking West Africans," 265; Asante, *Pan-African Protest*, 45; Bush, *Imperialism, Race and Resistance*, 222–26.

48. Asante, *Pan-African Protest*, 62–63. Featherstone, "Black Internationalism, Subaltern Cosmopolitanism, and the Spatial Politics of Antifascism," 1412.

49. Ewing, "Caribbean Labour Politics in the Age of Garvey," 36. Harris, *African-American Reactions to War in Ethiopia*, 63.

50. John Hope Franklin, quoted in Weisbord, *Ebony Kinship*, 97.

51. Nkrumah, *Autobiography of Kwame Nkrumah*, 22.

52. Du Bois, "Inter-Racial Implications of the Ethiopian Crisis," 88.

53. Harris, *United States and the Italo-Ethiopian Crisis*, 10.

54. Mallett, *Mussolini in Ethiopia*, 27; Strang, *Collision of Empires*. On (unmet) hopes for a "pan-colored" alliance against Italy, see Clarke, "An Alliance of the 'Colored' Peoples: Ethiopia and Japan."

55. Brantlinger, *Dark Vanishings*, 1.

56. There is an absence of scholarly literature on the "White Atlantic," but there are tantalizing references to it in Mills, "Unwriting and Unwhitening the World," 210; Stam and Shohat, *Race in Translation*, xv.

57. Chaplin, *Blood and Ink*, 29.

58. Chaplin, *Blood and Ink*, 39.

59. Chaplin, *Blood and Ink*, 47, 51, 35.

60. Chaplin, *Blood and Ink*, 106.

61. Bernhard, "Hitler's Africa in the East," 2–3.

62. Quoted in Harris, *United States and the Italo-Ethiopian Crisis*, 45.

63. Woodson, *Anthems, Sonnets, and Chants*, 167.

64. Asante, *Pan-African Protest*, 53, 172, 190.

65. Asante, *Pan-African Protest*, 53.

66. Goswami, "Imaginary Futures and Colonial Internationalisms," 1475; "Rambling Talks," *SLWN*, May 9, 1936. These critiques reflect what Getachew describes as the "burdened membership" in the League endured by these three states. Getachew, *Worldmaking after Empire*, 19.

67. As Robbie Shilliam has put it, many came to see their defense of "Ethiopia's sovereignty as part of their own liberation struggle against . . . [the] global colonial order." Shilliam, "Intervention and Colonial-Modernity," 1137.

68. "Après 35 ans de luttes contre l'oppression coloniale," *Africa*, December 1, 1935.

69. "Après 35 ans de luttes contre l'oppression coloniale."

70. In this context, see Putnam, "Ethiopia Is Now," 419–44. Postcolonial scholars have often highlighted the sense of *now* invoked by anticolonial temporalities. See Chakrabarty, *Provincializing Europe*, 8.

71. Du Bois, "Inter-Racial Implications of the Ethiopian Crisis," 88.

72. Rogers, *Real Facts about Ethiopia*, 2.

73. Rogers, *Real Facts about Ethiopia*, 2.

74. Rogers, *Real Facts about Ethiopia*, 7, 2.

75. Rogers, *Real Facts about Ethiopia*, 3.

76. Ewing, "Caribbean Labour Politics in the Age of Garvey," 36.

77. Quoted in Derrick, *Africa's Agitators*, 334.

78. Asante, *Pan-African Protest*, 179.

79. Buell, *Native Problem in Africa*, 819–52; Brown, *Economic History of Liberia*, 174–208; Sundiata, *Black Scandal*; Gershoni, *Black Colonialism*; Christy, "Pawning of Human Beings in Liberia," 169–74. For the House of Lords debate following the publication of the report, see Parl. Deb. H.L., 16 March 1932, vol. 83, c913.

80. Reeve, *Black Republic*, 9, 46.

81. Reeve, *Black Republic*, 178.

82. "The Rising Star of Liberia," *SLWN*, June 9, 1928.

83. Moses, *Golden Age of Black Nationalism*, 35. Delaney reversed his position by 1859, "making friendly overtures towards the Liberians." Moses, *Golden Age of Black Nationalism*, 35.

84. On Liberia's role in pan-Africanism, see Gershoni, *Black Colonialism;* Harris, *Global Dimensions of the African Diaspora;* Sundiata, *Black Scandal;* Hickey, "Positive Perspectives on Independent Africa"; Saha, "Romance of Nationhood." One key exception to the language of parody was Buell, *Native Problem in Africa.*

85. De La Rue, *The Land of the Pepper Bird,* 209.

86. Bush, *Imperialism, Race and Resistance,* 265; Coleman, *Nigeria,* 216.

87. Parl. Deb. H.L., 25 April 1934, vol. 91, cc724–5.

88. Olender, *Race and Erudition,* xix.

89. Robinson, "DuBois and Black Sovereignty," 44. Robinson's article attacks Du Bois for these positions. Robinson argues that, "blinded by the elitism characteristic of his class's prerogative," Du Bois "fell prey to American colonialism"; Robinson, "DuBois and Black Sovereignty," 39. Azikiwe, *Liberia in World Politics,* 221.

90. Ayoob, "Inequality and Theorizing in International Relations," 27–48.

91. Derrick, *Africa's Agitators,* 300.

92. Quoted in Robinson, "DuBois and Black Sovereignty," 43. Du Bois later explained: "I know what European imperialism has done to Asia and Africa; but, nevertheless, I had not then lost faith in the capitalist system, and I believed that it was possible for a great corporation, headed by a man of vision, to go into a country with something more than the mere ideal of profit." Robinson, "DuBois and Black Sovereignty," 46.

93. "Rambling Talks," *SLWN,* September 9, 1931.

94. "The Black Republic of Liberia and the White Civilised Nations of the World," *SLWN,* August 29, 1931. The newspaper also pointed out, in an article of the same title published on September 12, 1931, the "farce" of European powers claiming to care about the self-determination of Liberian "natives" when the inhabitants of Britain's West African colonies continued to live under colonial rule.

95. "The Black Republic of Liberia and the White Civilised Nations of the World," *SLWN,* August 29, 1931.

96. "The Black Republic of Liberia and the White Civilised Nations of the World."

97. "The Black Republic of Liberia and the White Civilised Nations of the World."

98. Brown, *Economic History of Liberia*, 65. The book was referred to by A. G. Hopkins thirty-two years later, in *An Economic History of West Africa*, 2, as a "neglected study" notable for its "careful research." An understudied figure, Brown was born in Missouri and had studied at Howard University and the University of Chicago before completing his doctorate at the London School of Economics. He later married Elsie Kaye, the daughter of a prominent English industrialist, converted to Islam while in Pakistan, and became director of the King's Mill in Huddersfield. See "Negro Expatriate Runs 900-Year Old Textile Firm," *Ebony*, June 1968.

99. Brown, *Economic History of Liberia*, 147.

100. Brown, *Economic History of Liberia*, 162.

101. Brown, *Economic History of Liberia*, 230.

102. Brown, *Economic History of Liberia*, 225.

103. Brown, *Economic History of Liberia*, 214.

104. Brown, *Economic History of Liberia*, 214.

105. Brown, *Economic History of Liberia*, 224.

106. On the idea of decolonization as a normative revolution, see Crawford, *Argument and Change in World Politics*. Patrick Wolfe observed that, though it was born in slavery, race in the United States "came into its own with slavery's abolition." After "the false dawn of Reconstruction, race intensified as a structure of social control." Wolfe, *Traces of History*, 77–78. Adom Getachew has pointed to the international parallels of the duplicitous expansion of citizenship to African Americans, drawing on Saidiya Hartman's concept of "burdened" citizenship. Getachew, *Worldmaking after Empire*, 19.

107. For an argument that dominant frameworks of progress and modernization in international decision-making are still "grounded in subtle notions of 'race,'" see Grovogui, "Come to Africa," 427.

108. Salt, "Ecological Chains of Unfreedom," 268.

109. The legal scholar Anthony Anghie has argued that the League of Nations mandates system, while claiming to offer a route to sovereignty for colonial territories, actually prolonged their subordination. It did so by expunging explicitly racist criteria for statehood only to replace those criteria with "scientific" language which, in fact, justified continued oversight and domination.

Anghie, *Imperialism, Sovereignty and the Making of International Law.* Though Haiti, Liberia, and Ethiopia were not mandates, since they had not been colonial territories before the First World War, a similar process saw the criteria for statehood shift in ways that rendered them nonsovereign.

110. Among many possible examples, see Guha, *History at the Limit of World-History;* Allen, *End of Progress.*

111. Scott, *Conscripts of Modernity,* 7.

112. Achille Mbembe rightly points out that there is "no longer a 'distinctive historicity' of these societies, one not embedded in times and rhythms heavily conditioned by European domination." Mbembe, *On the Postcolony,* 9.

113. Neither are all conceptions of "development" alike—a point made forcefully by Thandika Mkandawire in his essay "African Intellectuals and Nationalism," 40.

114. On "the impossibility of black sovereignty," see Salt, *Unfinished Revolution,* 94; Getachew, *Worldmaking after Empire,* 52; Glover, "'Flesh Like One's Own,'" 237. Nisancioglu's "Racial Sovereignty" gives a detailed theoretical account of the relationship between race and sovereignty.

115. Kobina Sekyi's unpublished manuscript, "The Parting of the Ways" (ca. 1922), and particularly chapter 3, "Our Brethren Abroad," focuses on Liberia and Haiti and the question of the African state. The manuscript is discussed in Langley, "Garveyism and African Nationalism," 10–13; an excerpt of chapter 3 is also published in Hill, *Marcus Garvey and Universal Negro Improvement Association Papers Papers,* 10:353–55.

116. Said, *Orientalism,* 8.

117. Bayly, *Birth of the Modern World,* 237.

118. In our contemporary order, the combination and flexibility of forms of hierarchical time continue to warn us against easy temporal fixes. For even the most well-meaning assaults on history can find themselves rearticulating the language of racializing differentiation. See Wilson, "Worlds beyond the Political?" In contemporary bordering, migration, and deportation regimes, for example, we find "surplus" and unwanted populations subject to multiple forms of differentiated time. Technologies of control might sometimes insist on such populations being lost in history. At other times, those technologies might subject the same populations to an "enforced orientation to the present." De Genova, "Migrant 'Illegality' and Deportability in Everyday Life," 427.

EPILOGUE

1. Chakrabarty, *Climate of History in a Planetary Age*, 3, 70. He adds, though, that the "planet" and the "globe" are paradoxically bridged by the idea of the Anthropocene. Chakrabarty draws partly on William Connolly's definition of the planetary as "a series of temporal force fields, such as climate patterns, drought zones, the ocean conveyor system, species evolution, glacier flows, and hurricanes." Connolly, *Facing the Planetary*, 7; see also Chakrabarty, *Climate of History in a Planetary Age*, 85–86; Kurki, *International Relations in a Relational Universe*, chap. 7. For a discussion of the scientific paradigm change that allows for this conception of the planetary to emerge, see Howe and Cronon, *Behind the Curve;* Weart, *Discovery of Global Warming.*

2. Apter, "Planetary Dysphoria."

3. Thacker, *In the Dust of This Planet*, 7.

4. Keil, "The Empty Shell of the Planetary," 5. The philosopher Michel Serres suggested in a similar vein that "mastery of the world must be replaced by the mastery of mastery." Quoted in Městrović, *Towards a New Orientation*, 47.

5. See Zúquete, *Identitarians.*

6. Khalili, *Foreign Office*, 2015, mixed media, https://www.bouchrakhalili.com/foreign-office/.

7. In his film *Two Meetings and a Funeral* (2017), for example, the artist Naeem Mohaiemen also shows empty buildings from the halcyon days of Third Worldism. See Folkerts, "Two Meetings and a Funeral."

8. Davis, "Introduction," 12.

9. An argument for the pressing importance of collective global action is recently advanced in Bratton, *Revenge of the Real.* Such world-directed action is what Toni Morrison describes as the "reconstruction of a world" and what Sylvia Wynter calls "creative and world constitutive activities." (both cited in McKittrick, *Demonic Grounds*, 32, 122.) The canon of African and Black environmental thought has yet to be comprehensively examined. Rare treatments include Smith, *African American Environmental Thought;* Behrens, "African Philosophy, Thought and Practice, and Their Contribution to Environmental Ethics"; Fabien, "African American Environmental Ethics."

10. In that sense it was both "lumping" *and* "splitting," terminology that Chakrabarty adopts to explain the disjuncture between postcolonial and environmentalist approaches to the world. "Lumpers," like environmentalists,

stress the essential oneness of the planet and the unifying fact of a shared terrestrial existence. Splitters," like most researchers in the humanities and especially postcolonial theorists, emphasize the hierarchies that divide the category of human. This is one reason, Chakrabarty suggests, that postcolonial theory has been insufficiently attentive to environmental questions. Chakrabarty, *Climate of History in a Planetary Age*, 17.

11. The best study of this fast-moving period remains Wallerstein, *Africa*. For background, see Esedebe, *Pan-Africanism;* and Geiss, *Pan-African Movement*. Getachew, in *Worldmaking after Empire*, examines the right to self-determination, regional federations, and the project for a New International Economic Order (NIEO) in light of the Black Atlantic anticolonial critique.

12. Robinson, *Black Marxism*, xxx.

13. Fanon, *Black Skin, White Masks*, 60.

14. Ruggie, "What Makes the World Hang Together?"

15. McCarthy, "Harlem Is Everywhere," 9; Gilroy, *Black Atlantic*.

16. See Fitzgerald, *Close to Home;* Mohan and Stokke, in "Participatory Development and Empowerment".

17. "Racial Unity," *GCL*, July 24–31, 1920.

18. Letter signed "Boisson" from La Sûreté Générale du Gouvernment Général de l'Afrique Occidentale Française, to Le Gouverneur Générale de l'Afrique Occidentale Française, Messieurs les Lieutenants Gouverneurs des Colonies du Groupe, and Monsieur l'Administrateur en chef Administrateur de la circonscription de Dakar, subject "Cri des Nègres," Dakar, November 1, 1935. 1E 16–6, Archives Nationales du Bénin, Porto Novo.

19. "Etat d'esprit des indigènes résident en France," April 29, 1927, 13 SLOT-FOM/1, Archives nationales d'outre-mer, Aix-en-Provence.

Bibliography

ARCHIVES

Archives nationales d'outre mer, Aix-en-Provence, France
    Service de liaison avec les originaires des territoires
    français d'outre-mer (SLOTFOM)
        Africa
        Le Colonisé
        Les Continents
        Le Courrier des Noirs
        Le Cri des Nègres (CDN)
        La Dépêche Africaine (LDA)
        Le Paria
        La Race Nègre (LRN)
        La Voix des Nègres
Archives nationales du Bénin, Porto Novo
British Library Newspaper Collection, London
    African Morning Post (AMP)
    The African Times and Orient Review (ATOR)
    The Gold Coast Leader (GCL)

The Gold Coast Nation
The Gold Coast Times
Sierra Leone Weekly News (SLWN)
Vox Populi
West Africa
West African Pilot (WAP)
Courtauld Institute of Art, London
Légitime Défense
Edinburgh University
The Negro World
Musée de l'Institut fondamental d'Afrique noire (IFAN), Dakar
L'A.O.F.: Écho de la Cote Occidentale D'Afrique
L'Ouest Africain Français
The National Archives (TNA) of the United Kingdom, London
Colonial Office (CO) Papers
Foreign Office Papers
War Office Papers
Public Records and Archives Administration Department of Ghana (PRAAD),
Accra
The Gold Coast Chronicle
The Gold Coast Leader (GCL)
The Gold Coast Nation
The Gold Coast Times
Public Records and Archives Administration Department of Ghana (PRAAD),
Cape Coast, Ghana
Kobina Sekyi Papers

PUBLISHED SOURCES

Abrahams, Peter. *The Coyaba Chronicles: Reflections on the Black Experience in the Twentieth Century.* Kingston: Ian Randle Publishers, 2004.

Adi, Hakim. "Bandele Omoniyi: A Neglected Nigerian Nationalist." *African Affairs* 90, no. 361 (1991): 581–605.

———. *West Africans in Britain, 1900–1960: Nationalism, Pan Africanism and Communism.* London: Lawrence and Wishart, 1998.

The African Law Reports: Sierra Leone Series. Edited by Alan Milner and Hugh Hurley. Dobbs Ferry, NY: Oceana Publications, 1950.

Agbosu, L. K. "The Origins of Forest Law and Policy in Ghana during the Colonial Period." *Journal of African Law* 27, no. 2 (1983): 169–87.

Ahearne, Jeremy, and John Speller, eds. "Pierre Bourdieu and the Literary Field." Special issue, *Paragraph* 35, no. 1 (2012).

Ainslie, Rosalynde. *The Press in Africa: Communications Past and Present.* London: Victor Gollancz, 1966.

Ajayi, J. F. Ade, and Michael Crowder. *History of West Africa.* Vol. 2. London: Longman, 1974.

Akpan, M. B. "Liberia and the Universal Negro Improvement Association: The Background to the Abortion of Garvey's Scheme for African Colonization." *Journal of African History* 14, no. 1 (1973): 105–27.

Alcoff, Linda Martín. *Visible Identities: Race, Gender, and the Self.* New York: Oxford University Press, 2005.

Alence, Rod. "The 1937–1938 Gold Coast Cocoa Crisis: The Political Economy of Commercial Stalemate." *African Economic History,* no. 19 (1990): 77–104.

Allen, Amy. *The End of Progress: Decolonizing the Normative Foundations of Critical Theory.* New York: Columbia University Press, 2016.

Allen, Susan Isabelle. *René Maran's Batouala Jazz-Text.* Bern: Peter Lang, 2015.

Ambaras, David R. *Japan's Imperial Underworlds: Intimate Encounters at the Borders of Empire.* Cambridge: Cambridge University Press, 2018.

Amin, Samir. *Accumulation on a World Scale: Unequal International Specialization and the International Flow of Capital.* New York: Monthly Review Press, 1974.

Anderson, Benedict. *Imagined Communities: Reflections on the Origin and Spread of Nationalism.* London: Verso, 2006.

———. *Under Three Flags: Anarchism and the Anti-Colonial Imagination.* London: Verso, 2005.

Anderson, Perry. *Zone of Engagement.* London: Verso, 1992.

Angelo, Hillary, and Kian Goh. "Out in Space: Difference and Abstraction in Planetary Urbanization." *International Journal of Urban and Regional Research* 45, no. 4 (2021): 732–44.

Anghie, Antony. *Imperialism, Sovereignty and the Making of International Law.* Cambridge: Cambridge University Press, 2008.

Apter, Emily. "Planetary Dysphoria." *Third Text* 27, no. 1 (2013): 131–40.

Arboleda, Martin. *Planetary Mine: Territories of Extraction under Late Capitalism*. Verso Books, 2020.

Arnold, A. James. "Beyond Postcolonial Césaire: Reading *Cahier d'un Retour au Pays Natal* Historically." *Forum for Modern Language Studies* 44, no. 3 (2008): 258–75.

Asante, S. K. B. "The Neglected Aspects of the Activities of the Gold Coast Aborigines Rights Protection Society." *Phylon* (1960–) 36, no. 1 (1975): 32–45.

———. *Pan-African Protest: West Africa and the Italo-Ethiopian Crisis, 1934–1941*. Legon History Series. London: Longman, 1977.

Aslanian, Sebouh David, Joyce E. Chaplin, Ann McGrath, and Kristin Mann. "AHR Conversation: How Size Matters: The Question of Scale in History." *American Historical Review* 118, no. 5 (2013): 1431–72.

Austin, Gareth. "Reciprocal Comparison and African History: Tackling Conceptual Eurocentrism in the Study of Africa's Economic Past." *African Studies Review* 50, no. 3 (2007): 1–28.

Ayoob, Mohammed. "Inequality and Theorizing in International Relations: The Case for Subaltern Realism." *International Studies Review* 4, no. 3 (2002): 27–48.

Azikiwe, Nnamdi. *Liberia in World Politics*. Westport, CT: Negro Universities Press, 1970.

———. *My Odyssey: An Autobiography*. London: C. Hurst and Co., 1970.

Baku, Kofi. "An Intellectual in Nationalist Politics: The Contribution of Kobina Sekyi to the Evolution of Ghanaian National Consciousness." PhD diss., University of Sussex, 1987.

Baldwin, James. *Collected Essays*. Edited by Toni Morrison. New York: Library of America, 1998.

———. "Princes and Powers." In *The Price of the Ticket*. New York: St Martin's Press, 1999.

Baldwin, James, and Raoul Peck. *I Am Not Your Negro*. London: Penguin Classics, 2017.

Balibar, Étienne, and Immanuel Wallerstein. *Race, Nation, Class: Ambiguous Identities*. 2nd ed. London: Verso, 2011.

Balthaser, Benjamin. *Anti-Imperialist Modernism: Race and Transnational Radical Culture*. Ann Arbor: University of Michigan Press, 2016.

Bartelson, Jens. *Visions of World Community*. Cambridge: Cambridge University Press, 2009.

Bateman, Fiona, and Lionel Pilkington, eds. *Studies in Settler Colonialism: Politics, Identity and Culture.* Basingstoke, UK: Palgrave MacMillan, 2011.

Bayly, C. A. *The Birth of the Modern World, 1780–1914: Global Connections and Comparisons.* Malden, MA: Wiley-Blackwell, 2004.

Behrens, Kevin. "African Philosophy, Thought and Practice, and Their Contribution to Environmental Ethics." PhD diss., University of Johannesburg, 2012.

Belich, James. *Replenishing the Earth: The Settler Revolution and the Rise of the Angloworld.* Oxford: Oxford University Press, 2009.

Bell, Duncan. *The Idea of Greater Britain: Empire and the Future of World Order, 1860–1900.* Princeton, NJ: Princeton University Press, 2007.

———. "Making and Taking Worlds." In *Global Intellectual History*, edited by Samuel Moyn and Andrew Sartori, 254–79. New York: Columbia University Press, 2013.

Bernal, Richard, Mark Figueroa, and Michael Witter. "Caribbean Economic Thought: The Critical Tradition." *Social and Economic Studies* 33, no. 2 (1984): 5–96.

Bernhard, Patrick. "Hitler's Africa in the East: Italian Colonialism as a Model for German Planning in Eastern Europe." *Journal of Contemporary History* 51, no. 1 (2016): 61–90.

Berry, Sara. "Hegemony on a Shoestring: Indirect Rule and Access to Agricultural Land." *Africa* 62, no. 3 (1992): 327–55.

———. "Supply Response Reconsidered: Cocoa in Western Nigeria, 1909–44." *Journal of Development Studies* 13, no. 1 (1976): 4–17.

Betts, Raymond F. *Assimilation and Association in French Colonial Theory, 1890–1914.* Lincoln: University of Nebraska Press, 2005.

Bhabha, Homi. "Of Mimicry and Man: The Ambivalence of Colonial Discourse." *October* 28 (1984): 125–33.

Bickford-Smith, Vivian. "The Betrayal of Creole Elites, 1880–1920." In *Black Experience and the Empire*, edited by Philip D. Morgan and Sean Hawkins, 194–227. Oxford: Oxford University Press, 2004.

Blain, Keisha N. *Set the World on Fire: Black Nationalist Women and the Global Struggle for Freedom.* Philadelphia: University of Pennsylvania Press, 2018.

Blain, Keisha N., and Tiffany M. Gill. *To Turn the Whole World Over: Black Women and Internationalism.* Champaign: University of Illinois Press, 2019.

Bledsoe, Adam, and Willie Jamaal Wright. "The Pluralities of Black Geographies." *Antipode* 51, no. 2 (2019): 419–37.

Bose, Sugata, and Kris Manjapra. *Cosmopolitan Thought Zones: South Asia and the Global Circulation of Ideas*. Basingstoke: Palgrave Macmillan, 2010.

Bourdieu, Pierre. *Pascalian Meditations*. Stanford, CA: Stanford University Press, 2000.

Brantlinger, Patrick. *Dark Vanishings: Discourse on the Extinction of Primitive Races, 1800–1930*. Ithaca, NY: Cornell University Press, 2003.

Bratton, Benjamin. *The Revenge of the Real: Politics for a Post-Pandemic World*. London: Verso Books, 2021.

Brennan, Timothy. *Borrowed Light: Vico, Hegel, and the Colonies*. Stanford, CA: Stanford University Press, 2014.

Brenner, Neil. "The Limits to Scale? Methodological Reflections on Scalar Structuration." *Progress in Human Geography* 25, no. 4 (2001): 591–614.

———. "The Urban Question: Reflections on Henri Lefebvre, Urban Theory and the Politics of Scale." *International Journal of Urban and Regional Research* 24, no. 2 (2000): 361–78.

Breuilly, John. *Nationalism and the State*. Manchester: Manchester University Press, 1993.

Brown, George William. *The Economic History of Liberia*. Washington, DC: Associated Publishers, 1941.

Brown, Wendy. "Wounded Attachments." *Political Theory* 21, no. 3 (1993): 390–410.

Buell, Raymond Leslie. *The Native Problem in Africa*. New York: Macmillan, 1928.

Bush, Barbara. *Imperialism, Race and Resistance*. London: Routledge, 1999.

Butler, Judith. *Bodies That Matter: On the Discursive Limits of "Sex."* New York: Psychology Press, 1993.

———. *The Psychic Life of Power: Theories in Subjection*. Stanford, CA: Stanford University Press, 1997.

Buzan, Barry, and George Lawson. *The Global Transformation: History, Modernity and the Making of International Relations*. Cambridge: Cambridge University Press, 2015.

Camiscioli, Elisa. *Reproducing the French Race: Immigration, Intimacy, and Embodiment in the Early Twentieth Century*. Durham, NC: Duke University Press, 2009.

Carby, Hazel V. *Race Men*. Cambridge, MA: Harvard University Press, 2009.

Carnegie, Charles V. "Garvey and the Black Transnation." *Small Axe* 5 (1999): 48–71.

Carr, Richard, and Bradley W. Hart. *The Global 1920s: Politics, Economics and Society*. New York: Routledge, 2016.

Casely Hayford, J. E. *Ethiopia Unbound: Studies in Race Emancipation*. London: Routledge, 2012.

———. *The Truth about the West African Land Question*. Hove, UK: Psychology Press, 1971.

Castor, Suzy. *L'occupation américaine d'Haïti*. Port-au-Prince: Société haïtienne d'histoire, 1988.

Césaire, Aimé. *Cahier d'un retour au pays natal*. Edited by F. Abiola Irele. Ibadan: New Horn Press, 1994.

———. *The Collected Poetry*. Translated by Clayton Eshleman and Annette Smith. Berkeley: University of California Press, 1983.

———. *Discourse on Colonialism*. New ed. New York: Monthly Review Press, 2000.

———. *Journal of a Homecoming / Cahier d'un retour au pays natal*. Translated by N. Gregson Davis. Durham, NC: Duke University Press Books, 2017.

———. *The Original 1939 Notebook of a* Return to the Native Land. Edited by A. James Arnold and Clayton Eshleman. Bilingual French-English ed. Middletown, CT: Wesleyan, 2013.

Chakrabarty, Dipesh. *The Climate of History in a Planetary Age*. Chicago: University of Chicago Press, 2021.

———. *Provincializing Europe: Postcolonial Thought and Historical Difference*. Princeton, NJ: Princeton University Press, 2000.

Chancy, Myriam J. A. *Framing Silence: Revolutionary Novels by Haitian Women*. New Brunswick, NJ: Rutgers University Press, 1997.

Chaplin, W. W. *Blood and Ink: An Italo-Ethiopian War Diary*. New York: Telegraph Press, 1936.

Chatterjee, Partha. *Empire and Nation: Selected Essays*. New York: Columbia University Press, 2010.

Childers, Kristen Stromberg. *Seeking Imperialism's Embrace: National Identity, Decolonization, and Assimilation in the French Caribbean*. Oxford: Oxford University Press, 2016.

Chimni, B. S. "Third World Approaches to International Law: A Manifesto." *International Community Law Review* 8, no. 1 (2006): 3–27.

Christy, Cuthbert. "Pawning of Human Beings in Liberia." *Journal of the Royal African Society* 30, no. 119 (1931): 169–74.

Clarke, J. Calvitt, III. "An Alliance of the 'Colored' Peoples: Ethiopia and Japan." In *Collision of Empires: Italy's Invasion of Ethiopia and Its International Impact*, edited by Bruce Strang, 231–60. Farnham: Ashgate, 2013.

Cole, Catherine M. *Ghana's Concert Party Theatre*. Bloomington: Indiana University Press, 2001.

Coleman, James S. *Nigeria: Background to Nationalism*. Berkeley: University of California Press, 1971.

Conboy, Katie, Nadia Medina, and Sarah Stanbury. *Writing on the Body: Female Embodiment and Feminist Theory*. New York: Columbia University Press, 1997.

Conklin, Alice L. *A Mission to Civilize: Republican Idea of Empire in France and West Africa, 1895–1930*. New ed. Stanford, CA: Stanford University Press, 2000.

Connolly, William E. *Facing the Planetary: Entangled Humanism and the Politics of Swarming*. Durham, NC: Duke University Press Books, 2017.

Conrad, Sebastian. *What Is Global History?* Princeton, NJ: Princeton University Press, 2016.

Constant, Isabelle, and Kahiudi C. Mabana. *Negritude: Legacy and Present Relevance*. Newcastle upon Tyne: Cambridge Scholars Publishing, 2009.

Cooper, Anna Julia. *A Voice From the South*. New York: Oxford University Press, 1990.

Cooper, Frederick. "Africa and the World Economy." *African Studies Review* 24, no. 2/3 (1981): 1–86.

———. *Citizenship between Empire and Nation: Remaking France and French Africa, 1945–1960*. Princeton, NJ: Princeton University Press, 2014.

Coronil, Fernando. "Towards a Critique of Globalcentrism: Speculations on Capitalism's Nature." *Public Culture* 12, no. 2 (2000): 351–74.

Cosgrove, Denis. *Apollo's Eye: A Cartographic Genealogy of the Earth in the Western Imagination*. Baltimore, MD: Johns Hopkins University Press, 2001.

Costello, Brannon. "Richard Wright's *Lawd Today!* and the Political Uses of Modernism." *African American Review* 37, no. 1 (2003): 39–52.

Crawford, Neta. *Argument and Change in World Politics: Ethics, Decolonization, and Humanitarian Intervention*. Cambridge: Cambridge University Press, 2002.

Cronon, Edmund D. *Black Moses: The Story of Marcus Garvey and the Universal Negro Improvement Association*. 2nd ed. Madison: University of Wisconsin Press, 1998.

Cronon, William. *Nature's Metropolis: Chicago and the Great West*. New York: W. W. Norton and Co., 2009.

Crosby, Alfred W. *Ecological Imperialism: The Biological Expansion of Europe, 900–1900*. Cambridge: Cambridge University Press, 2004.

Crowder, Michael. *Colonial West Africa: Collected Essays*. London: Routledge, 2013.

———. "Indirect Rule: French and British Style." *Africa* 34, no. 3 (1964): 197–205.

———. *Senegal: A Study in French Assimilation Policy*. London: Oxford University Press, 1962.

Cudjoe, Seth Dzifanu. *Aids to African Autonomy: A Review of Education and Politics in the Gold Coast*. London: College Press, 1950.

Currie, Mark. *About Time: Narrative, Fiction and the Philosophy of Time*. Edinburgh: Edinburgh University Press, 2007.

Dalleo, Raphael. *American Imperialism's Undead: The Occupation of Haiti and the Rise of Caribbean Anticolonialism*. Repr. ed. Charlottesville: University of Virginia Press, 2016.

Dan Izevbaye, S. "West African Literature in English: Beginnings to the Mid-Seventies." In *The Cambridge History of African and Caribbean Literature*, vol. 2, edited by F. Abiola Irele and Simon Gikandi, 472–503. Cambridge: Cambridge University Press, 2000.

Dash, J. Michael. *Haiti and the United States: National Stereotypes and the Literary Imagination*. 2nd ed. New York: Macmillan, 1997.

Davidson, Basil. *Black Star: A View of the Life and Times of Kwame Nkrumah*. Oxford: James Currey, 2007.

Davis, Angela. "Introduction." In *How Europe Underdeveloped Africa*, by Walter Rodney, 11–14. London: Verso Books, 2018.

Dawahare, Anthony. *Nationalism, Marxism, and African American Literature between the Wars: A New Pandora's Box*. Jackson: University Press of Mississippi, 2002.

De Genova, Nicholas P. "Migrant 'Illegality' and Deportability in Everyday Life." *Annual Review of Anthropology* 31 (2002): 419–47.

De Graft-Johnson, J. W. *Towards Nationhood in West Africa: Thoughts of Young Africa Addressed to Young Britain*. London: Headley Brothers, 1928.

De La Rue, Sidney. *The Land of the Pepper Bird*. New York: Knickerbocker Press, 1930.

Dennis, John Alfred. "The René Maran Story: The Life and Times of a Black Frenchman, Colonial Administrator, Novelist and Social Critic, 1887–1960." PhD diss., Stanford University, 1986.

Dequidt, Georges, and Georges Forestier. "Les aspects sanitaires du probleme de l'immigration en France." *Revue d'hygiene* 48 (1926).

Derickson, Kate. "Masters of the Universe." *Environment and Planning D: Society and Space* 36, no. 3 (2018): 556–62.

Derrick, Jonathan. *Africa's Agitators: Militant Anti-Colonialism in Africa and the West, 1918–1939*. London: Hurst, 2008.

Detweiler, Frederick German. *The Negro Press in the United States*. Chicago: University of Chicago Press, 1922.

Dewitte, Philippe. *Mouvements Nègres en France, 1919–1939*. Paris: L'Harmattan, 2004.

Digby-Junger, Richard. "*The Guardian, Crisis, Messenger,* and *Negro World*: The Early-20th-Century Black Radical Press." *Howard Journal of Communications* 9, no. 3 (1998): 263–82.

DiGiacomo, Mark. "The Assertion of Coevalness: African Literature and Modernist Studies." *Modernism/Modernity* 24, no. 2 (2017): 245–62.

Dorman, Jacob S. "Skin Bleach and Civilization: The Racial Formation of Blackness in 1920s Harlem." *Journal of Pan African Studies* 4, no. 4 (2011): 47–80.

Doty, Roxanne Lynn. *Imperial Encounters: The Politics of Representation in North-South Relations*. Minneapolis: University Of Minnesota Press, 1996.

Douglass, Frederick. "The Color Line." *North American Review* 132, no. 295 (1881): 567–77.

Dove, Mabel. *Selected Writings of a Pioneer West African Feminist*. Edited by Stephanie Newell and Audrey Gadzekpo. Nottingham: Trent Editions, 2004.

Drayton, Richard. "Federal Utopias and the Realities of Imperial Power." *Comparative Studies of South Asia, Africa and the Middle East* 37, no. 2 (2016): 401–6.

Drumont, Édouard. *La fin d'un monde: Étude psychologique et sociale*. Paris: Albert Savine, 1889.

Duara, Prasenjit. "The Regime of Authenticity: Timelessness, Gender, and National History in Modern China." *History and Theory* 37, no. 3 (1998): 287–308.

Dubey, Madhu. *Black Women Novelists and the Nationalist Aesthetic.* Bloomington: Indiana University Press, 1994.

Du Bois, W. E. B. *Darkwater: Voices from within the Veil.* New York: Harcourt, Brace and Howe, 1920.

———. "Inter-Racial Implications of the Ethiopian Crisis: A Negro View." *Foreign Affairs* 14, no. 1 (1935): 82–92.

———. *W. E. B. Du Bois on Asia: Crossing the World Color Line.* Jackson: University Press of Mississippi, 2005.

———. *The World and Africa* and *Color and Democracy.* Edited by Henry Louis Gates. Oxford: Oxford University Press, 2014.

———. *Writings.* Edited by Nathan I. Huggins. New York: Library of America, 1987.

Edwards, Brent Hayes. *The Practice of Diaspora: Literature, Translation, and the Rise of Black Internationalism.* Cambridge, MA: Harvard University Press, 2003.

———. "Review: The Ethnics of Surrealism." *Transition,* no. 78 (1998): 84–135.

Elkins, Caroline, and Susan Pedersen. "Introduction." In *Settler Colonialism in the Twentieth Century,* edited by Caroline Elkins and Susan Pedersen, 1–21. New York: Routledge, 2005.

———, eds. *Settler Colonialism in the Twentieth Century.* New York: Routledge, 2005.

Ellis, Mark. *Race, War, and Surveillance: African Americans and the United States.* Bloomington: Indiana University Press, 2001.

Emenyònu, Ernest. *The Rise of the Igbo Novel.* Oxford: Oxford University Press, 1978.

Escobar, Arturo. "Beyond the Third World: Imperial Globality, Global Coloniality and Anti-Globalisation Social Movements." *Third World Quarterly* 25, no. 1 (2004): 207–30.

Esedebe. *Pan-Africanism.* 2nd ed. Washington, DC: Howard University Press, 1994.

Etkind, Alexander. *Internal Colonization: Russia's Imperial Experience.* Hoboken, NJ: John Wiley and Sons, 2013.

Ewing, Adam. *The Age of Garvey: How a Jamaican Activist Created a Mass Movement and Changed Global Black Politics*. Princeton, NJ: Princeton University Press, 2014.

———. "Caribbean Labour Politics in the Age of Garvey, 1918–1938." *Race and Class* 55, no. 1 (July 2013): 23–45.

Ezra, Elizabeth. *The Colonial Unconscious: Race and Culture in Interwar France*. Ithaca, NY: Cornell University Press, 2000.

Fabian, Johannes. *Time and the Other: How Anthropology Makes Its Object*. New York: Columbia University Press, 2014.

Fabien, Vanessa. "African American Environmental Ethics: Black Intellectual Perspectives 1850–1965." PhD diss., University of Massachusetts Amherst, 2017.

Fanon, Frantz. "Antillais et Africains." *Esprit*, no. 223 (February 1955): 261–69.

———. *Black Skin, White Masks*. Translated by Charles Lam Markmann. London: Pluto Press, 2008.

———. *Toward the African Revolution: Political Essays*. New York: Grove Press, 1969.

———. *The Wretched of the Earth*. Translated by Richard Philcox. New York: Grove Press, 2004.

Fauvelle, François-Xavier. *The Golden Rhinoceros: Histories of the African Middle Ages*. Translated by Troy Tice. Princeton, NJ: Princeton University Press, 2018.

Featherstone, David. "Black Internationalism, Subaltern Cosmopolitanism, and the Spatial Politics of Antifascism." *Annals of the Association of American Geographers* 103, no. 6 (2013): 1406–20.

Federici, Silvia. *Caliban and the Witch*. New York: Autonomedia, 2004.

Ferguson, Niall. *Empire: How Britain Made the Modern World*. London: Penguin, 2004.

Ferreira da Silva, Denise. "Globality." *Critical Ethnic Studies* 1, no. 1 (2015): 33–38.

Fitzgerald, Jennifer. *Close to Home: Local Ties and Voting Radical Right in Europe*. Cambridge: Cambridge University Press, 2018.

Fitzpatrick, Martin, and Peter Jones. *The Reception of Edmund Burke in Europe*. London: Bloomsbury, 2017.

Folkerts, Hendrick. "Two Meetings and a Funeral: A Conversation between Naeem Mohaiemen and Hendrik Folkerts." *Metropolis M.*, February 15, 2018.

Ford, Lisa. *Settler Sovereignty: Jurisdiction and Indigenous People in America and Australia, 1788–1836.* Harvard Historical Studies, 166. Repr. ed. Cambridge, MA: Harvard University Press, 2011.

Foucault, Michel. *Ethics: Subjectivity and Truth.* Vol. 1. Edited by Paul Rabinow. New York: New Press, 1997.

Frankel, Jeffrey. "Cocoa in Ghana: The Cocoa Farmers, Cocoa Marketing Board, and Elasticity of Supply." Paper, MIT, 1974. https://scholar.harvard.edu/files/frankel/files/cocoa_in_ghana_01.pdf.

Gallicchio, Marc. *The African American Encounter with Japan and China: Black Internationalism in Asia, 1895–1945.* Chapel Hill: University of North Carolina Press, 2000.

Garvey, Amy Jacques, ed. *More Philosophy and Opinions of Marcus Garvey.* London: Routledge, 1977.

Garvey, Marcus. *The Tragedy of White Injustice.* New York: Haskell House, 1927.

Gates, Henry Louis, and Gene Andrew Jarrett, eds. *The New Negro: Readings on Race, Representation, and African American Culture, 1892–1938.* Princeton, NJ: Princeton University Press, 2007.

Geddes, John, and James Robertson. *The New Testament: Translated out of the Latin Vulgate, Newly Revised, with Annotations, Etc.* Preston: Preston and Heaton, 1812.

Geiss, Imanuel. *Pan-African Movement: History of Pan-Africanism in America, Europe and Africa.* New York: Holmes and Meier, 1975.

Gellner, Ernest. *Nations and Nationalism.* 2nd ed. Malden, MA: Wiley-Blackwell, 2006.

Gérard, Albert S. *European-Language Writing in Sub-Saharan Africa.* Amsterdam: John Benjamins Publishing, 1986.

Gershoni, Yekutiel. *Black Colonialism: The Americo-Liberian Scramble for the Hinterland.* Boulder, CO: Westview, 1985.

Getachew, Adom. *Worldmaking after Empire: The Rise and Fall of Self-Determination.* Princeton NJ: Princeton University Press, 2019.

Getachew, Adom, and Jennifer Pitts. "Introduction." In *W. E. B. Du Bois: International Writings.* Cambridge: Cambridge University Press, 2020.

Giladi, Amotz. "The Elaboration of Pan-Latinism in French Intellectual Circles, from the Turn of the Nineteenth Century to World War I." *Journal of Romance Studies* 14, no. 1 (March 1, 2014): 56–72.

Gilleard, C. J., and Paul Higgs. *Ageing, Corporeality and Embodiment*. Key Issues in Modern Sociology. New York: Anthem Press, 2013.

Gilpin, Robert. *War and Change in World Politics*. Cambridge: Cambridge University Press, 1981.

Gilroy, Paul. *Against Race: Imagining Political Culture beyond the Color Line*. Cambridge, MA: Harvard University Press, 2001.

———. *The Black Atlantic: Modernity and Double Consciousness*. London: Verso, 1993.

———. "Black Fascism." *Transition*, no. 81/82 (2000): 70–91.

Girvan, Norman. "Caribbean Dependency Thought Revisited." *Canadian Journal of Development Studies / Revue canadienne d'études du développement* 27, no. 3 (2006): 328–52.

Glover, Kaiama L. "'Flesh Like One's Own': Benign Denials of Legitimate Complaint." *Public Culture* 29, no. 2 (82) (2017): 235–60.

———. *Haiti Unbound: A Spiralist Challenge to the Postcolonial Canon*. Liverpool: Liverpool University Press, 2011.

Gocking, Roger S. "J. E. Casely Hayford." In *Encyclopedia of African History*. Vol. 1, edited by Kevin Shillington, 223–25. Abingdon: Taylor and Francis, 2005.

Godden, Richard. "'Absalom, Absalom!,' Haiti and Labor History: Reading Unreadable Revolutions." *ELH* 61, no. 3 (1994): 685–720.

Goebel, Michael. *Anti-Imperial Metropolis: Interwar Paris and the Seeds of Third World Nationalism*. New York: Cambridge University Press, 2015.

Gómez, Nicolás Wey. *The Tropics of Empire: Why Columbus Sailed South to the Indies*. Cambridge, MA: The MIT Press, 2008.

Gong, Gerrit W. *The Standard of "Civilization" in International Society*. Oxford: Oxford University Press, 1984.

Goodman, Nelson. *Ways of Worldmaking*. Indianapolis, IN: Hackett Publishing, 1978.

Goswami, Manu. "Imaginary Futures and Colonial Internationalisms." *American Historical Review* 117, no. 5 (2012): 1461–85.

———. *Producing India: From Colonial Economy to National Space*. Chicago: University of Chicago Press, 2004.

Goyal, Yogita. "Africa and the Black Atlantic." *Research in African Literatures* 45, no. 3 (2014): v–xxv.

Graves, John L. "The Social Ideas of Marcus Garvey." *Journal of Negro Education* 31, no. 1 (1962): 65–74.

Greenhalgh, P. A. L. *West African Diamonds, 1919–1983: An Economic History.* Manchester: Manchester University Press, 1985.

Greenhouse, Carol J. *A Moment's Notice: Time Politics across Cultures.* New York: Cornell University Press, 1996.

Grier, Beverly. "Pawns, Porters, and Petty Traders: Women in the Transition to Cash Crop Agriculture in Colonial Ghana." *Signs: Journal of Women in Culture and Society* 17, no. 2 (1992): 304–28.

Grimshaw, Anna, ed. *The C. L. R. James Reader.* Oxford: Wiley-Blackwell, 1992.

Grossberg, Lawrence. "On Postmodernism and Articulation: An Interview with Stuart Hall." *Journal of Communication Inquiry* 10, no. 2 (2016): 45–60.

Grovogui, Siba N. *Beyond Eurocentrism and Anarchy: Memories of International Order and Institutions.* New York: AIAA, 2006.

———. "Come to Africa: A Hermeneutics of Race in International Theory." *Alternatives* 26, no. 4 (2001): 425–48.

Guernsey, Brandon L. "Lamine Senghor's *La violation d'un pays* as a Precursor to Cultural Nationalism." *Journal of the African Literature Association* 8, no. 2 (2014): 94–109.

Guha, Ranajit. *History at the Limit of World-History.* New York: Columbia University Press, 2003.

Hahn, Steven. *The Political Worlds of Slavery and Freedom.* Cambridge, MA: Harvard University Press, 2009.

Hall, Kim Q. *Feminist Disability Studies.* Bloomington: Indiana University Press, 2011.

Hall, Stuart. "Cultural Identity and Diaspora." In *Identity: Community, Culture, Difference,* edited by Jonathan Rutherford, 222–37. London: Lawrence and Wishart, 1990.

———. "Race, Articulation, and Societies Structured in Dominance." In *Black British Cultural Studies: A Reader,* edited by Houston A. Baker Jr., Manthia Diawara, and Ruth H. Lindeborg, 16–60. Chicago: University of Chicago Press, 1996.

Hanretta, Sean. "'Kaffir' Renner's Conversion: Being Muslim in Public in Colonial Ghana." *Past and Present* 210, no. 1 (2011): 187–220.

Haraway, Donna J. *Manifestly Haraway*. Minneapolis: University of Minnesota Press, 2016.

Harold, Claudrena N. *The Rise and Fall of the Garvey Movement in the Urban South, 1918–1942*. New York: Routledge, 2009.

Harper, Tim. *Underground Asia: Global Revolutionaries and the Assault on Empire*. Cambridge, MA: Harvard University Press, 2020.

Harris, Brice. *The United States and the Italo-Ethiopian Crisis*. Stanford, CA: Stanford University Press, 1964.

Harris, David. *Sierra Leone: A Political History*. London: Hurst, 2013.

Harris, Joseph E. *African-American Reactions to War in Ethiopia, 1936–1941*. Baton Rouge: Louisiana State University Press, 1994.

———. *Global Dimensions of the African Diaspora*. Washington, DC: Howard University Press, 1993.

Hartman, Saidiya. "The Anarchy of Colored Girls Assembled in a Riotous Manner." *South Atlantic Quarterly* 117, no. 3 (2018): 465–90.

———. *Scenes of Subjection: Terror, Slavery, and Self-Making in Nineteenth-Century America*. Oxford: Oxford University Press, 1997.

———. *Wayward Lives, Beautiful Experiments*. London: Serpent's Tail, 2019.

Headley, John M. "The Sixteenth-Century Venetian Celebration of the Earth's Total Habitability: The Issue of the Fully Habitable World for Renaissance Europe." *Journal of World History* 8, no. 1 (1997): 1–27.

Heidegger, Martin. *The Fundamental Concepts of Metaphysics: World, Finitude, Solitude*. Bloomington: Indiana University Press, 1995.

Helgesson, Stefan. "Radicalizing Temporal Difference: Anthropology, Postcolonial Theory, and Literary Time." *History and Theory* 53, no. 4 (2014): 545–62.

Hesse, Barnor. "Racialized Modernity: An Analytics of White Mythologies." *Ethnic and Racial Studies* 30, no. 4 (2007): 643–63.

Hickey, Dennis C. "Positive Perspectives on Independent Africa: Ethiopia, Liberia, and the American Popular Press, 1920–1935." *Africana Journal* 17 (1998): 257–70.

Higashida, Cheryl. *Black Internationalist Feminism: Women Writers of the Black Left, 1945–1995*. Champaign: University of Illinois Press, 2011.

Hill, Robert A., ed. *The Marcus Garvey and Universal Negro Improvement Association Papers*. Vol. 1, *1826–August 1919*. Berkeley: University of California Press, 1983.

————, ed. *The Marcus Garvey and Universal Negro Improvement Association Papers*. Vol. 2, *27 August 1919–31 August 1920*. Berkeley: University of California Press, 1983.

————, ed. *The Marcus Garvey and Universal Negro Improvement Association Papers*. Vol. 6, *The Caribbean Diaspora, 1910–20*. Durham, NC: Duke University Press, 2011.

————, ed. *The Marcus Garvey and Universal Negro Improvement Association Papers*. Vol. 10. Berkeley: University of California Press, 2006.

Hill, Robert A., and Barbara Bair, eds. *Marcus Garvey: Life and Lessons*. Berkeley: University of California Press, 1992.

Hofmeyr, Isabel, and Derek R. Peterson. "The Politics of the Page: Cutting and Pasting in South African and African-American Newspapers." *Social Dynamics* 45, no. 1 (2019): 1–25.

Holmes, Alexander Baron, IV. "Economic and Political Organizations in the Gold Coast 1920–1945." PhD diss., University of Chicago, 1972.

Hopkins, A. G. "Economic Aspects of Political Movements in Nigeria and in the Gold Coast 1918–1939." *Journal of African History* 7, no. 1 (1966): 133–52.

————. *An Economic History of West Africa*. London: Longman, 1973.

Howard, Rhoda. "Differential Class Participation in an African Protest Movement: The Ghana Cocoa Boycott of 1937–38." *Canadian Journal of African Studies / Revue Canadienne Des Études Africaines* 10, no. 3 (1976): 469–80.

Howe, Joshua P., and William Cronon. *Behind the Curve: Science and the Politics of Global Warming*. Repr. ed. Seattle: University of Washington Press, 2016.

Howitt, Richard. "Scale." In *A Companion to Political Geography*, edited by John A. Agnew, Katharyne Mitchell, and Gerard Toal, 132–57. Hoboken, NJ: John Wiley and Sons, 2008.

————. "Scale and the Other: Levinas and Geography." *Geoforum* 33, no. 3 (2002): 299–313.

Hurtado, Albert L., William Cronon, and Howard R. Lamar. *Intimate Frontiers: Sex, Gender, and Culture in Old California*. Albuquerque: University of New Mexico Press, 2016.

Hutchings, Kimberly. *Time and World Politics: Thinking the Present*. Manchester: Manchester University Press, 2015.

Iliffe, John. *Africans: The History of a Continent*. Cambridge: Cambridge University Press, 2017.

Irele, F. Abiola, and Biodun Jeyifo, eds. *The Oxford Encyclopedia of African Thought.* 2 Vols. Oxford: Oxford University Press, 2010.

Jacobson, Matthew Frye. *Whiteness of a Different Color.* Cambridge, MA: Harvard University Press, 1999.

Jagmohan, Desmond. "Between Race and Nation: Marcus Garvey and the Politics of Self-Determination." *Political Theory* 48, no. 3 (2020): 271–302.

James, C. L. .R. *The Black Jacobins.* New York: Vintage Books, 1989.

James, Leslie. "Transatlantic Passages: Black Identity Construction in West African and West Indian Newspapers, 1935–1950." In *African Print Cultures: Newspapers and Their Publics in the Twentieth Century,* edited by Derek R. Peterson, Emma Hunter, and Stephanie Newell, 49–74. Ann Arbor: University of Michigan Press, 2016.

———. "What We Put in Black and White: George Padmore and the Practice of Anti-Imperial Politics." PhD diss., London School of Economics and Political Science, 2012.

Jenkins, Raymond George. "Gold Coast Historians and Their Pursuit of the Gold Coast Pasts, 1882–1917: An Investigation into Responses to British 'Cultural Imperialism' by Intellectuals of the Christianised, Commericial Communities of the Townships of the Southern Gold Coast, during the Years of British Imperial Conquest and Early Occupation, 1874–1919." PhD diss., University of Birmingham, 1985.

Jennings, Eric T. "Writing Madagascar Back into the Madagascar Plan." *Holocaust and Genocide Studies* 21, no. 2 (2007): 187–217.

Johnson, G. Wesley. *The Emergence of Black Politics in Senegal: The Struggle for Power in the Four Communes, 1900–1920.* Stanford, CA: Hoover Institution on War, Revolution, and Peace, Stanford University Press, 1971.

Joseph, Celucien L. *Thinking in Public: Faith, Secular Humanism, and Development in Jacques Roumain.* Eugene, OR: Wipf and Stock Publishers, 2017.

Joseph-Gabriel, Annette K. *Reimagining Liberation: How Black Women Transformed Citizenship in the French Empire.* Champaign: University of Illinois Press, 2019.

Jun, Helen Heran. *Race for Citizenship: Black Orientalism and Asian Uplift from Pre-Emancipation to Neoliberal America.* New York: New York University Press, 2011.

Kamola, Isaac A. *Making the World Global: US Universities and the Production of the Global Imaginary.* Durham, NC: Duke University Press Books, 2019.

Kaussen, Valerie. *Migrant Revolutions: Haitian Literature, Globalization, and U.S. Imperialism*. Lanham, MD: Lexington Books, 2007.

Kay, Cristóbal. *Latin American Theories of Development and Underdevelopment*. London: Routledge, 2010.

Keene, Edward. *Beyond the Anarchical Society: Grotius, Colonialism and Order in World Politics*. Cambridge: Cambridge University Press, 2002.

Keil, Roger. "The Empty Shell of the Planetary: Re-Rooting the Urban in the Experience of the Urbanites." *Urban Geography* 39, no. 10 (2018): 1589–1602.

Kelley, Robin D. G. "'But a Local Phase of a World Problem': Black History's Global Vision, 1883–1950." *Journal of American History* 86, no. 3 (1999): 1045–77.

———. "Introduction." In *Black, Brown, and Beige: Surrealist Writings from Africa and the Diaspora*, edited by Franklin Rosemont and Robin D. G. Kelley, 1–21. Austin: University of Texas Press, 2010.

———. *Race Rebels: Culture, Politics, and the Black Working Class*. New York: Free Press, 1996.

Kesteloot, Lilyan. *Black Writers in French: A Literary History of Negritude*. Translated by Ellen Conroy Kennedy. Washington, DC: Howard University Press, 1991.

Khalfa, Jean. "Aimé Césaire, *Cahier d'un retour au pays natal*." In *Twentieth-Century French Poetry: A Critical Anthology*, edited by Hugues Azérad and Peter Collier, 123–32. Cambridge: Cambridge University Press, 2010.

Kimble, David. *A Political History of Ghana: The Rise of Gold Coast Nationalism, 1850–1928*. Oxford: Clarendon Press, 1963.

Klinke, Ian. "Chronopolitics: A Conceptual Matrix." *Progress in Human Geography* 37, no. 5 (2013): 673–90.

Knowlton, Steven A. "'Show Me the Race or the Nation without a Flag, and I Will Show You a Race of People without Any Pride': The Flags of Black Nationalist Organizations as Disambiguating Responses to Polysemic National Symbols." *Raven: A Journal of Vexillology* 24 (2017): 27–61.

Kolchin, Peter. "Whiteness Studies: The New History of Race in America." *Journal of American History* 89, no. 1 (2002): 154–73.

Koselleck, Reinhardt. *Futures Past: On the Semantics of Historical Time*. New York: Columbia University Press, 2004.

Koskenniemi, Martti. *The Gentle Civilizer of Nations: The Rise and Fall of International Law, 1870–1960*. Cambridge: Cambridge University Press, 2002.

Krausz, Tamás. *Reconstructing Lenin: An Intellectual Biography*. New York: New York University Press, 2015.

Kurki, Milja. *International Relations in a Relational Universe*. Oxford: Oxford University Press, 2020.

Kurtz, Hilda E. "Scale Frames and Counter-Scale Frames: Constructing the Problem of Environmental Injustice." *Political Geography* 22, no. 8 (2003): 887–916.

Kwon, Nayoung Aimee. *Intimate Empire: Collaboration and Colonial Modernity in Korea and Japan*. Durham, NC: Duke University Press, 2015.

Lake, Marilyn, and Henry Reynolds. *Drawing the Global Colour Line: White Men's Countries and the International Challenge of Racial Equality*. Cambridge: Cambridge University Press, 2008.

Langley, J. Ayodele. "Garveyism and African Nationalism." *Race and Class* 11, no. 2 (1969): 157–72.

———. *Ideologies of Liberation in Black Africa*. London: Rowman and Littlefield, 1979.

Larmer, Miles, and Baz Lecocq. "Historicising Nationalism in Africa." *Nations and Nationalism* 24, no. 4 (2018): 893–917.

Lazarus, Neil. *The Postcolonial Unconscious*. Cambridge: Cambridge University Press, 2011.

Lee, Christopher J. "Jus Soli and Jus Sanguinis in the Colonies: The Interwar Politics of Race, Culture, and Multiracial Legal Status in British Africa." *Law and History Review* 29, no. 2 (2011): 497–522.

Lee, Emily S. *Living Alterities: Phenomenology, Embodiment, and Race*. Albany, NY: SUNY Press, 2014.

Lefebvre, Henri. *La production de l'espace*. Paris: Éditions Anthropos, 1974.

———. "Reflections on the Politics of Space." Translated by Michael J. Enders. *Antipode* 8, no. 2 (1976).

Lemelle, Sidney, and Robin D. G. Kelley, eds. *Imagining Home: Class, Culture and Nationalism in the African Diaspora*. London: Verso, 1994.

Levine, Robert S. *Martin R. Delany: A Documentary Reader*. Chapel Hill: University of North Carolina Press, 2003.

Lewis, Mary Dewhurst. *The Boundaries of the Republic: Migrant Rights and the Limits of Universalism in France, 1918–1940*. Stanford, CA: Stanford University Press, 2007.

Lewis, Rupert. *Marcus Garvey: Anti-Colonial Champion*. Trenton, NJ: Africa World Press, 1988.

Liauzu, Claude. *Aux origines des tiers-mondismes: Colonisés et anticolonialistes en France*. Paris: L'Harmattan, 2000.

Lloyd, David. "The Indigent Sublime: Specters of Irish Hunger." *Representations* 92, no. 1 (2005): 152–85.

———. *Under Representation: The Racial Regime of Aesthetics*. New York: Fordham University Press, 2018.

Lunn, Joe H. *Memoirs of the Maelstrom: A Senegalese Oral History of the First World War*. Portsmouth, NH: Heinemann, 1999.

Lynch, Hollis R. "Edward W. Blyden: Pioneer West African Nationalist." *Journal of African History* 6, no. 3 (1965): 373–88.

Macharia, Keguro. *Frottage: Frictions of Intimacy across the Black Diaspora*. New York: New York University Press, 2019.

Magee, Gary B. *Empire and Globalisation: Networks of People, Goods and Capital in the British World, c. 1850–1914*. Cambridge: Cambridge University Press, 2010.

Makalani, Minkah. *In the Cause of Freedom: Radical Black Internationalism from Harlem to London, 1917–1939*. Chapel Hill: University of North Carolina Press, 2011.

Malela, Buata B. *Les écrivains afro-antillais à Paris (1920–1960): Stratégies et postures identitaires*. Lettres du sud. Paris: Karthala, 2008.

Mallett, Robert. *Mussolini in Ethiopia, 1919–1935: The Origins of Fascist Italy's African War*. Cambridge: Cambridge University Press, 2015.

Mamdani, Mahmood. *Citizen and Subject: Contemporary Africa and the Legacy of Late Colonialism*. Princeton Studies in Culture/Power/History. Princeton, NJ: Princeton University Press, 1996.

Marable, Manning. *Malcolm X: A Life of Reinvention*. London: Penguin, 2011.

———. *W. E. B. Du Bois: Black Radical Democrat*. London: Routledge, 2015.

Maran, René. *Batouala*. Translated by Adele Szold Seltzer. New York: Thomas Seltzer, 1922.

———. *Batouala: Véritable roman nègre*. Paris: Albin Michel, 1921.

Marke, Charles. *The Origin of Wesleyan Methodism in Sierra Leone*. London: Charles and Kelly, 1913.

Marston, Sallie A. "The Social Construction of Scale." *Progress in Human Geography* 24, no. 2 (2000): 219–42.

Marston, Sallie A., John Paul Jones III, and Keith Woodward. "Human Geography without Scale." *Transactions of the Institute of British Geographers* 30, no. 4 (2005): 416–32.

Martin, Guy. *African Political Thought*. New York: Palgrave Macmillan, 2012.

Marx, Karl. *Capital*. Vol. 1. Translated by Ben Fowkes. London: Penguin Classics, 1992.

Massey, Doreen B. *Spatial Divisions of Labor: Social Structures and the Geography of Production*. Hove, UK: Psychology Press, 1995.

Matera, Marc. *Black London: The Imperial Metropolis and Decolonization in the Twentieth Century*. Oakland: University of California Press, 2015.

Matera, Marc, Misty L. Bastian, and Susan Kingsley Kent. *The Women's War of 1929: Gender and Violence in Colonial Nigeria*. Cheltenham, UK: Palgrave Macmillan, 2011.

Matthews, Sean. "Change and Theory in Raymond Williams's Structure of Feeling." *Pretexts: Literary and Cultural Studies* 10, no. 2 (2001): 179–94.

May, Vivian M. "'It Is Never a Question of the Slaves': Anna Julia Cooper's Challenge to History's Silences in Her 1925 Sorbonne Thesis." *Callaloo* 31, no. 3 (2008): 903–18.

M'bayo, Tamba E. "W. E. B. Du Bois, Marcus Garvey, and Pan-Africanism in Liberia, 1919–1924." *The Historian* 66, no. 1 (2004): 19–44.

Mbembe, Achille. *Critique of Black Reason*. Translated by Laurent Dubois. Durham, NC: Duke University Press Books, 2017.

———. *Necropolitics*. Durham, NC: Duke University Press Books, 2019.

———. *On the Postcolony*. Berkeley: University of California Press, 2001.

———. "The Society of Enmity." *Radical Philosophy* 200 (December 2016): 23–35.

McCarthy, Jesse. "Harlem Is Everywhere." *Dissent* 65, no. 2 (2018): 6–13.

McClintock, Anne. *Imperial Leather: Race, Gender, and Sexuality in the Colonial Contest*. London: Routledge, 2013.

McKay, Claude. *A Long Way from Home*. Edited by Gene Andrew Jarrett. New Brunswick, NJ: Rutgers University Press, 2007.

McKittrick, Katherine. *Demonic Grounds: Black Women and the Cartographies of Struggle*. Minneapolis: University Of Minnesota Press, 2006.

McKittrick, Katherine, and Clyde Woods, eds. *Black Geographies and the Politics of Place*. Toronto: South End Press, 2007.

McPherson, Alan. "Personal Occupations: Women's Responses to U.S. Military Occupations in Latin America." *The Historian* 72, no. 3 (2010): 568–98.

Melville, Herman. *Redburn: His First Voyage*. New York: Harper and Brothers, 1850.

Merchant, Carolyn. *The Death of Nature: Women, Ecology, and the Scientific Revolution*. New York: HarperOne, 2019.

Meredith, David. "The Colonial Office, British Business Interests and the Reform of Cocoa Marketing in West Africa, 1937–1945." *Journal of African History* 29, no. 2 (1988): 285–300.

Mĕstrović, Matko. *Towards a New Orientation*. Cambridge: Cambridge Scholars Publishing, 2012.

Mgbako, Ofole. "'My Blackness Is the Beauty of This Land': Racial Redefinition, African American Culture, and the Creation of the Black World in South Africa's Black Consciousness Movement." *Safundi* 10, no. 3 (2009): 305–34.

Mies, Maria. *Patriarchy and Accumulation on a World Scale: Women in the International Division of Labour*. London: Zed Books, 1998.

Mignolo, Walter. *The Darker Side of Western Modernity: Global Futures, Decolonial Options*. Durham, NC: Duke University Press, 2011.

Miller, Christopher L. *Nationalists and Nomads: Essays on Francophone African Literature and Culture*. Chicago: University of Chicago Press, 1998.

Millet, Kethly. *Les paysans haïtiens et l'occupation américaine d'Haïti, 1915–1930*. La Salle, Haïti: Collectif Paroles, 1978.

Mills, Charles W. "Unwriting and Unwhitening the World." In *Race and Racism in International Relations: Confronting the Global Colour Line*, edited by Alexander Anievas, Nivi Manchanda, and Robbie Shilliam, 203–16. London: Routledge, 2014.

Mkandawire, Thandika. "African Intellectuals and Nationalism." In *African Intellectuals: Rethinking Politics, Language, Gender and Development*, edited by Thandika Mkandawire, 10–55. New York: Zed Books, 2005.

Mohan, Giles, and Kristian Stokke. "Participatory Development and Empowerment: The Dangers of Localism." *Third World Quarterly* 21, no. 2 (2000): 247–68.

Mohanram, Radhika. *Black Body: Women, Colonialism, and Space*. Minneapolis: University of Minnesota Press, 1999.

Moretti, Franco. "Conjectures on World Literature." *New Left Review* 2, no. 1 (2000): 54–68.

Moses, Wilson Jeremiah. *Creative Conflict in African American Thought*. New York: Cambridge University Press, 2004.

———. *The Golden Age of Black Nationalism, 1850–1925*. Oxford: Oxford University Press, 1988.

Mottier, Véronique. "Eugenics and the State: Policy-Making in Comparative Perspective." In *The Oxford Handbook of the History of Eugenics*, edited by Alison Bashford and Philippa Levine, 134–53. Oxford: Oxford University Press, 2010.

Mudimbe, V. Y. "African Gnosis Philosophy and the Order of Knowledge: An Introduction." *African Studies Review* 28, no. 2/3 (1985): 149–233.

Mueller, Justin. "Temporality, Sovereignty, and Imperialism: When Is Imperialism?" *Politics* 36, no. 4 (2016): 428–40.

Mukonoweshuro, Eliphas G. *J. E. Casely Hayford*. Lanham, MD: University Press of America, 1993.

Murphy, David. "Defending the 'Negro Race': Lamine Senghor and Black Internationalism in Interwar France." *French Cultural Studies* 24, no. 2 (2013): 161–73.

———. "Tirailleur, facteur, anticolonialiste: La courte vie militante de Lamine Senghor (1924–1927)." Cahiers d'histoire. *Revue d'histoire critique*, no. 126 (2015): 55–72.

Muthu, Sankar. *Enlightenment against Empire*. Princeton, NJ: Princeton University Press, 2003.

Mwangi, Evan. *Africa Writes Back to Self: Metafiction, Gender, Sexuality*. Albany, NY: SUNY Press, 2010.

Nairn, Tom. *Faces of Nationalism: Janus Revisited*. London: Verso, 1998.

Narayan, John. "British Black Power: The Anti-Imperialism of Political Blackness and the Problem of Nativist Socialism." *Sociological Review* 67, no. 5 (2019): 945–67.

———. "Huey P. Newton's Intercommunalism: An Unacknowledged Theory of Empire." *Theory, Culture and Society* 36, no. 3 (2019): 57–85.

Nardal, Paulette. *Beyond Negritude: Essays from Woman in the City*. Translated by T. Denean Sharpley-Whiting. Albany, NY: SUNY Press, 2009.

Newell, Stephanie. *The Forger's Tale: The Search for Odeziaku*. Athens: Ohio University Press, 2006.

————. *The Power to Name: A History of Anonymity in Colonial West Africa.* Athens: Ohio University Press, 2013.

Nisancioglu, Kerem. "Racial Sovereignty." *European Journal of International Relations* 26, no. S1 (2020): 39–63.

Nkrumah, Kwame. *The Autobiography of Kwame Nkrumah.* Edinburgh: Thomas Nelson and Sons, 1959.

Noiriel, Gerard, and Charles Tilly. *The French Melting Pot: Immigration, Citizenship and National Identity.* Translated by Geoffroy De Laforcade. Minneapolis: University of Minnesota Press, 1996.

Noland, Carrie. *Voices of Negritude in Modernist Print: Aesthetic Subjectivity, Diaspora, and the Lyric Regime.* New York: Columbia University Press, 2015.

Noyes, John K. *Herder: Aesthetics against Imperialism.* Toronto: University of Toronto Press, 2015.

Obiechina, Emmanuel. *An African Popular Literature: A Study of Onitsha Market Pamphlets.* Cambridge: Cambridge University Press, 1973.

————. *Culture, Tradition and Society in the West African Novel.* Cambridge: Cambridge University Press, 1975.

Okrent, Daniel. *The Guarded Gate: Bigotry, Eugenics and the Law That Kept Two Generations of Jews, Italians, and Other European Immigrants out of America.* New York: Simon and Schuster, 2019.

Olaniyan, Tejumola, and James H. Sweet. "Introduction." In *The African Diaspora and the Disciplines,* edited by Moyo Okediji, Tejumola Olaniyan, and James H. Sweet, 1–17. Bloomington: Indiana University Press, 2010.

Olender, Maurice. *Race and Erudition.* Cambridge, MA: Harvard University Press, 2009.

Omu, Fred I. A. *Press and Politics in Nigeria, 1880–1937.* London: Longman, 1978.

Padmore, George. *How Britain Rules Africa.* London: Wishart, 1936.

Palumbo-Liu, David, Bruce Robbins, and Nirvana Tanoukhi. *Immanuel Wallerstein and the Problem of the World: System, Scale, Culture.* Durham, NC: Duke University Press, 2011.

Pamphile, Léon Dénius. *La croix et le glaive: L'église catholique et l'occupation américaine d'Haïti.* Port-au-Prince: Éditions des Antilles, 1991.

————. *L'éducation en Haiti sous l'occupation américaine 1915–1934.* Port-au-Prince: Imprimerie des Antilles, 1988.

Patterson, Tiffany Ruby, and Robin D. G. Kelley. "Unfinished Migrations: Reflections on the African Diaspora and the Making of the Modern World." *African Studies Review* 43, no. 1 (2000): 11–45.

Pedersen, Susan. *The Guardians: The League of Nations and the Crisis of Empire.* Oxford: Oxford University Press, 2015.

Perry, Jeffrey B. *Hubert Harrison: The Voice of Harlem Radicalism, 1883–1918.* New York: Columbia University Press, 2010.

———, ed. *A Hubert Harrison Reader.* Middletown, CT: University Press of New England, 2008.

Peterson, Derek R., and Emma Hunter. "Print Culture in Colonial Africa." In *African Print Cultures: Newspapers and Their Publics in the Twentieth Century,* edited by Stephanie Newell, Emma Hunter, and Derek R. Peterson, 1–49. Ann Arbor: University of Michigan Press, 2016.

Pitts, Jennifer. *Boundaries of the International: Law and Empire.* Cambridge, MA: Harvard University Press, 2018.

Plummer, Brenda Gayle. "The Afro-American Response to the Occupation of Haiti, 1915–1934." *Phylon* (1960–) 43, no. 2 (1982): 125–43.

———. "Garveyism in Haiti during the US Occupation." *Journal of Haitian Studies* 21, no. 2 (2015): 68–87.

———. *Haiti and the United States: The Psychological Moment.* United States and the Americas. Athens: University of Georgia Press, 1992.

Putnam, Aric. "Ethiopia Is Now: J. A. Rogers and the Rhetoric of Black Antico- lonialism during the Great Depression." *Rhetoric and Public Affairs* 10, no. 3 (2007): 419–44.

———. *The Insistent Call: Rhetorical Moments in Black Anticolonialism, 1929–1937.* Amherst: University of Massachusetts Press, 2012.

Putnam, Lara. "Circum-Atlantic Print Circuits and Internationalism from the Peripheries in the Interwar Era." In *Print Culture Histories Beyond the Metropo- lis,* edited by James J. Connolly, Patrick Collier, Frank Felsenstein, Kenneth R. Hall, and Robert G. Hall, 215–43. Toronto: University of Toronto Press, 2016.

Quayson, Ato. *Strategic Transformations in Nigerian Writing: Orality and History in the Work of Rev. Samuel Johnson, Amos Tutuola, Wole Soyinka and Ben Okri.* Oxford: James Currey, 1997.

Quinn-Judge, Sophie. *Ho Chi Minh: The Missing Years, 1919–1941*. London: C. Hurst and Co. Publishers, 2003.

Rancière, Jacques. "The Politics of Literature." *SubStance* 33, no. 1 (2004): 10–24.

Rao, Rahul. *Third World Protest: Between Home and the World*. Oxford: Oxford University Press, 2010.

Reeve, Henry Fenwick. *The Black Republic, Liberia: Its Political and Social Conditions To-Day*. London: H. F. and G. Witherby, 1923.

Renault, Matthieu. "Toward a Counter-Genealogy of Race: On C. L. R. James." Translated by Patrick King. *Viewpoint Magazine*, September 16, 2015.

Renda, Mary A. *Taking Haiti: Military Occupation and the Culture of U.S. Imperialism, 1915–1940*. Chapel Hill: University North Carolina Press, 2001.

Reza, Alexandra. "African Anticolonialism as Cosmonationalism." Master's thesis, Oxford University, 2015.

Rhodes, Cecil. *The Last Will and Testament of Cecil John Rhodes: With Elucidatory Notes to Which Are Added Some Chapters Describing the Political and Religious Ideas of the Testator*. Making of Modern Law. London: "Review of Reviews" Office, 1902.

Riley, Shannon Rose. *Performing Race and Erasure: Cuba, Haiti, and US Culture, 1898–1940*. London: Palgrave Macmillan, 2016.

Robbins, Bruce. "Single? Great? Collective?: On Allegory and Ideology." *South Atlantic Quarterly* 119, no. 4 (2020): 789–98.

Roberts, Stephen H. *The History of French Colonial Policy, 1870–1925*. London: Frank Cass, 1963.

Robinson, Cedric. *Black Marxism: The Making of the Black Radical Tradition*. New ed. Chapel Hill: University of North Carolina Press, 2000.

———. "DuBois and Black Sovereignty: The Case of Liberia." *Race and Class* 32, no. 2 (1990): 39–50.

Roediger, David. *Black on White: Black Writers on What It Means to Be White*. New York: Knopf Doubleday, 2010.

———. *Class, Race and Marxism*. London: Verso, 2017.

———. *The Wages of Whiteness: Race and the Making of the American Working Class*. Haymarket. London: Verso, 2007.

Rogers, J. A. *The Real Facts about Ethiopia*. Baltimore, MD: Black Classic Press, 1982.

Rohdie, Samuel. "The Gold Coast Aborigines Abroad." *Journal of African History* 6, no. 3 (1965): 389–411.

Rolinson, Mary G. *Grassroots Garveyism: The Universal Negro Improvement Association in the Rural South, 1920–1927.* Chapel Hill: University of North Carolina Press, 2007.

Roll, Jarod. "Garveyism and the Eschatology of African Redemption in the Rural South, 1920–1936." *Religion and American Culture* 20, no. 1 (2010): 27–56.

Rose, Tricia. "'Fear of a Black Planet': Rap Music and Black Cultural Politics in the 1990s." *Journal of Negro Education* 60, no. 3 (1991): 276–90.

Rosenberg, Clifford. *Policing Paris: The Origins of Modern Immigration Control between the Wars.* Ithaca, NY: Cornell University Press, 2006.

Rosenberg, Emily S. "Ordering Others: US Financial Advisers in the Early Twentieth Century." In *Haunted by Empire: Geographies of Intimacy in North American History*, edited by Ann Laura Stoler, 405–27. Durham, NC: Duke University Press, 2006.

———, ed. *A World Connecting: 1870–1945.* Cambridge, MA: Belknap Press, 2012.

Rosenboim, Or. *The Emergence of Globalism: Visions of World Order in Britain and the United States, 1939–1950.* Princeton, NJ: Princeton University Press, 2017.

Ross, Rodney A. "Black Americans and Haiti, Liberia, the Virgin Islands, and Ethiopia, 1929–1936." PhD Thesis, University of Chicago, 1975.

Roumain, Jacques. *When the Tom-Tom Beats: Selected Prose and Poems.* Translated by Joanne Fungaroli and Ronald Sauer. Washington, DC: Azul Editions, 1995.

Rowell, Charles H. "An Interview with Brent Hayes Edwards." *Callaloo* 22, no. 4 (1999): 784–97.

Ruggie, John Gerard. "What Makes the World Hang Together? Neo-Utilitarianism and the Social Constructivist Challenge." *International Organization* 52, no. 4 (1998): 855–85.

Saada, Emmanuelle. *Empire's Children: Race, Filiation, and Citizenship in the French Colonies.* Chicago: University of Chicago Press, 2012.

Sagna, Olivier. "Des pionniers méconnus de l'indépendance: Africains, Antillais et luttes anti-colonialistes dans aa France de l'entre-deux-guerres (1919–1939)." PhD diss., Paris 7, 1986.

Saha, Santosh. "The Romance of Nationhood: An Investigation of the Attitudes of Educated Africans toward Liberia, 1847–1980." PhD diss., Kent State University, 1993.

Said, Edward W. *Culture and Imperialism*. London: Vintage, 1994.

———. *Orientalism*. 25th anniversary ed. with 1995 afterword. London: Penguin Books, 2003.

Salt, Karen. "Ecological Chains of Unfreedom: Contours of Black Sovereignty in the Atlantic World." *Journal of American Studies* 49, no. 2 (2015): 267–86.

———. *The Unfinished Revolution: Haiti, Black Sovereignty and Power in the Nineteenth-Century Atlantic World*. Liverpool: Liverpool University Press, 2019.

Samuels, Warren J., Jeff E. Biddle, and John B. Davis. *A Companion to the History of Economic Thought*. Hoboken, NJ: John Wiley and Sons, 2008.

Sartre, Jean Paul. *Black Orpheus*. Translated by S. W. Allen. New York: Présence Africaine, 2001.

Satter, Beryl. "Marcus Garvey, Father Divine and the Gender Politics of Race Difference and Race Neutrality." *American Quarterly* 48, no. 1 (1996): 43–76.

Schmidt, Hans. *The United States Occupation of Haiti, 1915–1934*. New Brunswick, NJ: Rutgers University Press, 1971.

Schneider, William H. *Quality and Quantity: The Quest for Biological Regeneration in Twentieth-Century France*. Cambridge History of Medicine. Cambridge: Cambridge University Press, 1990.

Schwarz, Bill. *The White Man's World*. Vol. 1 of *Memories of Empire*. Oxford: Oxford University Press, 2013.

Scott, David. *Conscripts of Modernity: The Tragedy of Colonial Enlightenment*. Durham, NC: Duke University Press, 2004.

Sekyi-Otu, Ato. *Fanon's Dialectic of Experience*. Cambridge, MA: Harvard University Press, 1997.

Senghor, Lamine. *La violation d'un pays*. Paris: Bureau d'editions, 1927.

Senghor, Léopold Sédar. *Liberté 1: Negritude et Humanisme*. Paris: Éditions du Seuil, 1964.

———. *Selected Poems of Léopold Sédar Senghor*. Edited by F. Abiola Irele. Cambridge: Cambridge University Press, 1977.

Shaloff, Stanley. "Press Controls and Sedition Proceedings in the Gold Coast, 1933–39." *African Affairs* 71, no. 284 (1972): 241–63.

Shannon, Magdaline W. *Jean-Price Mars, the Haitian Elite and the American Occupation, 1915–35*. London: Palgrave Macmillan, 1997.

Sharpley-Whiting, Tracy Denean. *Negritude Women*. Minneapolis: University of Minnesota Press, 2002.

Shaw, Martin. *Theory of the Global State: Globality as an Unfinished Revolution.* Cambridge: Cambridge University Press, 2000.

Shepard, Todd. *The Invention of Decolonization: The Algerian War and the Remaking of France.* Ithaca, NY: Cornell University Press, 2008.

———. *Sex, France, and Arab Men, 1962–1979.* Chicago: University of Chicago Press, 2018.

Sherwood, Marika. *Origins of Pan-Africanism: Henry Sylvester Williams, Africa, and the African Diaspora.* New York: Routledge, 2010.

Shilliam, Robbie. "Intervention and Colonial-Modernity: Decolonising the Italy/Ethiopia Conflict through Psalms 68:31." *Review of International Studies* 39, no. 5 (2013): 1131–47.

———. "What about Marcus Garvey? Race and the Transformation of Sovereignty Debate." *Review of International Studies* 32, no. 3 (2006): 379–400.

Simms, Rupe. "Western Christianity: A Nationalist Ideology in African Political History." *Griot* 23, no. 2 (2004): 16–30.

Skinner, Quentin. "Meaning and Understanding in the History of Ideas." *History and Theory* 8, no. 1 (1969): 3–53.

Slate, Nico. *Colored Cosmopolitanism: The Shared Struggle for Freedom in the United States and India.* Cambridge, MA: Harvard University Press, 2012.

Smethurst, James Edward. *The New Red Negro: The Literary Left and African American Poetry, 1930–1946.* Oxford: Oxford University Press, 1999.

Smith, Anthony D. *Nationalism: Theory, Ideology, History.* Cambridge: Polity Pres, 2001.

Smith, Kimberly K. *African American Environmental Thought: Foundations.* Lawrence: University Press of Kansas, 2019.

Smith, Neil. "Contours of a Spatialized Politics: Homeless Vehicles and the Production of Geographical Scale." *Social Text*, no. 33 (1992): 55–81.

———. "Geography, Difference and the Politics of Scale." In *Postmodernism and the Social Sciences*, edited by Joe Doherty, Elspeth Graham, and Mo Malek, 57–79. London: Palgrave Macmillan UK, 1992.

Smith, William Gardner. "The Negro Writer: Pitfalls and Compensations." *Phylon* (1940–1956) 11, no. 4 (1950): 297–303.

Snyder, Louis Leo. *Macro-Nationalisms: A History of the Pan-Movements.* Westport, CT: Greenwood Press, 1984.

Solanke, Ladipo. *United West Africa, or Africa at the Bar of the Family of Nations.* London: African Publication Society, 1969.

Spengler, Oswald. *The Hour of Decision.* Translated by Charles Francis Atkinson. London: George Allen and Unwin, 1934.

Spiegler, J. S. "Aspects of Nationalist Thought among French-Speaking West Africans, 1921–1939." PhD diss., University of Oxford, 1968.

Spillers, Hortense J. "Mama's Baby, Papa's Maybe: An American Grammar Book." *Diacritics* 17, no. 2 (1987): 65–81.

Spiro, Jonathan. *Defending the Master Race: Conservation, Eugenics, and the Legacy of Madison Grant.* Burlington: University of Vermont Press, 2008.

Spitzer, Leo. *The Creoles of Sierra Leone: Responses to Colonialism, 1870–1945.* Madison: University of Wisconsin Press, 1975.

———. *Lives in Between: Assimilation and Marginality in Austria, Brazil, and West Africa, 1780–1945.* Cambridge: Cambridge University Press, 1990.

Spitzer, Leo, and LaRay Denzer. "I. T. A. Wallace-Johnson and the West African Youth League." *International Journal of African Historical Studies* 6, no. 3 (1973): 413–52.

Spivak, Gayatri Chakravorty. "Three Women's Texts and a Critique of Imperialism." *Critical Inquiry* 12, no. 1 (1985): 243–61.

Stam, Robert, and Ella Shohat. *Race in Translation: Culture Wars around the Postcolonial Atlantic.* New York: New York University Press, 2012.

Steiner, Zara. *The Triumph of the Dark: European International History 1933–1939.* Repr. ed. Oxford: Oxford University Press, 2013.

Stepan, Nancy Leys. "Race, Gender, Science and Citizenship." In *Cultures of Empire: Colonizers in Britain and the Empire in the Nineteenth and Twentieth Centuries, A Reader,* edited by Catherine Hall, 61–87. New York: Routledge, 2000.

Stephens, Michelle Ann. *Black Empire: The Masculine Global Imaginary of Caribbean Intellectuals in the United States, 1914–1962.* Durham, NC: Duke University Press, 2005.

Stephens, Ronald J., and Adam Ewing, eds. *Global Garveyism.* Gainesville: University Press of Florida, 2019.

Stoddard, Lothrop. *The French Revolution in San Domingo.* Boston: Houghton Mifflin Company, 1914.

————. *The Rising Tide of Color against White World-Supremacy.* London: Chapman and Hall, 1920.

Stoler, Ann Laura. "Tense and Tender Ties: The Politics of Comparison in North American History and (Post) Colonial Studies." *Journal of American History* 88, no. 3 (2001): 829–65.

Stovall, Tyler. "The Color Line behind the Lines: Racial Violence in France during the Great War." *American Historical Review* 103, no. 3 (1998): 737–69.

————. *White Freedom: The Racial History of an Idea.* Princeton, NJ: Princeton University Press, 2021.

Strang, Bruce, ed. *Collision of Empires: Italy's Invasion of Ethiopia and Its International Impact.* Farnham: Ashgate, 2013.

Sundiata, I. K. *Black Scandal: America and the Liberian Labor Crisis, 1929–1936.* Philadelphia: Institute for the Study of Human Issues, 1980.

Sweeney, Carole. *From Fetish to Subject: Race, Modernism, and Primitivism, 1919–1935.* Westport, CT: Greenwood Publishing, 2004.

Swyngedouw, Erik. "Globalisation or 'Glocalisation'? Networks, Territories and Rescaling." *Cambridge Review of International Affairs* 17, no. 1 (2004): 25–48.

Taylor, Christopher. *Empire of Neglect: The West Indies in the Wake of British Liberalism.* Durham, NC: Duke University Press, 2018.

Taylor, Griffith. "The Distribution of Future White Settlement: A World Survey Based on Physiographic Data." *Geographical Review* 12, no. 3 (1922): 375–402.

Taylor, Peter J. "A Materialist Framework for Political Geography." *Transactions of the Institute of British Geographers* 7, no. 1 (1982): 15–34.

Taylor, Ula Y. "'Negro Women Are Great Thinkers as Well as Doers': Amy Jacques-Garvey and Community Feminism, 1924–1927." *Journal of Women's History* 12, no. 2 (2000): 104–26.

Terrell, Mary Church. *A Colored Woman in a White World.* New York: G. K. Hall, 1996.

Thacker, Eugene. *In the Dust of This Planet.* Horror of Philosophy, 1. London: John Hunt Publishing, 2011.

Thakur, Vineet, Alexander E. Davis, and Peter Vale. "Imperial Mission, 'Scientific' Method: An Alternative Account of the Origins of IR." *Millennium* 46, no. 1 (September 1, 2017): 3–23.

Thomas, Martin. *The French Empire between the Wars: Imperialism, Politics and Society.* Manchester: Manchester University Press, 2000.

Thompson, Virginia. *French West Africa*. London: Allen and Unwin, 1958.

Tinsley, Omise'eke Natasha. "Black Atlantic, Queer Atlantic: Queer Imaginings of the Middle Passage." *GLQ: A Journal of Lesbian and Gay Studies* 14, no. 2–3 (2008): 191–215.

Tooze, Adam. "The War of the Villages: The Interwar Agrarian Crisis and the Second World War." In *The Cambridge History of the Second World War*. Vol. 3, *Total War: Economy, Society and Culture*, edited by Michael Geyer and Adam Tooze, 385–412. Cambridge: Cambridge University Press, 2015.

Tosh, John. *A Man's Place: Masculinity and the Middle-Class Home in Victorian England*. New Haven, CT: Yale University Press, 2008.

Tumblety, Joan. *Remaking the Male Body: Masculinity and the Uses of Physical Culture in Interwar and Vichy France*. Oxford: Oxford University Press, 2012.

van Munster, Rens, and Casper Sylvest. *The Politics of Globality since 1945: Assembling the Planet*. London: Routledge, 2016.

Veracini, Lorenzo. *Settler Colonialism: A Theoretical Overview*. Basingstoke, UK: Palgrave Macmillan, 2010.

Véron, Kora. "Césaire at the Crossroads in Haiti: Correspondence with Henri Seyrig." *Comparative Literature Studies* 50, no. 3 (2013): 430–44.

Vincent, Theodore G. *Black Power and the Garvey Movement*. Baltimore: Black Classic Press, 2006.

Vinson, Robert Trent. *The Americans Are Coming!: Dreams of African American Liberation in Segregationist South Africa*. Athens: Ohio University Press, 2012.

———. "'Sea Kaffirs': 'American Negroes' and the Gospel of Garveyism in Early Twentieth-Century Cape Town." *Journal of African History* 47, no. 2 (2006): 281–303.

Viswanathan, Gauri, ed. *Power, Politics, and Culture: Interviews with Edward Said*. New York: Vintage, 2007.

Vitalis, Robert. *White World Order, Black Power Politics: The Birth of American International Relations*. Ithaca, NY: Cornell University Press, 2015.

Von Eschen, Penny M. *Race against Empire: Black Americans and Anticolonialism, 1937–1957*. Ithaca, NY: Cornell University Press, 1997.

Vucetic, Srdjan. *The Anglosphere: A Genealogy of a Racialized Identity in International Relations*. Stanford, CA: Stanford University Press, 2011.

Wallerstein, Immanuel. *Africa: The Politics of Independence and Unity*. Lincoln: University of Nebraska Press, 2005.

————. *The Modern World-System: Capitalist Agriculture and the Origins of the European World-Economy in the Sixteenth Century*. Vol. 1. Repr. ed. Berkeley: University of California Press, 2011.

Walsh, John Patrick. *Free and French in the Caribbean: Toussaint Louverture, Aimé Césaire, and Narratives of Loyal Opposition*. Bloomington: Indiana University Press, 2013.

Walter, Dierk. *Colonial Violence: European Empires and the Use of Force*. London: C. Hurst and Co., 2017.

Watson, Cicely. "Birth Control and Abortion in France since 1939." *Population Studies* 5, no. 3 (1952): 261–86.

Watson, Hilbourne A. "Raciology, Garveyism and the Limits of Black Nationalism in the Caribbean Diaspora." *Shibboleths: A Journal of. Comparative Theory* 2, no. 2 (2008): 85–95.

Weart, Spencer R. *The Discovery of Global Warming*. Cambridge, MA: Harvard University Press, 2008.

Weheliye, Alexander G. *Habeas Viscus: Racializing Assemblages, Biopolitics, and Black Feminist Theories of the Human*. Durham, NC: Duke University Press, 2014.

Weisbord, Robert G. *Ebony Kinship: Africa, Africans, and the Afro-American*. Westport, CT: Greenwood Press, 1973.

Weiss, Holger. *Framing a Radical African Atlantic*. Leiden: Brill, 2013.

————. "The Making of an African Bolshevik: Bankole Awoonor Renner in Moscow, 1925–1928." *Ghana Studies* 9, no. 1 (2006): 177–220.

Westermann, D. "Review: Towards Nationhood in West Africa by I. W. de Graft Johnson." *Journal of the International African Institute* 2, no. 4 (1929): 431–32.

Whitlock, Gillian. *The Intimate Empire: Reading Women's Autobiography*. London: A and C Black, 2000.

Wigger, Iris. *The "Black Horror on the Rhine": Intersections of Race, Nation, Gender and Class in 1920s Germany*. London: Palgrave Macmillan UK, 2017.

Wilder, Gary. *Freedom Time: Negritude, Decolonization, and the Future of the World*. Durham, NC: Duke University Press, 2015.

————. *The French Imperial Nation-State: Negritude and Colonial Humanism between the Two World Wars*. New ed. Chicago: University of Chicago Press, 2005.

Williams, Eric. *Capitalism and Slavery*. Chapel Hill: University of North Carolina Press, 1944.

Williams, Raymond, and Michael Orrom. *Preface to Film*. London: Film Drama, 1954.

Wilson, Henry Summerville. *Origins of West African Nationalism*. London: Palgrave Macmillan, 2016.

Wilson, Kalpana. "Worlds beyond the Political? Post-Development Approaches in Practices of Transnational Solidarity Activism." *Third World Quarterly* 38, no. 12 (2017): 2684–702.

Winkiel, Laura. *Modernism, Race and Manifestos*. Cambridge: Cambridge University Press, 2008.

Wintz, Cary D. *African American Political Thought, 1890–1930: Washington, Du Bois, Garvey and Randolph*. London: Routledge, 2015.

Wolfe, Patrick. *Settler Colonialism and the Transformation of Anthropology: The Politics and Poetics of an Ethnographic Events*. London: Continuum, 1999.

———. *Traces of History: Elementary Structures of Race*. London: Verso, 2015.

Woodson, Jon. *Anthems, Sonnets, and Chants: Recovering the African American Poetry of the 1930s*. Columbus: Ohio State University Press, 2011.

Wright, Richard. "Foreword." In *Pan-Africanism or Communism?*, by George Padmore, 11–14. London: Dobson Books, 1956.

———. *Lawd Today!* London: A. Blond, 1965.

Wynter, Sylvia. "Sambos and Minstrels." *Social Text*, no. 1 (1979): 149–56.

———. "Unsettling the Coloniality of Being/Power/Truth/Freedom: Towards the Human, after Man, Its Overrepresentation—An Argument." *CR: The New Centennial Review* 3, no. 3 (2003): 257–337.

Wyse, Akintola. *H. C. Bankole-Bright and Politics in Colonial Sierra Leone, 1919–1958*. Cambridge: Cambridge University Press, 2003.

Young, M. Crawford. "Nationalism, Ethnicity, and Class in Africa: A Retrospective (Nationalisme, ethnicité et classe en Afrique: Une rétrospective)." *Cahiers d'Etudes Africaines* 26, no. 103 (1986): 421–95.

Younis, Musab. "The Grand Machinery of the World: Race, Global Order and the Black Atlantic." PhD diss., University of Oxford, 2017.

———. "Race, the World and Time: Haiti, Liberia and Ethiopia (1914–1945)." *Millennium: Journal of International Studies* 46, no. 3 (2018): 352–70.

———. "'United by Blood': Race and Transnationalism during the Belle Époque." *Nations and Nationalism* 23, no. 3 (2017): 484–504.

Zachernuk, Philip Serge. *Colonial Subjects: An African Intelligentsia and Atlantic Ideas.* Charlottesville: University of Virginia Press, 2000.

———. "Of Origins and Colonial Order: Southern Nigerian Historians and the 'Hamitic Hypothesis' c. 1870–1970." *Journal of African History* 35, no. 3 (1994): 427–55.

Zarakol, Ayşe, ed. *Hierarchies in World Politics.* Cambridge: Cambridge University Press, 2017.

Zúquete, José Pedro. *The Identitarians: The Movement against Globalism and Islam in Europe.* Notre Dame, IN: University of Notre Dame Press, 2018.

Index

Aborigines Rights Protection Society
(ARPS), 50–51
Africa, 83, 108, 143–44
"Africa and the World Economy"
(Cooper), 185n33
African Morning Post, 63–64, 67–68, 121,
197n69
African Times and Orient Review (ATOR),
32–33, 42
African World, 91–92
Afro-American, 137, 139
Aids to African Autonomy (Cudjoe), 121–22
Algeria: participation in politics, 75–77;
World War I troops, 23–24
Ali, Dusé Mohamed, 32, 64, 94, 208n79
Anglo-Fanti, The (Sekyi), 183n10
anticolonialism: patriarchy of, 14, 123–27,
154; reactionary, 12; scholarship on,
19–20. *See also* body; economics of
exploitation; global scale of Black

anticolonialism; space; time and
temporality
Antilles: assimilation of, 75–76; and
colonial ideology, 203n31
antisemitism, 26, 83, 96, 171n93
A.O.F., 80–81
Appollian gaze, described, 3, 9–10. *See
also* global scale of Black
anticolonialism
"Are Moroccans and Algerians Negroes?"
(Garvey), 23–24, 27–28
ARPS (Aborigines Rights Protection
Society), 50–51
articulation, 13
Asante, S. K. B., 142
assimilation, 41–43, 73, 75–77, 83–88, 131
atavism, racial, 134–39, 146, 147
ATOR (African Times and Orient Review),
32–33, 42
Awoonor-Renner, Kweku Bankole, 64

257

Azikiwe, Nnamdi: as editor, 18–19, 63–64; as leader, 154; on Liberia, 51, 132, 148; *Liberia in World Politics*, 50, 148; *My Odyssey*, 132; *Renascent Africa*, 51; on South Africa, 121

Baldwin, James, 98–99
Barau, Jean, 214n44
Batilliat, Marcel, 200n89
Batouala (Maran), 111–12
Bethune, Mary Beth, 208n94
Black Jacobins, The (James), 136
Black Panther Party, 46, 177n47
Black planet, 99
Black Republic, Liberia, The (Reeve), 146–47
Black Skin, White Masks (Fanon), 98, 104
Black Star Line, 37
Blanchitude. See Whiteness
Blinkards, The (Sekyi), 91, 182n9
Bloch, Jean-Richard, 198n82
Blyden, E. W., 17, 57, 58, 59, 184n12
body: in Black French writing, 103–15, 127; body scale connecting to global scale, 5, 8, 104, 123, 125–27; body scale in Black Atlantic writings, 103–15; corporeality of economic exploitation, 69; and gender, 14, 123–27; instability of and White settlement, 100–104, 106–9, 115–22; labored body, 103, 111–15, 123; loneliness of, 103, 110–11, 114–15, 123; nature and Black body, 107; scholarship on, 111, 123, 125; theft of, 126; as trapped or confined, 62, 69, 104; in West African writing, 103–4, 115–23, 127
"Bois d'ébène" (Roumain), 113–14
Britain: citizenship, 187n51; racial policy in British-occupied West Africa, 73–74;

and White prestige, 90; World War II appeasement, 140. *See also* indirect rule
British Nationality Act of 1948, 187n51
Brown, George W., 150–52
Butler, Judith, 5, 126

Cadet, Eliézer, 138
Cahier d'un retour au pays natal (Césaire), 94–95, 97–98, 110, 113
Cameroon, mandate in, 138
Capitalism and Slavery (Williams), 136
Casely Hayford, Gladys May, 183n11
Casely Hayford, J. E., 55, 57–63
CDRN (Comité de défense de la race Nègre), 192n14
Césaire, Aimé: and assimilation, 84, 85; and body, 113, 114, 115; *Cahier d'un retour au pays natal*, 94–95, 97–98, 110, 113; on class, 193n21; *Discourse on Colonialism*, 12, 122, 193n21; on Haiti, 136; *La Tragédie du roi Christophe*, 136; *L'Étudiant Noir*, 84; and loneliness of body, 110; *Toussaint Louverture*, 136; on Whiteness, 94–95, 97–98
Chakrabarty, Dipesh, 156
Chamberlain, Joseph, 90
Chaplin, William Watts, 141
Chicago Defender, 17, 137
citational techniques, 49–50, 53–54, 59, 122, 127, 139
citizenship: British, 187n51; declinist writings and US, 96; and flags, 35; French, 96; versus subjecthood, 61
Clarke, Edward Young, 26–27
class: and economic exploitation, 58, 78–79; and economics writing in West Africa, 56

climate crisis, 6

cocoa industry and crisis, 63, 65–66, 68, 197n69

Code de la famille, 73

Colored Woman in a White World, A (Terrell), 97

colorism and Garvey, 26, 40–43

"Color Line, The" (Douglass), 95–96

Comet, 19, 64, 94, 120, 196n51

Comité de défense de la race Nègre (CDRN), 192n14

Comité d'études coloniales, 193n16

communism: and Black intelligentsia, 16; and Black writing in France, 77–80, 83, 84; and scholarship on West African economic writing, 56–57, 70; and Scottsboro, 83; and West African writing on exploitation, 63–65, 70

Congress of Black Writers and Artists, 98–99

conjugation: of time, 130; of Whiteness, 42–44; of world, 12–14

Conklin, Alice, 87

Cooper, Anna Julia, 115, 124

Cooper, Frederick, 185n33

cosmopolitanism, Black, 25, 28, 33–34, 40, 41

"Cracker in the Caribbean, The" (Harrison), 136–37

Cudjoe, S. D., 121–22

Danquah, J. B., 191n94

Darkwater (Du Bois), 97

Davies, H. O., 145

Davis, Angela, 157

Davis, Henrietta Vinton, 35

Decline of the West, The (Spengler), 96

declinist writing, 73, 95–96, 98–99

decolonization: versus anticolonialism, 8–9, 21; independence as goal, 85; scholarship on, 169n85; and sovereignty, 147, 152

Defence of the Ethiopian Movement, A (Omoniyi), 53

Defferre, Paul, 80

de Graft-Johnson, J. W., 50–53

Delaney, Martin, 147

de la Rue, Sidney, 147

Dequidt, Georges, 71–72, 88

Desroy, Annie, 214n43

diaspora: ambiguities of, 27; in *ATOR*, 33; as product of globality, 9; and time, 211n6

Discourse on Colonialism (Césaire), 12, 122, 193n21

Domination et colonization (Harmand), 87

Douglass, Frederick, 95–96

Doysié, Abel, 198n81

Drumont, Edouard, 96

Du Bois, W. E. B.: on cocoa crisis, 66; and cosmopolitanism, 41; *Darkwater*, 97; and Garvey, 40–41; on invasion of Ethiopia, 140, 144; on labor, 79; and Maran, 205n46; *Souls of Black Folk*, 97; on sovereignty of Liberia, 148; "The Souls of White Folk," 97; on Whiteness, 41, 97

Duboscq, André, 199n82

Ducoudray, Gustave, 94

dysphoria: planetary, 156–57; postcolonial, 157

Economic History of Liberia, The (Brown), 150–52

economics of exploitation: and Casely Hayford, 57–63; and class

economics of exploitation *(continued)*
beneficiaries, 58, 78–79; and cocoa
crisis, 63, 65–66, 68; corporeality of,
69; and extirpation threat, 54, 114; and
Garveyism, 39–40; and Liberia, 150–52;
and militarism, 67, 69; scholarship on,
56; as structure of world, 56; in West
African writing, 47–50, 53–70, 104; and
White prestige, 91–93
Edwards, Brent Hayes, 27, 81, 162n16,
167n58, 170n86, 172n98, 203n31
Egypt and League of Nations, 211n13
elimininationism, 108–9, 131
environmentalism: and climate crisis, 6;
and postcolonialism, 156–57
epidermalization, 5, 104
Ethiopia: invasion of, 108, 132, 138–45,
168n68; modernity of, 141–42;
sovereignty of, 45–46, 131–33, 140,
142–45, 152–54
eugenics, 71–73, 87
exploration and understanding of the
world, 10
extinction discourse, 44, 141
extirpation threat: and body in Black
French writing, 105–15, 127; and body
in West African writing, 115–23, 127;
and economic exploitation, 54, 114;
elimininationism, 108–9, 131; and
eugenics in France, 71–73, 87; and
Garveyism, 31, 41–44; and invasion of
Ethiopia, 108; and planetary dysphoria, 156–57; in Solanke, 54; and White
settlement, 100, 101, 102, 106–9, 115–22

Fagunwa, D. O., 182n9
Fanon, Frantz: *Black Skin, White Masks*,
98, 104; on body as hemmed in, 62; on

class, 80; on decolonization, 21; on
epidermalization, 5, 104; on restruc-
turing world, 158
Fanti National Constitution, The (Sarbah), 55
Faulkner, Thomas, 146
Faure, Emile, 79
Ferris, W. H., 39
Fiawoo, Ferdinand Kwasi, 182n9
financial receivership: and Haiti, 134, 135;
and Liberia, 132, 134, 146, 151
flags: Black Panther Party, 177n47;
Liberty League, 34; UNIA, 34–35, 36
folktales, 183n10
Ford, James W., 67
Foreign Office (2015), 157
Forest Bill, 59
Forestier, Georges, 71–72, 88
Foucault, Michel, 11, 201n11
France: citizenship in, 96; and eugenics,
71–73, 87; and immigration, 71–73, 75,
82–83, 87–88, 96; population manage-
ment in, 72–73, 87; use of African
troops in World War I, 23–24, 87;
White settlement of colonies, 106–7;
World War II appeasement, 108
France, Black writing in: on body, 103–15,
127; on settlement, 117; time and
temporality in, 128–29; on Whiteness,
73, 75–88, 94–96, 97–98
French Communist Party (PCF), 77–80
French Revolution in San Domingo, The
(Stoddard), 134–35
Froude, James Anthony, 134

Garcia, Elie, 132, 138
Garvey, Amy Ashwood, 185n26
Garvey, Marcus: "Are Moroccans and
Algerians Negroes?," 23–24, 27–28; and

Haiti: Haitian Revolution, 136; interest in, 131–33; occupation of, 83, 132, 134, 135–39; sovereignty of, 45–46, 131–39, 152–54

Hands Off Abyssinia, 139

Harding, Warren G., 198n80

Harmand, Jules, 87

Harrison, Hubert: and conjugation, 13–14; and cosmopolitanism, 33; and flags, 34, 40; and global focus, 2; on Haiti, 136–37; on Stoddard, 199n88; on violence, 200n90

Heidegger, Martin, 166n57

Heline, Theodore, 120

Histoire Sommaire de la Civilisation (Ducoudray), 94

Ho Chi Minh, 36

Holly, Theodora, 213n42

Houénou, Kojo Tovalou, 105

Hour of Decision, The (Spengler), 96

Hudicourt, M. Pierre, 137

Hudicourt, Theresa, 138

I Am Not Your Negro (2017), 200n97

illiteracy and newspapers, 30, 168n73

immigration: France, 71–73, 75, 82–83, 87–88, 96; US, 198n80

imperialism: global scale of, 3; global scale of anticolonialism as reaction to, 3–4, 12. *See also* assimilation; economics of exploitation; politics of racial exploitation; White settlement

indirect rule: and Casely Hayford, 60–61; and color bar, 73, 118; as differential or capricious, 18, 62, 188n58; and economic exploitation, 57, 60–61; and White prestige, 92; and White settlement, 118, 119

International African Friends of Abyssinia, 139

International Commission of Women of the Darker Races, 138

internationalism: and Black Panthers, 46; and Garveyism, 29, 33–34, 45–46; and Harrison, 33; relation to nationalism, 8–9, 20–22, 29; as term, 21

International Trade Union Committee of Negro Workers, 64

Italy: invasion of Ethiopia, 108, 132, 138–45, 168n68; invasion of Libya, 141; and White settlement in Africa, 206n61

James, C. L. R., 136, 139

Japan: and Garvey, 35, 36; settlement in Manchuria, 206n61; and Solanke, 54–55

Jews: antisemitism, 26, 83, 96, 171n93; and Madagascar, 108

Johnson, Samuel, 184n12

Johnson-Reed Immigration Act, 198n80

Joint Resolutions on the Negro Question, 107

Jones, E. N., 131

Kenya, White settlement in, 101, 107

Kerr, Philip (Lord Lothian), 117–18

Khalili, Bouchra, 157

Kimble, David, 190n79

King, C. D. B., 180n90

Kouyaté, Tiemoko Garan, 81, 83, 108, 109, 192n14, 193n21

Ku Klux Klan, 26–27

La blanche négresse (Valcin), 214n43

labor and the body, 103, 111–15, 123

Ménil, René, 109–10, 123
militarism: of colonialism, 83; and
    economic exploitation, 67, 69; and
    Garveyism, 37–39
mining industry, 151, 187n43, 189n76
Mirault, Jospeh, 138
modernity: and Ethiopia, 141–42; and
    Haiti, 133–34, 136, 139
Mohaiemen, Naeem, 219n7
Moody, Josephine, 124–26
Morand, Paul, 81–83
Moses, Wilson J, 29
Muret, Maurice, 198n81
My Odyssey (Azikiwe), 132

NAACP, 137, 138
Nardal, Paulette, 81, 83–84
nationalism: and Black Panthers, 46; and
    Black writing on French imperialism,
    73, 77–78, 85; and Casely Hayford, 57;
    and Garveyism, 29, 37–39, 45–46;
    relation to internationalism, 8–9,
    20–22, 29; scholarship on, 85, 171n92;
    as term, 21; and time, 129; and UNIA,
    34–40; and West African political
    writing, 54, 190n79
Native Life in South Africa (Plaatje), 115
nègre term, 114
Negritude, 75, 105, 110, 112, 199n87
Negro Worker, 67
Negro World: "Are Moroccans and
    Algerians Negroes?" (Garvey), 23–24,
    27–28; Black cosmopolitanism in, 25,
    28; and economics of oppression,
    39–40; founding of, 30; globality of,
    25–29, 31–32, 45–46, 168n73; on Haiti,
    136–37, 138; influence of, 30, 63, 190n79;
    and Maran, 205n46; and militarism,

37, 38; nationalism and international-
    ism in, 22; precursors to, 32–33; and
    UNIA flag, 34; on Whiteness, 41–45
"Neige sur Paris" (Senghor), 110
Nemours, Alfred Auguste, 143–44
New Journal and Guide, 137
New Negro, 14
newspapers: ephemerality of, 20; global
    impact of, 17–18, 30, 50, 159; as
    planetary system, 50; precarity of,
    17–18; surveillance and concern about,
    30–31, 159. *See also* France, Black
    writing in; West African writing
New Times and Ethiopian News, 139
Nigeria: African participation in politics,
    188n58; pan-Africanism of expatriates,
    191n96
Nkrumah, Kwame, 140
Nwana, Pita, 182n9

Ocansey, Alfred John, 63, 64
Odeziaku, 207n68
Omoniyi, Bandele, 53
Onitsha market literature, 183n10
"Open Letter to the Negroes of the
    World" (Solanke), 53–54
optimism in post–World War I writing,
    2–3
"Our White Friends," 91–93

Padmore, George, 64, 121, 148, 207n72
Pan-African Congress, 1, 3
pan-Africanism: challenges of, 15; global
    scale of, 9; and invasion of Ethiopia,
    140, 142–43, 145; and occupation of
    Haiti, 138; versus pan-nationalism, 21;
    rise of, 15, 87; and sovereignty, 133, 147;
    and state boundaries, 70, 158–59

Third Worldism: decline of, 157; and invasion of Ethiopia, 145

time and temporality: conjugation of time, 130; as deliberately unstable in Black Atlantic writing, 129–30; and diaspora, 211n6; and immobilization, 4, 130; and nationalism, 129; and the present/now, 129, 144; and racial atavism, 134–39, 146, 147; scholarship on, 210n5; of sovereignty of Ethiopia, 132–33, 140, 142–45, 152–54; of sovereignty of Haiti, 132–39, 152–54; of sovereignty of Liberia, 132–33, 146–54; and technologies of control, 218n118; and White settlement, 119–20, 131

Toussaint Louverture (Césaire), 136

Towards Nationhood in West Africa (de Graft-Johnson), 50–53

tragedy, Liberia as, 149–52

travel, 15, 16

Two Meetings and a Funeral (2017), 219n7

Union Intercoloniale, 80, 193n16

United Gold Coast Convention (UGCC), 52

United Negro Improvement Association (UNIA): flag, 34–35, 36; and Liberia, 180n90; and racial classification, 23; slogans, 32; and sovereignty, 37–39, 45, 46. See also *Negro World*

United States: and American writing on Haiti occupation, 136–38; and American writing on Whiteness, 95–97, 98–99; declinist writings and race policy, 96; extirpation threat from White settlement, 107–8; immigration policy, 198n80; and invasion of Ethiopia, 140, 141, 142; and Liberia, 132, 134; occupation of Haiti, 83, 132, 134, 135–39; and Scottsboro boys, 83; White settlement of, 120. See also Garveyism

United States of Africa, 70

United West Africa (or Africa) at the Bar of the Family of Nations (Solanke), 51, 54, 67

Vacher de Lapouge, Georges, 71

Vaillant-Couturie, Paul, 202n22

Valcin, Virgile, 214n43

violence: of colonial exploration and discovery, 10; and extirpation threat from White settlement, 107–8, 120–21; and labored body, 112–15; militarism and Garveyism, 37–39; militarism of colonization, 83

Voice, 33

von Puttkamer, Jesko, 52, 184n19

Wachuku, J. A., 66–67

Wallace-Johnson, I. T. A., 64

Wallerstein, Immanuel, 7, 195n41

Washington, Booker T., 176n36

WASU, 53

Weltanschauung (worldview), 166n57

Weltbild (world-picture), 166n57

West Africa, 61, 115

West African Pilot, 63, 65, 66–67, 69, 120, 121

West African Students' Union (WASU), 52, 53

West African writing: body in, 103–4, 115–23, 127; citational techniques, 49–50, 53–54, 59, 122, 127, 139; economics of racial exploitation in, 47–50, 53–70, 104; on history, 183n12; and invasion of Ethiopia, 142–43; politics of racial exploitation in, 47–55, 60–62; Whiteness in, 88–94, 98

Founded in 1893,
UNIVERSITY OF CALIFORNIA PRESS
publishes bold, progressive books and journals
on topics in the arts, humanities, social sciences,
and natural sciences—with a focus on social
justice issues—that inspire thought and action
among readers worldwide.

The UC PRESS FOUNDATION
raises funds to uphold the press's vital role
as an independent, nonprofit publisher, and
receives philanthropic support from a wide
range of individuals and institutions—and from
committed readers like you. To learn more, visit
ucpress.edu/supportus.